Political Ideology and Voting Behavior
in the Age of Jackson

INTERDISCIPLINARY APPROACHES TO HISTORY SERIES
Gerald E. Stearn, editor

Political Ideology and Voting Behavior in the Age of Jackson

JOEL H. SILBEY

Cornell University

PRENTICE-HALL, INC., Englewood Cliffs, New Jersey

Library of Congress Cataloging in Publication Data

SILBEY, JOEL H.
 Political ideology and voting behavior in the age
of Jackson.

 (Interdisciplinary approaches to history series)
 Bibliography: p.
 1. Political parties—United States—History.
2. Elections—United States—History. 3. Voting—
United States—History. 4. United States—Politics
and government—1815–1861. I. Title. II. Series.
JK2260.S49   324′.2   72-11828
ISBN   0-13-685644-6 (pbk)

Printed in the United States of America

10 9 8 7 6 5 4 3 2 1

PRENTICE-HALL INTERNATIONAL, INC., London
PRENTICE-HALL OF AUSTRALIA, PTY. LTD., Sydney
PRENTICE-HALL OF CANADA, LTD., Toronto
PRENTICE-HALL OF INDIA PRIVATE LIMITED, New Delhi
PRENTICE-HALL OF JAPAN, INC., Tokyo

To Victoria and David

contents

4
New Sources and New Interpretations, 47

A. SOURCES

B. INTERPRETATIONS

Political Ideology and Voting Behavior
in the Age of Jackson

1

quantification and the study of american politics in the age of jackson

Throughout most of its history, the United States has been a mass participation society. Extensive popular involvement in frequent elections has existed as long as the nation itself. Although there have been some persistent restrictions on the right of suffrage, particularly in our early history, voting privileges have generally been widely extended. Certainly since the early nineteenth century most adult white males could vote on a regular basis if they chose to, hold office if they could be nominated and elected, and participate in all of the activities making up the American political culture.

This act of voting—deciding who should be president, congressman, senator, governor, mayor or city councilman—is a form of social comment in a democracy. As people vote they reveal something about themselves, their expectations, their attitude toward the government, their own personal situation, and the social divisions and tensions within their society. In the years since the depression of 1929, for example, there has been a persistent tendency for groups at the lower end of the socioeconomic income scale to vote overwhelmingly Democratic, regardless of residence, race, religion, or previous partisan choice. Similarly, upper class voters have usually supported the Republicans. Both have done so apparently in response to their memories of conditions during the depression years and the policies of the Democratic administrations of the New Deal years, which brought certain relief and redress to the lower classes in the society, often at some expense to those higher on the social scale.[1] On the other hand, there have been occasional deviations from the class pattern of contemporary voting behavior. In 1960, for example, millions of voters who usually supported Democratic candidates switched to the Republicans. Most of the switchers were from deeply religious Protestant groups in a year when the Democratic candidate was a Catholic; apparently there existed a religious tension in the society strong enough to weaken both the importance of other issues and the bonds of party loyalty.

In both cases the way people cast their ballots revealed certain of their attitudes about the society, its leadership, and the government. For that reason the nature of popular voting behavior has consistently interested not only political scientists but historians as well. Descriptions of the great political battles, every presidential election, and many lesser contests abound in our historical literature. Nor have historians stopped at description. They have also explored the reasons underlying each specific result, seeking revelations about the character of a single incident, complex of events, particular period, or the general nature of political and social conflict in America.

Although there has never been total agreement, most American historians have, until recently, espoused a "Progressive" view of the nature of human behavior. They argued that, in politics, as Charles Beard wrote, "economics explains the mostest." Most of the time men pursue a clearly perceived, rationally defined self-interest rooted in their economic status.[2] Inevitably, one historian has written, the haves and the have-nots in our society "must possess differing ideologies and must oppose each other because of their economic background."[3] As a result, a persistent class conflict between the underprivileged and overprivileged has determined the nature and shape of political confrontation in America. The arena of struggle was the ballot box, where competing systems of belief came into contact in fights over government leadership and policies. The results of elections demonstrated the power and distribution of different economic forces and the saliency of real economic issues to the people of the United States.

The years of Andrew Jackson's dominant role in American politics demonstrated clearly to the Progressive historians the importance of economic class conflict in American history. Frederick Jackson Turner

---

[1] The nature of contemporary voting behavior is analyzed in Angus Campbell, et al., *The American Voter* (New York, 1960), and, by the same authors, *Elections and the Political Order* (New York, 1966).

[2] Quoted in John Higham, et al., *History* (Englewood Cliffs, N.J., 1965), p. 230.

[3] Robert Berkhofer, *A Behavioral Approach to Historical Analysis* (New York, 1969), p. 157.

argued, for example, that in the first quarter of the nineteenth century, the small farmers and pioneers on the western frontier challenged the political domination of a more aristocratic seacoast, where wealthy groups fought back to preserve their enormous inherited political power.[4] In the 1820s the democratic masses began to win significant victories, particularly at the state level. They swept good democrats into office, gained control of many states, and began to draft more liberal state constitutions, clearing away many undemocratic survivals of an earlier time. In particular, they removed property restrictions on popular voting, the major weapon of the upper classes against them. In the 1820s, they also found a national champion in Andrew Jackson. Turning out to vote for him and his associates in massive numbers they succeeded in bringing down the entrenched forces of upper class conservatism. In the massive democratic upheaval that was the presidential election of 1828, thousands of newly enfranchised poor whites went to the polls for the first time to support their champion and to bring down "the House of Have."[5]

Political parties played a crucial role in this upheaval. They were the respositories of the contending belief systems shaped by economic differences in the society. The Democrats were "the party of poverty and numbers, and the Whigs the party of property and talents" according to a standard textbook in American history.[6] The parties' leadership, rhetoric, and policy stances all reflected their particular orientation. The Whigs were led by the wealthiest members of the community, the Democrats by rougher elements. Party platforms revealed the different material needs of the contending economic classes. The Whigs supported an economic program—national bank, protective tariff, federal aid for internal improvements—that would aid their material interests. The Democrats strongly opposed such aid to monopoly power and special interest. The voters responded to these appeals and cast their votes along class lines.

The progressive vision of Jacksonian political history dominated American historiography in the first half of the twentieth century. In 1945, Arthur M. Schlesinger, Jr. gave it its most forceful and brilliant articulation in his *The Age of Jackson*. As the epigraph to the work Professor Schlesinger quoted George Bancroft's statement: "the feud between the capitalist and laborer, the House of Have and the House of

---

4 See Frederick Jackson Turner, *The Frontier in American History* (New York, 1920). The Jacksonian era is covered in his *The United States, 1830–1850, The Nation and its Sections* (New York, 1935).

5 The quotation is from George Bancroft, Jacksonian political leader and democratic historian.

6 Samuel Eliot Morison and Henry Steele Commager, *The Growth of the American Republic* (New York, 4th edition, revised and enlarged, 1956), pp. 554–55.

Want, is as old as social union, and can never be entirely quieted. . . ."[7] The remainder of the book forcefully developed the theme, particularly emphasizing the crucial role of the urban lower classes in creating the Jacksonian democratic political revolution.

Professor Schlesinger's arguments, and the Progressive synthesis generally, were based primarily on a wide reading in the surviving literary evidence from the Age of Jackson. Elaborate discussions of electoral strategy, voter attitudes, and campaign issues abounded in surviving newspapers, partisan pamphlets, political speeches, and the letters exchanged between political leaders. All of these often contained rich veins of economic consciousness and class appeal. The air was filled with demands for radical change and political democracy on one side, conservative defenses of the status quo on the other. Historians reading through these materials, selecting and underscoring those that seemed most representative of the time, were obviously particularly impressed with the class quality of Jacksonian rhetoric.

Despite the pervasiveness of the progressive interpretation of the nature of politics in the Jacksonian era, there had always been some challenge to it. A number of historians played up less democratic aspects of the Jacksonian coalition and questioned the credentials of the Old Hero himself as a leader of the common man. These attitudes, the minor theme in Jacksonian historiography in the 1920s and 1930s, became strongly articulated and more widely accepted in the post-World War II period. But even when the Progressives were challenged, the challenge came from within traditional historiographic methodology, and an essentially economic component remained at the core of the new argument. The re-reading of documents indicated to one group of historians that the Jacksonian movement was quite different from the Progressive description. Marvin Meyers underscored the ambiguity of the surviving documents. The Jacksonians, he pointed out, expressed many reactionary ideas as well as progressive sentiments in a confused and confusing era of change. Many revisionist historians questioned whether the "common man fighting for democracy" theme was even relevant at all. The United States was, in the view of Louis Hartz and Richard Hofstadter, something close to a consensual society, free of the kinds of class conflicts stressed by the Progressives. In fact, the Jacksonians, Bray Hammond argued, were not fighting at the ballot box to expand political freedom at all. They were primarily business entrepreneurs in a rapidly developing economy. Their mobilization of voters behind demands for reform originated in their desire to further their own economic interests. The fight against the Bank of the United States, for

---

[7] Arthur M. Schlesinger, Jr., *The Age of Jackson* (Boston, 1945), epigraph.

example, was led by state bankers anxious to free their operations from the restraints of centralized banking, not to promote democratic tendencies in the society—an interpretation that contrasted sharply with Arthur Schlesinger's belief that liberalism in America (including Jacksonianism) "has been ordinarily the movement on the part of other sections of society to restrain the power of the business community."[8]

Differences of this type strikingly raised, even more forcefully than usual, the nagging question of whether the political culture of the age was being correctly understood, and whether it could not be read with more precision and fewer differences of opinion. In answer, some historians have been attracted to methodological advances in other disciplines, particularly approaches designed to further the precise measurement and explanation of electoral behavior. Quantitative analysis of voting—the amassing and correlating of large amounts of electoral and social data about the electorate—has become, in the last two decades, an increasingly sophisticated and widely used tool of analysis among political scientists and sociologists. They have systematically polled individuals as to their partisan preferences and cross-tabulated the responses with a number of social and economic characteristics of the voters. The results of their research produced some important new ideas about the nature of political ideology and individual partisan choice.

At first, the primary emphasis of this research was in contemporary politics. But a number of political scientists and historians also analyzed election returns stretching far back into the American past. Beginning with relatively simple statistical examinations of trends and patterns in popular voting returns, they expanded them to include more sophisticated quantitative methods and more and more available social data from early censuses, economic compilations, church records, and state and local statistical publications. They also adopted computers in order to handle the massive amounts of numerical data they found. Finally, they read widely in the substantive research findings about contemporary political processes seeking clues to the nature of individual electoral behavior. The results of their work ultimately posed a thoroughgoing challenge to the work of previous students of the Jacksonian political structure.

Their most important challenge was methodological. They argued that the heavy reliance by earlier historians on documentary material was inadequate as a means of understanding mass political behavior. Surviving documents are usually only the fragmentary residue of the evidence that any society produces about itself. There can be, therefore, some crucial problems for the historian in the material. He does not know at

[8] *Ibid.,* p. 505.

first glance where the opinions and explanations offered in a particular document lie in the spectrum of opinion in a society. Does the document explain the actions and attitudes of a majority, an influential policy-making group, or a person in position to know what is actually happening? Or is it, rather, the opinion of a less important or knowledgeable group, or even of an isolated fringe in the political spectrum? Without discerning this carefully we can be seriously misled about the nature of policy making, public opinion, and political motivation. Often documents are written, speeches drafted, and remarks recorded to mislead and misinform. More often, because an observer himself was misinformed or misled, his statement standing alone will misdirect the viewer. Finally, there often survive many contradictory points of view in the material that can be used to argue a number of different and sharply conflicting viewpoints. Which of these correctly reports opinion or underlying causes? These are important problems that historians have usually resolved by using their imaginative insight based on their own wide reading and deep knowledge of a period. No matter how much they may know about a period, however, their insight is subjectively, not objectively, based. Without precise, empirical evidence, even the best informed insights remain potentially incorrect and subject to conflicting interpretations.

Most important of all, the opinions and behavior of the elite who produce most of the surviving documents of any age are not necessarily representative of the attitudes of the mass electorate. It is very possible that the better educated, more involved business and political leaders in the community had a clearer perception of economic issues and of their own material interests, for instance, than did the rest of the voters. They may have, therefore, joined particular political parties and cast their ballots in response to something such as Jackson's war on the Bank. But it is dangerous to read into their actions similar reasoning and behavior on the part of the mass electorate. The latter's involvement in and knowledge about such issues may not have been as clear cut, and other matters may have been more influential in determining their political actions. The only way to discover this is to pay less attention in the first instance to surviving rhetoric and to concentrate, instead, on determining precisely how most people actually voted.

The best indicators we have of mass political attitudes and behavior are the extensive surviving election returns and social data from the Jacksonian period. Such statistics, Lee Benson argued, are the only sources historians have from which inferences can be drawn directly about mass, not elite opinion. They allow historians to measure aspects of that opinion with precise and verifiable data, not fertile intuition alone. Election returns are the surviving record of the actual political choices of all voters, free from the bias of the investigator or the possible unrepresentativeness of other material. Benson's commitment to "a more diligent empiricism" in research led him to compile and analyze extensive amounts of quantitative evidence in order to reinterpret Jacksonian Democracy. In a pathbreaking article and then in a major monograph, *The Concept of Jacksonian Democracy: New York as a Test Case,* Benson manipulated quantities of voting returns and demographic data to demonstrate, first, their usefulness in understanding why the electorate acted as it did, and then, what that in turn revealed about the political character of the era.[9]

The use of statistics in political history was not new. Before World War I, Frederick Jackson Turner had used popular voting returns, economic data, and geographic materials in his studies of frontier politics; Dixon Ryan Fox discovered in election data evidence that urban workers and small farmers worked together to oust the upper classes from political power in New York State in the Jacksonian period; and Ulrich B. Phillips and Arthur C. Cole correlated votes for the Whig party with the more wealthy areas of the Southern states and established a relationship which seemed to confirm the importance of class conflict in ante-bellum politics. Others followed their example in the years since.[10] What was new was the increased sophistication of quantitive analysis in political history. The earlier use of election and demographic statistics suffered from a number of weaknesses. It was never systematic: historians generally selected and concentrated on a relatively few elections (usually presidential contests) without trying to incorporate all available electoral data in their analysis. They usually treated elections in isolation from one another, often not catching, therefore, continuities and changes in the patterns of behavior from election to election. Furthermore, by concentrating primarily on presidential elections they overlooked the significant electoral shifts which often occurred in off-year contests. They also concentrated on the returns from large scale electoral units losing, thereby, significant insight into group voting behavior. If a county went Whig by 55 percent to 45 percent, for example, this told us little unless we could locate precisely where in the

9 The quotation is from John William Ward, "The Age of the Common Man," in *Reconstructing The American Past,* ed. John Higham (New York, 1962), p. 96. Benson's thoughts on these matters were first presented in "Research Problems in American Political Historiography," in *Common Frontiers of the Social Sciences,* ed. Mirra Komarovsky (Glencoe, Ill., 1955), pp. 113–83. Much of this essay is reprinted in Chapter 4 below. Also see Lee Benson, "An Approach to the Scientific Study of Past Public Opinion," *Public Opinion Quarterly,* XXXI (Winter, 1967–1968), 522–67, especially 560–62.

10 Richard Jensen, "American Election Analysis: A Case History of Methodological Innovation and Diffusion," in *Politics and the Social Sciences,* ed. Seymour Martin Lipset (New York, 1969).

county each party got its votes. Analyzing election returns by relatively more socially homogeneous minor civil divisions such as wards, townships, and precincts, can reveal much more about the social basis of voting behavior than can the more heterogeneous larger units of analysis. Most of all, earlier historians related their voting returns primarily to the economic characteristics of the units involved. They did not examine other possible social variables to see if another and stronger relationship to the voting patterns perhaps existed. Their "design of proof . . . [was] logically fallacious," Lee Benson noted, "because it assumes that the relationship between two variables can be discovered without considering the possible influence of other variables."[11] Modern historians using quantitative data have sought to overcome these deficiencies by collecting all available voting returns and correlating them with all surviving descriptive social and economic data.

Nothing in the quantitative revolution in political history eliminates the need to use traditional historical sources. Quantitative evidence, by itself, does not explain why a particular distribution of the vote occurred as it did. It is, at best, a substantial clue to the reasons underlying mass behavior. The historian must still reconstruct those reasons from the surviving documentary evidence he has always used. But this reconstruction is quite different from traditional approaches to the written record. Obviously, the best way to establish either a document's representativeness or its correctness in discussing mass behavior is to compare it with a precise description of what mass opinion actually was, free from the bias of contemporary writers and the historian's own imperfect intuition. If the actual distribution of the vote belies a document's explanation it must be reconsidered as to its meaning no matter who wrote it. On the other hand, once the actual vote distribution has been established, many things may be revealed in the documents that might have been glossed over, ignored, or misunderstood.

It was not only quantitative methods that political historians borrowed from the social scientists. They were also aided in defining their problems and understanding the implication of the patterns they uncovered by research results in current political analysis. Electoral behavior is complex, and an individual's vote in a particular election flows from a number of sources. Students of electoral behavior have, for example, discovered a persistent structural pattern in popular voting. Most of the time, the same groups vote for the same party in election after election regardless of changes in candidates, the rise of new issues, and the apparent importance of cataclysmic events. Second, the knowledge voters

[11] Lee Benson, *Turner and Beard, American Historical Writing Reconsidered* (Glencoe, 1960), p. 154.

possess about specific issues in a given election is usually quite low. The rational discussion of the great national issues in extensive campaigns apparently has minimal impact on subsequent electoral behavior. Rather, voters appear primarily to follow tradition and past habits of partisan identification when they cast their ballots.

Nor, for large parts of our history, have voting patterns followed economic class lines. Many voters of similar class and occupation vote quite differently from each other and always have. At the same time, dissimilar economic groups frequently vote together. Extensive interviewing of voters as well as research into past voting patterns has highlighted the primary importance of social and psychological variables such as religious affiliation and party identification in shaping contemporary voting behavior. The value structure of the basic groups to which individual voters belong and with which they identify is more influential in shaping voting choice than any well-formulated conceptions of the issues currently being discussed. These values originate in the experiences of different groups within American society, the shared perspectives toward the world that develop out of these experiences, and, most crucially, the recurring clashes between different groups espousing conflicting norms that have characterized American history. "Members of the same primary groups," one study has argued, "characteristically vote alike, think alike on issues, and affiliate with the same party."[12] The most potent primary group is the family where views about the world are first conditioned; then come the values of the larger community in which the family lives and operates. Association within family and community leads to political socialization—the absorption of attitudes toward other groups and individuals that spill over into politics.

Analysis of voting data from the different eras of American history has brought into sharp focus the particular importance of clashing religious and ethnic perspectives in shaping group values and attitudes toward politics. "Every ethnic group," Lawrence Fuchs has written, "has its own distinctive style of cognition, perception, feeling, and behavior. . . ."[13] Due to clashing perspectives between different ethnic groups and their persistent social competition throughout American history, political confrontation has followed, most noticeably at the ballot box. Economic differences within the society have occasionally influenced voting behavior, but more often they have been subordinate to persistent cultural tensions except in periods of intense economic dislocations such as the 1890s and 1930s. But even in such periods of sharp economic conflict in politics, cultural differences still influenced much voting behavior.

[12] Herbert McClosky and Harold E. Dahlgren, "Primary Group Influence on Party Loyalty," *American Political Science Review*, LIII (September, 1958), 758.
[13] Lawrence Fuchs, ed., *American Ethnic Politics* (New York, 1968), p. 6.

The political party system is central to the shaping of these group perspectives within the voting universe. The parties are the repositories and reflectors of the belief systems of the different social groups. Parties developed as institutions designed to organize and channel the many competing groups and ideas in a complex society into manageable units to contest elections. The various ethnocultural and socioeconomic conflicts shaping political attitudes in the society became built into the different party coalitions. Over time the parties took on the aura of their component groups, each reflecting in its program and rhetoric major aspects of the norms and values of its constituent groups. Parties are broad, symbolic institutions to most voters, standing for or against their values, needs, and desires within the society. As a result, a deep attachment to a particular party becomes rooted among most voters, and this party identification survives issues, catastrophes, changes of residence, and the emergence of new forces in politics. Thus, the most powerful and clearest indicator of voting behavior in any election is party identification—the pre-existing partisan preference of each individual voter.[14]

Stimulated by the promise of these findings and methodological advances for their own work, a number of American historians have used quantitative evidence to reinterpret Jacksonian Democracy. Several have constructed systematic time series of election results to determine what the overall patterns were, the location of each party's support, and when and among which groups shifts occurred. Some of these studies have been remarkably simple in method. J. R. Pole and Richard McCormick, for example, have reported on patterns of suffrage eligibility and turnout to determine the contribution of the Jacksonians to the freeing of the common man. McCormick, among others, has also investigated whether or not the lower economic classes actually voted for Jackson and the Democrats. Other historians have used more complex quantitative methodology and more wide-ranging data sources. Conscious of the many influences affecting individual political choice, and critical of the earlier tendency to relate only economic characteristics to voting behavior, they have correlated election returns with a wide range of available material, including religious affiliation, national background, the previous political habits of voters, and the size and location of their home areas, as well as their economic class and occupation. This effort in multivariate analysis has led a number of scholars into the world of computer technology and sophisticated statistical formulae in search of possible relationships between these group characteristics and voting behavior. The results of

---

[14] Robert Lane, *Political Life, Why and How People Get Involved in Politics* (New York, paperback edition, 1965), pp. 299–300.

their efforts, as the selections included below indicate, have produced a number of striking revisions in our understanding of the Jacksonian era. Although many historians have remained cautious about any extensive use of quantitative analysis in political history, certainly, if nothing else, the adoption of quantitative techniques has enriched our ability to deal with an important and challenging historical problem.

2

---

political development
in the united states,
1790-1840

Inauguration Day, 1829 was tumultuous. Thousands of people descended on the White House grounds to celebrate Andrew Jackson's decisive victory over John Quincy Adams, nearly injuring the new president in their fervor and doing some considerable damage to physical property. These frenetic events, which horrified some observers and delighted others, symbolized the culmination of a half century of American political development under the Constitution. Two political parties had vigorously contested for the highest office in the nation, more than one million voters in twenty-four states had cast ballots, and each candidate had received substantial support from devoted adherents. A man whom some considered violent, uncouth, and rustic, but whom others thought of as a tribune of the common people, had successfully challenged the leader of the eastern establishment.

Fifty years before, the political situation had not been as energetic, as organized, as large scale, or as complex. Colonial politics had had its share of political conflicts between vigorously contesting social groups, bitter political rhetoric, and sharp electoral confrontation. But relatively few people had been involved in these battles. In most colonies, laws severely restricted the number of citizens who could vote. In addition, the institutions of American politics were undeveloped. The parties and factions of colonial America were impermanent, transient things, largely controlled by a few upper class families and leaders. Above all, there was no national focus or identity to a political culture traditionally centered in many different local arenas.

The roots of the nineteenth-century political structure lay in developments since the ratification of the Constitution. The establishment of a national political arena alongside the older local ones gave an important national focus to politics. The continuation of local conflicts, the strong national program pushed by Alexander Hamilton in the 1790s, and our involvement in the world war between Britain and France all stimulated bitter electoral politics. For the first time there was need for national political organizations to coordinate the resulting battles for national office. Between 1790 and 1815 the Republican and Federalist parties emerged, developed programs and distinct policy orientations, and built up electoral organizations to harness the multitude of conflicting groups in a complex political system.

This system was never static. New sources of political conflict developed constantly, ranging from increased tensions between different ethnocultural groups to intense disagreements over economic policies. Immigration from a variety of sources was a major stimulant of discord. In the 1790s, British migrants and French refugees, people with long standing hostility to one another, both settled in the United States. German religious pietists, English dissenting sects, and Irish Catholics also found themselves living side by side with their traditional Anglo–Saxon, Protestant enemies in a political system in which all of them could participate. Battles over restrictive immigration legislation, the rights of aliens to vote, and state laws limiting certain religious or national practices brought these differences into the political arena. The spread of the great Protestant religious revival in the early years of the nineteenth century, coinciding with increased Catholic immigration, intensified cultural perceptions and sharpened political hostilities between different religious and nationality groups.

The potential for economic conflict stemmed from a number of problems produced by the rapid, often chaotic growth of the nation. The United States was an unequal society. Differentiated land holdings, occupations, and geographic considerations separated Americans into various economic classes. Other inequalities existed due to the differing stages of economic development in different areas. Some regions with a high degree of commercial development, superior natural resources, or well-developed transportation networks needed little promotional aid from the political system. Other places, not as well endowed, demanded government aid to stimulate their growth. Conflicts erupted over all of these things—land prices and land distribution, state promotional laws and subsidies, tariff protection, and government aid for transportation improvements. The far-reaching depression of 1819 dramatically sharpened these conflicts. Political battles erupted in state capitals and in Washington as different groups pressured the political system to provide redress and promote recovery.

At the same time that new social and economic cleavages were developing, the number of participants in the American political structure sharply increased. Since the Revolution there had been challenges to traditional limitations, such as property qualifications, on the right of suffrage. These restrictions began to ease significantly in the early nineteenth century as a number of states revised their constitutions. In New York State, for example, the new constitution, drafted in 1821, allowed a white adult male to vote if he paid taxes or was eligible for militia service. Under the previous constitution a citizen had had to own £ 100 worth of property in order to vote for governor. In addition, a number of states also improved their electoral machinery and procedures to promote easier participation. As a result of these changes there now existed side by side in the political system a potential for political conflict, a continuous focus on the ballot box, and a steady expansion of the number of people involved at all levels.

Despite the persistence of political conflict on the American scene and the growth of the political arena, the first national party system had not taken deep root. By 1815 the Federalist party no longer functioned effectively as a national opposition. Contests for national offices temporarily lost much of their significance as the basic focus of political conflict returned to the states. But events after 1819, particularly between 1824 and 1828, restored an important degree of nationality to American politics. The fight for the presidency took on renewed importance and national political institutions once more developed, this time in permanent form.

The policies of John Quincy Adams's government particularly stimulated the growth of powerful opposition forces. The president's strong stands on economic issues and questions of national power alienated and drove into opposition all of those who saw themselves adversely affected by Adams's nationalist ideology. Determined to oust him from the presidency, they sought a potent alternative candidate. They found one in Andrew Jackson, a Tennessee planter, military hero, and longtime state political leader. Jackson's striking military successes against the British in the War of 1812 and against the Indians in the South and Southwest had won him widespread popular support for the presidency. In 1824, although he won more popular votes than anyone else in a four-way race, his lack of a majority in the electoral college threw the contest into the House of Representatives. There an alliance among unfriendly politicians caused his defeat. Jackson and his followers savagely attacked this "corrupt bargain" between oligarchic political bosses and joined with the opponents of Adams's policies in a well-organized appeal to the people to right the wrong of 1824. Four years later they were successful.

With Jackson in the presidency, political conflict did not decrease. In the months and years after his tumultuous inaugural, Jackson also proved to be a strong president with an evolving program that provoked intense opposition. Differences over the tariff, Indian affairs, the authority of the central government, and the role of the president in shaping policies all contributed to the continuing growth of bitter political divisions in the country. Perhaps the greatest surge forward for the opposition occurred during the Bank war of 1832–1834 when factional rivalries in many states hardened into bitter two-party conflict. The war on the bank was not popular where banking remained undeveloped or there was great economic need for such an institution. But, even more, the issue came to symbolize a wide range of developing political cleavages stimulated by Jackson's strong stands and inflexible determination to have his way.

Nor was this all. Issues inspired by Jackson's policies were dramatic, and they importantly affected voter behavior. But other issues, particularly the residue of long-existing local, cultural, and sectional conflicts continued potent and added to this intense political atmosphere. In the North a widespread anti-masonic movement reinvigorated a range of tensions within the society. Similarly, another great Protestant revival in the early thirties intensified hatred between Protestants and Roman Catholics. In New York City in the thirties and forties, a nativist movement challenged the right of immigrants to enter freely into American society and politics.

In campaign after campaign, such social and economic divisions were the basic stuff of electoral politics. National political parties once more emerged to channel these conflicts and organize the mass of voters for political activity. As the parties grew in importance, few political groups escaped becoming part of this developing two-party system. The Democrats and Whigs each assiduously promoted their own cause, competed for all available votes, and absorbed almost all of the issues and battles on the political landscape. By the time Jackson left office, well-organized political coalitions stood amidst a large electorate as the centerpieces of political conflict, each taking different issue stances and each representing different groups and beliefs in the society—differences repeatedly revealed on election day.

The sources of political conflict in Jacksonian America were many, and the policies advocated and beliefs articulated varied. But when individual voters cast their ballots on election day they brought some kind of order to this diversity. They defined themselves and their beliefs about what the crucial issues of the society were as clearly as anyone ever did. What did their voting behavior say about their beliefs? What issues and differences—economics, ethnocultural distinctions, the great national conflicts, or other matters—most affected their behavior? What was the role of Jackson and his party in the liberalization of the political structure? What impact did the infusion of lower class voters have on Jackson's electoral successes? Finally, what do the answers to these questions reveal about the political ideology and belief system of the age and the nature of Jacksonian Democracy? The following material turns to explore these issues.

3

traditional sources and traditional interpretations

A wealth of literary evidence—the letters of political leaders, personal memoirs of politicians, accounts by contemporary observers of the political scene, reports of legislative debates, official government documents, newspapers, partisan pamphlets, platforms, and campaign biographies—survives for the Jacksonian era. As we have noted, historians from Frederick Jackson Turner in the 1890s, to Arthur Schlesinger, Jr., in the 1940s have drawn upon these materials to portray the political culture of the era in terms of an epic struggle between an encrusted aristocracy of wealth and power and the emerging mass political movement behind Andrew Jackson. Certainly, much of the rhetoric contained in these sources supported such an interpretation. Shrill denunciations of the "House of Have" by the "House of Want" (as George Bancroft, Jacksonian politician and historian, put it), permeated Democratic party literature in such crises as the Bank War and in multitudes of election campaigns. Contemporary newspapers often analyzed election results in terms of class voting, and upper class sources expressed discomfort at the raging sociopolitical revolution they perceived going on around them.

But, whatever the rhetoric, the vital problem of linking these descriptions, written by a relatively few men, to actual patterns of mass behavior and ideology could not be done by literary evidence alone. A number

17

of historians did confront this problem by adding mass electoral and
social data to their literary evidence. But their methods were unsystem-
atic, and their technology inadequate for the analysis necessary. Most
of all, even those who employed quantitative data began with assumptions rising out of their literary sources. In his *The Decline of the Aristocracy in the Politics of New York, 1790–1840* (New York, 1918), for
example, Dixon Ryan Fox carefully related the economic composition of
New York City voting districts to their voting records to demonstrate
lower class support for the Democratic party, Whig support among the
wealthy. But Fox and others who did similar quantitative explorations
never fully investigated to see if other characteristics (for instance the
ethnocultural composition of an area) exhibited a stronger relationship
with voting patterns than did economic class. The power of the democratic rhetoric and the heavy reliance on literary sources remained the
common shaping theme of Jacksonian historiography. Some examples
of these sources are included in the following selections.

A. SOURCES

1. NEW YORK EVENING POST (1834)
   "The Division of Parties"

The editorials and news columns of contemporary newspapers
provide dramatic descriptions and suggestive insights into the political
affairs of their day. The *New York Evening Post,* edited by William
Cullen Bryant, was a leading, and often quoted, spokesman of radical
Democracy in New York City during the Jacksonian era. In 1834, at the
height of the bitter debates over the Bank of the United States, the paper
summed up its perception of the nature of American politics and provided a nice synthesis of the class conflict view of political divisions.
Reprinted from the issue of November 4, 1834.

Since the organization of the Government of the United States the
people of this country have been divided into two great parties. One of
these parties has undergone various changes of name; the other has continued steadfast alike to its appellation and to its principles and is now,
as it was at first, the *Democracy.* Both parties have ever contended for
the same opposite ends which originally caused the division, whatever
may have been, at different times, the particular means which furnished
the immediate subject of dispute. The great object of the struggles of
the Democracy has been to confine the action of the General Government within the limits marked out in the Constitution; the great object
of the party opposed to the Democracy has ever been to overleap those

boundaries and give to the General Government greater powers and a wider field for their exercise. The doctrine of the one party is that all power not expressly and clearly delegated to the General Government remains with the States and with the people; the doctrine of the other party is that the vigor and efficacy of the General Government should be strengthened by a free construction of its powers. The one party sees danger from the encroachments of the General Government; the other affects to see danger from the encroachments of the States.

This original line of separation between the two great political parties of the Republic, though it existed under the old Confederation and was distinctly marked in the controversy which preceded the formation and adoption of the present Constitution, was greatly widened and strengthened by the project of a National Bank, brought forward in 1791. This was the first great question which occurred under the new Constitution to test whether the provisions of that instrument were to be interpreted according to their strict and literal meaning; or whether they might be stretched to include objects and powers which had never been delegated to the General Government and which consequently still resided with the States as separate sovereignties.

The proposition of the Bank was recommended by the Secretary of the Treasury on the ground that such an institution would be "of primary importance to the prosperous administration of the finances, and of the greatest utility in the operations connected with the support of public credit." This scheme, then, as now, was opposed on various grounds; but the constitutional objection constituted then, as it does at the present day, the main reason of the uncompromising and invincible hostility of the Democracy to the measure. They considered it as the exercise of a very important power which had never been given by the States or the people to the General Government and which the General Government could not therefore exercise without being guilty of usurpation. Those who contended that the Government possessed the power effected their immediate object; but the controversy still exists. And it is of no consequence to tell the Democracy that it is now established by various precedents and by decisions of the Supreme Court that this power is fairly incidental to certain other powers expressly granted; for this is only telling them that the advocates of free construction have, at times, had the ascendancy in the Executive and Legislative and, at all times, in the Judiciary Department of the Government. The Bank question stands now on precisely the same footing that it originally did; it is now, as it was at first, a matter of controversy between the two great parties of this country, between parties as opposite as day and night, between parties which contend, one for the consolidation and enlargement of the powers of the General Government, and the other for strictly limiting that Government to the objects for which it was instituted and to the exercise of the means with which it was entrusted. The one party is for a popular government; the other for an aristocracy. The one party is composed, in a great measure, of the farmers, mechanics, laborers, and other producers of the middling and lower classes, according to the common gradation by the scale of wealth, and the other of the consumers, the rich, the proud, the privileged, of those who, if our Government were converted into an aristocracy, would become our dukes, lords, marquises, and baronets. The question is still disputed between these two parties; it is ever a new question; and whether the democracy or the aristocracy shall succeed in the present struggle, the fight will be renewed whenever the defeated party shall be again able to muster strength enough to take the field. The privilege of self-government is one which the people will never be permitted to enjoy unmolested. Power and wealth are continually stealing from the many to the few. There is a class continually gaining ground in the community who desire to monopolize the advantage of the Government, to hedge themselves round with exclusive privileges and elevate themselves at the expense of the great body of the people. These, in our society, are emphatically the aristocracy; and these, with all such as their means of persuasion or corruption or intimidation can move to act with them, constitute the party which are now struggling against the democracy for the perpetuation of an odious and dangerous moneyed institution.

Putting out of view, for the present, all other objections to the United States Bank,—that it is a monopoly, that it possesses enormous and overshadowing power, that it has been most corruptly managed, and that it is identified with political leaders to whom the people of the United States must ever be strongly opposed—the constitutional objection alone is an insurmountable objection to it.

The Government of the United States is a limited sovereignty. The powers which it may exercise are expressly enumerated in the Constitution. None not thus stated, or that are not "necessary and proper" to carry those which are stated into effect, can be allowed to be exercised by it. The power to establish a bank is not expressly given; neither is it incidental; since it cannot be shown to be "necessary" to carry the powers which are given, or any of them, into effect. That power cannot therefore be exercised without transcending the constitutional limits.

This is the *democratic* argument stated in its briefest form. The *aristocratic* argument in favor of the power is founded on the dangerous heresy that the Constitution says one thing and means another. That "necessary" does not mean *necessary* but simply *convenient*. By a mode of reasoning not looser than this it would be easy to prove that our Government ought to be changed into a monarchy, Henry Clay crowned king, and the opposition members of the Senate made peers of the realm; and power, place, and perquisites given to them and their heirs forever.

2. | SAMUEL J. TILDEN
"The Address of the Convention to the Democratic Young Men of the County of Columbia," (1833)

　　　Campaign documents also survive in abundance from the 1830s. Each party extensively utilized pamphlets, reprints of speeches and platforms, and handbills as an important means of mobilizing popular support in election campaigns. Historians have often milked these documents for what they reveal about the political attitudes of the parties and the people being addressed. The following was drafted by young Samuel J. Tilden, just becoming involved in New York State politics in 1833, as one part of the Democratic party's war against the Bank. Reprinted from John Bigelow, *The Life of Samuel J. Tilden* (New York, 1895), I, 39–41.

What is it which has hung for ages like an incubus upon England, repressing the rising spirit of freedom, and paralyzing every effort to ameliorate her political condition, which, at this moment, exerts an influence over her far more mighty than that of her hereditary aristocracy, and, in truth, sways her destinies? A heartless, soulless moneyed power—a tyranny sternly inexorable and unrelenting, when, as in the recent glorious struggles for reform, even the monarch and many of the titled nobility were ready to yield something to the just complaints of an oppressed people. And can we be insensible to the rapid and fearful strides which the same power is making in our own country? Are not monopolies and corporations springing up like hydras in every part of the nation? Are they not obtaining an alarming ascendency over our legislative bodies, and over the people themselves? Is not the most mighty and dangerous of them now convulsing the country by its struggles for continued existence? Has it not already arrayed the rich as an associated class in its support? Has it not assailed the purity of the press, the fidelity of our representatives, and the freedom of our elections, the three great pillars which support the noble superstructure of American liberty? Has it not betrayed the just authority of Congress, and, with reckless audacity, dared to dictate to us the choice of our rulers? Has it not, by its control over the currency and business of the country, spread far and wide dismay, misery, and ruin, that it might coerce and intimidate the people to an acquiescence in its wishes? Has it not engaged in an organized effort virtually to rob the mechanics and working classes of the right of suffrage, by driving them from the employment upon which they and their families depend for subsistence, unless they would surrender this dearest birthright of freemen to the dictation of those who, by means of their wealth, possess an accidental power over them? And if it be successful in effecting a recharter, is any one so infatuated as to hope that, when the time for another renewal recurs, its application can be resisted? If Andrew Jackson, with a long life of glorious public service, with a degree of popularity and public confidence never enjoyed before save by the Father of his Country, and sustained by a party numerous, united, and powerful almost beyond example—if he is unequal to the conflict, who shall hereafter dare encounter its peril and hazard? or who, having the patriotism and the firmness to make the attempt, can have the slightest chance of success? No, fellow-citizens, this contest can never be refought. Give to the bank extended existence, postpone the struggle now when you are better prepared to meet it than you can expect ever again to be, allow the bank to inweave itself more closely with our commercial system, and to strengthen its alliance with the wealth of the nation,—and every effort to resist its power hereafter will be fruitless. In practice, it will be perpetual. It will exist forever, the centre and stronghold of the money power. New exclusive privileges will soon be demanded. The means now employed to effect its designs, if once successful, will again be resorted to and be again successful. It will assemble around it all the rich and aristocratic, giving unity to their efforts and wielding their energies, till finally, as with advancing time wealth accumulates and poverty becomes more excessive, A MONEYED ARISTOCRACY will hold undisputed sway over this now free and happy people.

3. | *Henry Horn to James K. Polk (1832)*

Perhaps the most utilized of all literary sources in political history are the surviving manuscripts of political leaders. The private letters exchanged among politicians often furnish clues as to how they viewed the world around them as well as their motivation for specific actions. Letters from constituents back home provide a means, albeit a very subjective one, of assessing the impact of specific issues and the direction of public opinion. In 1832, James K. Polk, future president of the United States, was a rising congressman from Tennessee; Henry Horn was a former Pennsylvania congressman, at that time Collector of the Port of Philadelphia. Reprinted from Herbert Weaver and Paul Bergeron, eds. *Correspondence of James K. Polk* (Nashville, 1969), I, 490–93. [Footnotes omitted.]

My Dear Sir   Philadelphia August 7 1832

I wrote you a line in Great haste immediately after our Town meeting in favour of the Veto, and enclosed at the same time one of our daily papers containing an account of the proceedings which were had on that occasion by which you may have formed some Idea of the State of our feelings here.

I am now happy in being able to say that the political aspect of our affairs is cheering and encouraging beyond my most sanguine hopes. Though fully aware of the fears and unchangeable character of the People of our State and of the Great difficulty which would be experienced even by the most adroit politicians in Shaking the confidence of the People in the measures of our Venerable friend the President, I nevertheless could not avoid the belief that the Change in the Tariff and the Veto upon the Bank would have operated in a degree to our Prejudice. But as the best digested theories and the Shrewdest calculations upon future events often fall before the unerring test of experience so in the present case the Result has baffled all Calculations upon the effect of the Tariff and the Bank on our State public opinion in regard to these Great national measures seems to have undergone a change that is truly astonishing. The tariff as modified is decidedly popular even the ultras who clammoured loudly against any change in our protective Sistem are obliged to acknowledge the Judiciousness of the change or to acquiesce in silence in a measure to which their opposition would be utterly useless. The Bank which we were told was an institution deeply seated in the affections of our People and so essential to our aggricultural, manufacturing and commercial prosperity I believe will be suffered to die without a tear of Sympathy from the Great Republican party of our State. The arristocracy it is true will as they always have done lament the loss of this powerful engine and will labour hard to save it from its fate. But we do not fear them; the people are awakened to a sense of their danger. The Key Note of preparation has been Sounded in the east and in the Western extremities of our State; it will be Responded to from every quarter and I feel the most perfect assurance that nothing can arrest the determined Spirit of our honest yeomanry to Sustain the President *Triumphantly* at the approaching Election against all factious opposition in whatever form it may present itself.

The Veto is Sustained now not merely upon the ground of the Presidents constitutional Right to exercise it but as one of the proudest acts in the Political life of that Venerable and patriotic Chief. The newspapers of our party I believe without exceptions have come out decidedly in favour of the measures of the administration. They are impeled into our Support by the irresistable current of Public opinion. The Editors with us are not the leaders but the mere Organs of the party and So long only as they faithfully and truly diseminate our Sentiments can they act with any efficiency among us. When they become recreant to the interests of their Legitimate Sovereigns the People they are dismissed from our Confidence and turned adrift to be picked up by those who are disposed to employ them and to pay them the wages of their iniquity. Such is now the condition of Our Inquirer (although we never Considered that paper as orthodox to our party). Since its appostacy it has been discharded by all true friends of the Administration and its Editor is treated with merited contempt. The Pennsylvanian, our new Jackson paper, is conducted with some ability and great energy. Its circulation however is as yet too limited. We hope it will obtain as it deserves an increase of subscribers. If it should be extensively circulated I am convinced it will prove a Valuable auxiliary to our cause.

The Sentinel which you Know from its connection with the Ingham faction had long been doubtful and equivocal in its character has now come out Boldly and decidedly in favour of the measures of the administration and of the Reelection of the President. This is one of the Strongest indications that our insidious opponents and lukewarm friends are now convinced that opposition to the Reelection of the President would be a fruitless effort on their part which must necessarily consign them to the Ranks of a beaten and broken down minority. What Course we Shall pursue in our city and County in Relation to our Congressional elections is as yet impossible to say. A few weeks will develope it. I am inclined to hope that both of my Colleagues will meet with a powerful opposition if not a defeat. Certainly the Col. cannot be returned again as he has taken refuge in the Ranks of the opposition. Not So with the Doctr; he is one of the most *decided Jackson men in the County.* If possible he goes even beyond you and I. What think you of this?

Although tired of Political life and entirely averse to leaving my family, my home and my business for a life at Washington I find it necessary that I should at least enter the political field as a Citizen (not as a candidate) and perform my tour of duty until the reelection of the President is consumated.

Our citizens are much alarmed and excited by the Rapid increase of that dreadful Scourge the Cholera among us. I am placed upon the Sanitary Committee which Subjects me to many truly distressing scenes. In the midst of which I cherish a lively hope of enjoying the pleasure of again greeting you at the Capitol in triumph.

HENRY HORN

4. | Charles A. Beard and Mary Beard
       | *"Jacksonian Democracy—A Triumphant*
       | *Farmer-Labor Party"*

Charles A. Beard brought to all of his many historical works a
determination to probe beneath the formal superstructure of politics to
the basic social and economic realities underlying the political conflicts
of an age. In his earlier works, particularly *An Economic Interpretation
of the Constitution of the United States* (1913), and *Economic Origins
of Jeffersonian Democracy* (1915), Beard was among the first historians
to utilize quantitative data to demonstrate that a powerful and recurrent
clash between different economic interest groups and classes formed the
real substance of political and constitutional controversy in American
society. He subsequently applied this same materialist conception of
political conflict to the whole of American history—albeit without much,
if any, further recourse to quantitative evidence. His reading of such
surviving rhetoric of the Jacksonian period as the Bank veto message
confirmed the picture drawn from these same sources by such historians
of the era as Frederick Jackson Turner, Dixon Ryan Fox, and Arthur M.
Schlesinger, Sr. Like them, he found the age's politics rooted in the surge
of democratic attitudes in American life emanating from the lower
reaches of the social order in both agricultural west and urban East, and
a long and bitter battle at the polls and in the legislature between these
democratic forces and a bitterly resistant upper class of the economic and
political order.

Although his discussion of actual voting is indirect and not specifically
stressed, Beard, in the following chapter from his monumental *The Rise
of American Civilization* (1927), written with his wife, effectively codifies
a generation's interpretation of the politics, suffrage patterns, and belief
system of the period. Only Arthur M. Schlesinger, Jr., a decade or so later,
added much of substance to the picture drawn by Beard and his contemporaries, and Schlesinger's propositions were built onto a structure
already clearly marked. Reprinted by permission of The Macmillan
Company from *The Rise of American Civilization* by Charles A. Beard
and Mary Beard, pp. 542–80. Copyright 1933 by The Macmillan Company, renewed 1961 by William Beard and Miriam Beard Vagts.

The creation of nine states beyond the mountains, accelerating the
steady movement of political power toward the West, was synchronous
with profound social changes on the seaboard—changes equally disturbing to eastern gentlemen of the old school in wigs, ruffles, knee breeches,
and silver buckles. While the widening agricultural area was sending an
ever-increasing number of representatives to speak for farmers upon the

floor of Congress, state after state on the Atlantic coast was putting ballots into the hands of laborers and mechanics whom the Fathers of the Republic had feared as Cicero feared the proletariat and desperate debtors of ancient Rome. Even Jefferson, fiery apostle of equality in the abstract, shrank at first from the grueling test of his own logic; not until long after the Declaration of Independence did he commit himself to the dangerous doctrine of manhood suffrage.

Expressing their anxieties in law, the framers of the first state constitutions, as we have noted, placed taxpaying or property qualifications on the right to vote. The more timid excluded from public office all except the possessors of substantial property; and those who stood aghast at the march of secularism applied religious tests that excluded from places of political trust Catholics, Jews, Unitarians, and scoffers who denied belief in hell. All people thus laid under the ban of the law they regarded as socially unsafe. "The tumultuous populace of large cities," ran the warning words of Washington, "are ever to be dreaded." In Jefferson's opinion also, "the mobs of the great cities" were "sores on the body politic."

Such was the prevailing view among the ruling classes of the time and it was founded on no mere theories of state. The conduct of the rioters in the days of the Stamp Act agitation, the fierce treatment meted out to Tories in the years of the Revolution, and the mass meetings of workingmen in New York and Philadelphia when the first state constitutions were being framed, all indicated that social forces of unknown power were stirring beneath the surface of society.

There was a brief period of peace and reaction while the Constitution was being launched but that was the calm before the storm. Washington had been safely installed only a few weeks when the alarm bell of the French Revolution gave the signal for an uprising of the sansculottes of the western world. Before long, in all the cities of the American seaboard, a movement for white manhood suffrage was in full swing. Indeed, the mechanics of Pennsylvania had already set an example in 1776 by forcing the adoption of a low taxpaying franchise which gave a broad popular base to the government and paved the way for a Jacobinical democracy. During Washington's first administration, in 1791, to be exact, Vermont came into the Union without property restrictions, and Delaware gave the ballot to all white men who paid taxes. Though reckoned among the conservative states, Maryland "shot Niagara" in 1809 by adopting manhood suffrage; and nine years later Connecticut, even less devoted to the quest for novelties, decided that all males who contributed a trivial sum to the support of the government could be trusted with the ballot.

The fire spread to Massachusetts. Into the state constitutional convention of 1820 strode radicals ready to strike down all the political privileges expressly accorded to property, raising anew the specter of Daniel Shays. Frightened at their demands, Daniel Webster, then in the prime of his manhood, and John Adams, at the close of his memorable career, joined in protesting against innovations. With his customary eloquence, Webster warned the convention that all the revolutions of history which had shaken society to its foundations had been revolts against property; that equal suffrage was incompatible with inequality in property; and that if adopted it would either end in assaults on wealth or new restraints upon democracy—a reaction of the notables. In spite of the fact that the argument was cogent, it did not rally the delegates as one man to the established bulwarks. The privileges of riches in the state senate were indeed retained but the straight property test for the suffrage was abandoned and a small taxpaying restriction adopted, merely to be swept away itself within a few years.

A similar contest took place in New York in 1821 when a band of Federalists in the constitutional convention argued, threatened, and raged to save the political rights of property, only to go down in defeat after gaining some petty concessions which were abolished within five years in favor of white manhood suffrage. From this struggle echoes were heard in Rhode Island where the mechanics of Providence, learning of Tammany's victory in New York, called for a similar unhorsing of the freeholders who ruled their own state. Unawed by their hue and cry, the conservatives stood firm while the tiny commonwealth founded by apostles of liberty was shaken by a long and stormy agitation over the rights of man. For nearly twenty years the tempest blew hard, provoking an armed uprising, known as Dorr's Rebellion, and culminating in the substitution of a taxpaying for the freehold qualification on the suffrage.

Still more obdurate were Virginia and North Carolina, notwithstanding the power of Jefferson's great name; the former would not let anybody but landowners vote until 1850; the latter did not surrender that restriction for six years more. But the delay was not so significant, for the growth of the western counties in those two states gave them each a population of small farmers who had no more love for the planters on the coast than the Irish mechanics of New York City had for the stockholders in the United States Bank. Thus it may be said that when the nineteenth century turned its first quarter, political power was slipping from the hands of seaboard freeholders, capitalists, and planters into the grip of frontier farmers—usually heavily in debt to the East for capital and credit—and into the hands of the working class of the industrial towns, already tinged with leveling doctrines from fermenting Europe.

As the cohorts of the new democracy marched in serried ranks upon the government, they inevitably modified the spirit and practice of American politics. First of all, they criticized the method of electing the President. Shrinking from the hubbub of popular agitations, the Fathers had sought to remove the choice of the chief magistrate as far as possible from the passions of the multitude; though impressed by the difficulties of the task they hoped to introduce a quiet, dignified procedure about as decorous as the selection of a college rector by a board of clerical trustees. To attain their end, they provided that the President of the United States and also the Vice-President should be carefully chosen by a small body of electors selected as the legislatures of the states might decide.

Given this choice, the legislatures, naturally greedy for power, proceeded to exercise the right themselves; but before long the new democracy was thundering at their doors, demanding the transfer of that sovereign prerogative to the voters at the polls. Slowly but surely the managers of politics yielded to the cry for the popular choice of the President; in 1824 only six states still allowed the legislatures to choose the presidential electors and eight years later but a single state, South Carolina, clung to the original mode. One of the great safeguards against the tyranny of majorities was now submerged in the tossing waves of democracy.

Yet the all-devouring populace was by no means satisfied with this gain, for the nomination of party candidates for President was still in the control of a small body of politicians known as the "congressional caucus." After the country divided into two parties, it became necessary for each of them to select its candidate in advance of the election; but of course the rank and file of its personnel could not assemble for that purpose in one forum, travel being tedious and expensive even for exalted officers. Accordingly the party members in Congress simply took upon themselves the high function. When the season for choosing the presidential candidate approached, the congressmen of each party met in caucus behind closed doors and agreed upon the dignitary to be put before the people. While the election of President and Vice-President was passing into popular control, the choice of candidates thus remained in the grip of a few managers in Washington.

To the new democracy this situation was intolerable and a roar of protest went up against it. In 1824, on the refusal of "old King Caucus" to nominate General Andrew Jackson, such a clatter was raised that never again did members of Congress dare officially to select the people's candidates for them. When the campaign of 1832 came around, there was substituted for the caucus an institution known as the nominating convention, an extra-legal party conference composed of faithful delegates chosen by local assemblies of loyal partisans. To be sure. Senators and Representatives were always prominent in the convention but they were now faced by hundreds of party agents "fresh from the people," as Jackson was wont to say.

In fact, the grand convention was mainly ruled by officeholders and aspirants for office. While the election of the President was vested in the people legally, the choice of candidates, in fact, passed from the congressional monopoly to professional politicians at large. This transfer was noted by many eminent observers, especially by those who failed to win a nomination; and soon the convention was denounced in the vivid terms formerly applied to the caucus. Nevertheless, the new party institution took root and flourished; by 1840 it seemed as rigidly fixed as the Constitution itself. It also became at the same time the accepted organ of party operation in the lower ranges of state and county politics. Men who refused to abide by its decisions were anathematized and treated like social pariahs.

The profits as well as the powers of public office now became objects of interest to the new democracy. "To the victors belong the spoils," a slogan of New York politicians, was elevated to the dignity of a national principle in the age of Andrew Jackson. And yet it would be a mistake to assume that the doctrine was a product of the period. To the statesmen of ancient Rome the emoluments of office and the plunder of the provinces were matters of prime concern; the hands of the righteous Cicero were far from spotless. The government of England in the era of the Georges was an immense aggregation of sinecures and profitable positions, the impeccable Pitt having his Newcastle to distribute pelf among the beggars of the better sort that swarmed around Parliament.

In colonial America, contests over lucrative posts filled official circles with petty rackets; the thrifty Franklin made the most of his opportunity as royal postmaster-general of America. Once independence was established, there were problems of statecraft to be considered. Even the virtuous Washington, placed by a sense of honor and private fortune above jobbery in public offices, could not ignore its function in party management. In making his first appointments, he was careful to choose friends rather than enemies of the new Constitution, although he occasionally tried to clip the wings of especially dangerous critics by giving them places in the administration; and, taught by experience the perils of doubters in his own household, he finally vowed that he would henceforth select only well-disposed persons for office, on the highly defensible theory that no government can rely on its foes for success. Jefferson was equally careful, when removals, resignations, and death occurred, to make selections with reference to party loyalty.

This practice the labor and agrarian democracy which later swept into power merely amplified by ousting a larger proportion of office-holders and by avowing more frankly that the sweets of place were among the joys of victory. To this doctrine, they added another, namely, rotation in office, demanding that terms be short so that more party workers could share in the delights of conquest. The bucolic openly admitted the purpose; while the sophisticated argued that long tenure made officers lazy, bureaucratic, and tyrannical.

In either form the new gospel weighed heavily with farmers who seldom saw as much as a hundred dollars cash in the course of a whole year and with mechanics who labored at the bench or forge for seventy-five cents a day. To them a chance at the public "trough," as the phrase ran in gross colloquialism, was to be welcomed gratefully on any axiom of ethics. Indeed, it was often difficult to distinguish, except in mathematical terms, between those who suffered from the taint of vulgarity in office-seeking and those who united public emoluments and private retainers in the higher ranges of the public service. Whatever the niceties of the occasion required, it was clear to all that the advent of the farmer-labor democracy was bound to work changes in the more decorous proceedings handed down from the Fathers.

The flow of time in which occurred these modifications in American political life carried off the heroic figures of the Revolution and left the race to the fleet men of a new generation. Washington died in 1799, still "first in the hearts of his countrymen," as Light Horse Harry Lee said in the funeral oration. Patrick Henry had already gone to his long home; Samuel Adams was soon to follow. In 1804, Alexander Hamilton, in the prime of life, was shot in a duel by Aaron Burr. John Adams and Thomas Jefferson, old and bent under the weight of years, trudged on in the dusty way until 1826, when they died within a few hours of each other on July 4, reconciled and at peace. Charles Carroll, last surviving signer of the Declaration of Independence, lived to turn the first sod for the Baltimore and Ohio Railway on July 4, 1828, and to see with dimmed eyes the outlines of a progressive future; but in four years he too was no more. James Madison, philosopher of the Constitution, kept up the good fight long enough to write a ringing protest against nullification in South Carolina; then death carried him off at the ripe old age of eighty-five.

When the election of 1824 arrived, there was no Father of the republic, in the vigor of manhood and crowned with the halo of a romantic age, able to take up the office laid down by Colonel Monroe. Time as ever was ruthless. The Virginia succession had come to an end. Even the Federalist party, founded by Hamilton and Washington, was out of the field—or rather incorporated as a disturbing factor in the all-embracing Republican party of Jefferson. The "era of good feeling" was closing;

buried or concealed hatreds were reviving. New men, looking to the future rather than to the past, were jostling one another for place and power in the forum, but none stood out head and shoulders above the others as the inevitable successor to Monroe.

Puzzled by this state of affairs, the congressional caucus nominated for the presidency W. H. Crawford of Georgia, a man of ability but not a commanding personality. Its decree was in regular form but it could not be enforced because, forsooth, three other candidates insisted on entering the lists. John Quincy Adams, son of the second President, regarded himself as heir apparent in virtue of his services as Secretary of State; while the frontier brought its hard fist down on the political table with emphasis, announcing the rights of Henry Clay of Kentucky and Andrew Jackson of Tennessee. "The wild men of the Mississippi region" could not be ignored but fortune postponed their mastery.

So divided were the returns from the polls that no one of the four had a majority of the presidential electors as required by the Constitution; Jackson stood at the top, Clay at the bottom. From this it followed that the election was thrown into the House of Representatives, where each state could cast only one vote—the vote of its delegation—and men elected in calmer days held the floor under the leadership of Clay as Speaker. Upon the trained ears of the old political dynasty, the cries of Jackson's hordes swarming into the lobbies sounded like the voices of willful fanatics. Bent on defeating them at all costs, Clay, whose small number of votes left him outside the pale, threw his strength heavily to the right and by skillful management won the presidency for Adams with the office of Secretary of State for himself, perhaps, as alleged, quite accidentally.

Though the roaring flood of the new democracy was now foaming perilously near the crest, the great dike of proscriptive rights still held, for Adams could no doubt give to the government the tone of the old régime. He called himself a Republican in politics, having turned against the Federalists and affiliated with the Jeffersonians in the days when the latter were regarded by the New England aristocracy as "a Jacobinical rabble." Nevertheless, he was no horny-handed farmer, aproned mechanic, or bold Indian fighter, dear to the rising electorate of the age. Educated at Harvard and in the politest circles of Europe, Adams viewed public service as a kind of *noblesse oblige* to be kept untainted by the vulgar odors of loot and spoils—a service capable of protecting democracy by efficient administration against the inroads of the plutocracy.

Besides being out of lockstep in matter of political patronage, he was opposed to flinging western land out to impecunious members of Congress, avid speculators, and gambling farmers. Looking to the long future, he believed in preserving the public domain as a great national treasury of resources to be wisely and honestly managed with a view to revenues for roads, canals, and education in letters, arts, and sciences. Besides anticipating by nearly a hundred years some of the most enlightened measures of conservation, Adams foresaw in a livid flash the doom of slavery in a social war.

By no possible effort could he become a Jacksonian "mixer"; like his illustrious descendant, Henry Adams, he was destined to wander in space without finding rest or peace. From the beginning to the end of his administration, misfortune dogged his steps. When he appointed Clay head of the State Department, the resentment of Jackson's party broke all bounds, worshipers of "Old Hickory," seeing in the appointment conclusive proof that a "corrupt bargain" had defeated their Hero. With a feeling of righteous indignation, they began to prepare for the next election, filling Adams' four years with torment by abuse and with chagrin by gathering in his friends as they fled from the sinking ship. In a tidal wave the country repudiated Adams at the next election.

The campaign of 1828 was marked by extreme rancor—a bitterness akin to that of 1800 when the Jeffersonian hordes drove the elder Adams from power. Metropolitan newspapers, the clergy, federal office-holders, manufacturers, and bankers were in general hotly in favor of reelecting Adams; the richest planters of the Old South preferred him to Jackson, even if they had little love for a New England Puritan himself. Against this combination were aligned the farmers, particularly those burdened with poverty and debts, and the mechanics of the towns who shouted their "Hurrah for Jackson!" with a gusto.

Passions of rank and place, rather than definite issues, divided the two factions and in the mad scramble for power both resorted to billingsgate of the most finished quality. Though garbed in the mantle of respectability, the Adams faction pictured Jackson, to use the terse summary of a recent historian, Claude Bowers, "as a usurper, an adulterer, a gambler, a cock-fighter, a brawler, a drunkard, and a murderer." It also turned on his wife, its national campaign committee even sinking so low as to send out bales of pamphlets attacking the moral character of his "dear Rachel" who, although she did smoke a pipe, was a woman of exemplary life. In this unsavory game, Jackson's faction, determined not to be outdone, portrayed Adams as a stingy Puritan, an aristocrat who hated the people, a corruptionist who had bought his own election, and a waster of the people's money on White House decorations; and accused Clay of managing Adams' campaign "like a shyster, pettifogging in a bastard suit before a country squire."

When the smoke of the fray had lifted, it was found that Adams had won nothing but the electoral votes of New England and not even all those; whereas Jackson had carried the rest of the Union, making an absolutely clean sweep in the South and West. The collapse of the

Adams party was terrible to behold. Gentlemen and grand dames of the old order, like the immigrant nobles and ladies of France fleeing from the sansculottes of Paris, could discover no consolation in their grief.

On March 4, 1829, a son of the soil rode into Washington to take the oath of office. All the Presidents before Andrew Jackson had come from families that possessed property and its cultural accompaniments. None had been compelled to work with his hands for a livelihood; all except Washington had received a college education. Jackson, on the other hand, born of poverty-stricken parents in the uplands of South Carolina, was of the earth earthy. It is not even known just how or when he got the barest rudiments of learning but it is certain that to the end of his life his language, if forceful and direct, was characterized by grammar strangely and wonderfully constructed.

In his youth Jackson had gone to the Tennessee frontier where, as a land speculator, horse trader, politician, and rural genius in general, he managed to amass a large estate and a goodly number of slaves. Tall and sinewy, he loved wrestling matches, fist fights, and personal quarrels. By way of settling one dispute, he killed a man in a duel and ever afterward treasured the pistol that performed the deed as a trophy to show his visitors. In an awful brawl with the Benton brothers, he himself received a bullet which remained imbedded in his flesh for many years as evidence of his hardihood. Whenever an Indian fight occurred in his neighborhood, he rushed to the front.

Elevated to the leadership of the local militia by his undoubted courage, Jackson won the passionate devotion of his men by sharing their hardships and perils. Already a local hero, he had leaped into national fame in 1815 by defeating a blundering and incompetent British general at the battle of New Orleans. Finally, he had added more laurels by wresting Florida from Spain, summarily hanging two English subjects, and stamping out warlike Indians on the border.

This son of the soil, transformed in the eyes of his devotees into a military figure comparable to Napoleon the Great, furnished excellent presidential timber for the new democracy. That his views on the tariff, internal improvements, and other current issues were nebulous in no way detracted from his immense and irresistible availability. He was from the West. He was a farmer—a slave owner, no doubt, but still a farmer. He had none of the unction that marked the politicians of the seaboard school and the mechanics could think of him as one of themselves.

Jackson's opponents, of course, sneered because he was rough in manner, smoked an old pipe, chewed tobacco profusely, told stories that could not be printed, loafed around with a week's bristles on his face, and wore soiled clothes. John Quincy Adams, who knew Jackson well, could hardly suppress his anguish when Harvard gave "the brawler from Tennessee" the degree of doctor of laws. It was not a pure accident that Jackson's chief regret at the end of his presidential course was "that he had never had an opportunity to shoot Clay or hang Calhoun." But the contempt of his enemies only endeared him the more to the masses, especially as all charges were discreetly counterbalanced by news that he regularly read the Bible, recited countless lines of Watts' doleful hymns, and asked the blessing at the table. Moreover, those who saw him dressed in his best, with his pipe and plug laid aside, bowing in his courtliest manner, concluded that the discreditable tales about him were partisan falsehoods.

When the day of Jackson's inauguration came, the city of Washington was jammed with crowds. From near and far thousands of his devoted followers had come to witness the spectacle—and in many cases to get jobs in the new administration. All the decorum of former days was rudely broken. Bowing right and left to cheering throngs, Jackson and his party walked from his hotel to the inaugural ceremonies. After taking the oath of office, he rode in his best military style down the Avenue to the White House, followed by a surging sea of worshippers.

On his arrival at the presidential residence the doors were thrown open to everybody and, if Webster is to be accepted as authority, the pushing idolators behaved like hoodlums, upsetting the punch bowls, breaking glasses, and standing in muddy boots on damask chairs to catch a glimpse of the people's Napoleon. "The reign of King Mob seemed triumphant," groaned Justice Story of the Supreme Court. Recalling the refinements of Jefferson, Mrs. Margaret Bayard Smith, a leader in the local social set, held her nose and wrote: "The noisy and disorderly rabble . . . brought to my mind descriptions I have read of the mobs in the Tuileries and at Versailles."

With utmost dispatch the business of government—and dividing the spoils—was begun. To aid him in the operation, Jackson chose two cabinets. The first, composed of the heads of departments, was filled with men of fair talent and some distinction; many a worse ministry has been assembled since. The second, known as the "Kitchen Cabinet," was made up of Isaac Hill, Amos Kendall, and other private advisers, who served as a collective agency to keep the king informed about the gossip of the capital and to keep the masses in good humor with news meet for their understanding.

As soon as the chiefs were installed, a survey of the gentlemen in federal berths commenced. "No damn rascal who made use of an office or its profits for the purpose of keeping Mr. Adams in or General Jackson out of power is entitled to the least leniency save that of hanging," wrote one of the President's applicants. "You may say to all our anxious

Adamsites that the Barnacles will be scraped clean off the Ship of State," declared a member of the kitchen sanhedrin. "Most of them have grown so large and stick so tight that the scraping process will doubtless be fatal to them."

Though the threats were terrifying, in fact the slaughter of the innocents was not as great as the opposition alleged. Indeed, many got only their just deserts; some of the tenants were found to be scoundrels, prosecuted, and convicted for fraudulent transactions while public servants, one of the "martyrs," a personal friend of Adams, being sent to prison for stealing from the Treasury. No doubt hundreds of old and faithful officers were ousted; but on the other hand hundreds were allowed to retain their places in spite of the severe pressure from the Jackson followers, begging for jobs.

It is therefore due to the memory of the President to say that, like Clive in India, he had reason to be proud of his moderation. To this judgment must be quickly joined the statement that Jackson started the custom of making wholesale removals in favor of party workers, giving high national sanction to the practice of bestowing the spoils upon the victors. A few intellectuals, such as James Russell Lowell, soon poured ridicule upon the system; many statesmen, especially those who had never had occasion to make use of it, denounced it; yet as time passed that form of political etiquette became more and more prevalent, hardening into prescription.

In addition to scraping barnacles from the Ship of State, Jackson gave energetic consideration to the political issues of the hour: the tariff, nullification, the Bank, internal improvements, and the disposal of western lands. All these questions were economic in character, presenting new phases of the struggle that had produced the colonial revolt against Great Britain, the reaction under Hamilton, and the swing to Jefferson. And their management involved the fortunes of the three marked sections into which the country was divided—the capitalistic Northeast, the planting South, and the farming regions beyond the seaboard—with the mechanics of the towns coming into the play whenever the aristocracy of wealth and talents was to be pommeled.

Each section had an outstanding champion who sought to make congressional combinations of power in the interest of his constituents. Daniel Webster, as Fisher, his biographer, tells us, was "the hope and reliance of the moneyed and conservative classes, the merchants, manufacturers, capitalists, and bankers." John C. Calhoun acted frankly as the mouthpiece of the planting aristocracy; he acknowledged it and was proud of it. Thomas Hart Benton of Missouri was the shouting spokesman of the western farmers and land speculators who were struggling to wrench the public domain from the grip of the government.

Happily placed between extremes, North and South, Henry Clay labored to construct a platform that would command the support of the eastern capitalists and the western farmers, unite hearts and make him President; but he failed to accomplish his design.

Into the lists Jackson entered as gladiator-at-large for the masses against the moneyed classes, declaring that the agricultural interest was "superior in importance" to all others and placing himself, as he said, at the head of "the humbler members of society—the farmers, mechanics, and laborers who have neither the time nor the means" of securing special favors for themselves. They heard him gladly and thought him their Sir Galahad.

If the tariff and land questions had stood alone, the Northeast and the West might have found it easier to draw together in 1830, but the old banking and currency issue that had plagued America since the days of George III was once more to the front in a virulent form. The second United States Bank, chartered for twenty years in 1816 to enable the Jeffersonians to finance their war, was becoming in the minds of western farmers and eastern mechanics the very citadel of tyrannical money power.

Radical Democrats had denounced it on principle from the beginning and their attacks steadily increased in animosity. Others acquired their views from practice. The notes of the Bank, sound throughout the Union, drove from circulation the paper currency of shaky institutions chartered by state politicians, thus inflaming village statesmen with anger against the "rich and well-born." Its managers were accused of showing favoritism to friendly politicians and of discriminating against the followers of Jackson in making loans; indeed a "psychic injury" of this character, alleged to have been inflicted on one of the President's friends, seems to have been the original source of his special rage against the Bank. The managers were likewise charged with using their power to contract the currency for the purpose of punishing their enemies, with giving retainers to some of their orators in Congress, and with spending corporate funds for campaign purposes. So the natural hostility of the masses to the plutocracy was intensified by dark and sinister rumors about a new "corrupt squadron."

That many of the charges against the Bank were groundless was later revealed by historical research. If some of Jackson's men were denied loans for business reasons, it was never proved that discriminations were made against Democratic politicians merely on account of their doctrinal views. If the Bank refused to be used by the brokers in spoils, its motive was economic rather than partisan. In the beginning at least, its president, Nicholas Biddle, it seems, tried to steer his way "on sound business lines" through the maze of politics.

After the war on the Bank commenced, however, both he and his colleagues laid hold of the various weapons at hand. From that time forward, the allegation that members of Congress received retainers from the Bank certainly rested on a substantial basis. In any case its mightiest spokesman in the Senate, Daniel Webster, was on the payroll of the corporation, a fact made clear in distant days by the publication of Biddle's letters and papers. In those documents it is recorded that, two weeks after the opening of a congressional session in which a battle royal was to be fought over its charter, Webster wrote to Biddle, shrewdly conveying the information that he had declined to take a case against the Bank and adding with charming frankness: "I believe my retainer has not been renewed or refreshed as usual. If it be wished that my relation to the bank should be continued, it may be well to send me the usual retainers."

Equally well established now is the charge that the Bank contracted its loans for the purpose of producing distress and breaking the back of the political opposition. Beyond all question, in the midst of the contest a term of financial stringency was deliberately inflicted on the country; Biddle, sure of his ground, declaring to the head of the Boston branch that "nothing but the evidence of suffering abroad will produce any effect in Congress." Webster himself, convinced that pressure on the populace would be useful, wrote to Biddle that "this discipline, it appears to me, must have very great effects on the general question of rechartering the Bank."

In fact, the private correspondence of the period now open to the student shows that the supporters and beneficiaries of the Bank had effected a strong union of forces for the purpose of controlling a large section of the press, dictating to politicians, frightening indifferent business men, and defying Jackson and his masses. "This worthy President," laughed Biddle, "thinks that because he has scalped Indians and imprisoned Judges, he is to have his way with the Bank. He is mistaken."

Pride was, nevertheless, riding for a fall. Jackson's anger, once aroused, was terrible to behold; it was the anger of the warrior rushing on his foe heedless of wounds and death, not the cold and calculating wrath of the counting house. Moreover, he had behind him the accumulating discontent of the agrarian and labor elements in the new democracy—an unrest which he steadily fanned into flame by very clever tactics. In his first message to Congress, Jackson attacked the Bank openly but not with might and main. In his second and third messages, he deftly referred to the subject, warily leaving the decision to "an enlightened people and their representatives."

If the opposition had maintained a discreet silence, a clash might have been avoided; but, boasting of its wisdom, it chose another course. The Bank was uneasy about the future: and Clay, sniffing the presidential air in 1832, decided to make an issue of it then and there. Though its charter had four more years to run, the Bank applied for a renewal and Congress, under the leadership of Clay, passed the bill granting the petition.

Jackson's reply to this defiance was a veto and a ringing message calling on the masses to support his position. Paying his respects to high sentiments, he took his stand by the Ark of the Covenant, declaring the Bank unconstitutional. Knowing full well that the Supreme Court had held otherwise a few years before, Jackson countered this uncomfortable verdict with the bald statement that each officer took the oath to support the Constitution as he understood it, not as it was understood by others— a doctrine that probably set all aged gentlemen in horsehair and robes trembling for the future of their country, while pleasing Old Hickory's followers immensely.

Having paid his homage to the auspices, Jackson got down to the meat of the matter: the alignment of economic forces. He called attention to the fact that the people of the western and southwestern states held only $140,000 worth of the twenty-eight millions of capital stock outstanding in private hands, whereas the capitalists of the middle and eastern states held more than thirteen millions. He pointed out that, of the annual profits of the Bank, $1,640,000 came from nine western states where little or none of the stock was held.

The moral lesson was obvious. It was an economic conflict that happened to take a sectional form: the people of the agricultural West had to pay tribute to eastern and foreign capitalists on the money they had borrowed to buy land, make improvements, and engage in speculation. Jackson did not shrink from naming the contestants. "The rich and powerful" were bending the acts of the government to their selfish purposes; the rich were growing richer under special privilege; "many of our rich men . . . have besought us to make them richer by acts of Congress. By attempting to gratify their desires, we have in the results of our legislation arrayed section against section, interest against interest, and man against man, in a fearful commotion which threatens to shake the foundations of our Union."

That was indeed a call to arms. The head of the Bank, Biddle, declared himself delighted with it. "It has all the fury of the unchained panther, biting the bars of his cage. It is really a manifesto of anarchy, such as Marat and Robespierre might have issued to the mob." The President's cheer leaders threw up their hats with sheer joy at the spectacle. Western farmers had been charged with seeking to avoid their honest debts; they had replied by asserting that the money they borrowed had been made by the printing presses of the Bank under government authority. Now Jackson embodied their theories and vehemence in a message. If there was any frosty philosopher present, looking serenely upon the battle, he has left us no memoirs.

In the election of 1832, after a campaign of unrestrained emotions, Jackson completely discomfited his opponent, Clay, and returned to the White House like a Roman conqueror with his victims at his chariot. The Bank had fought him; thinking in terms of war, the President proceeded to fight back. Its charter had four years of legal life remaining; the law could not be repealed by military decree; so other means of attack were found. Acting as head of the administration, Jackson ordered the Secretary of the Treasury to deposit no more federal revenues in the Bank or any of its branches and to withdraw in the payment of bills the government's cash already in its vaults. Besides this he distributed the national funds among state banks, remembering to reward those which had correct political affiliations—institutions which became known as "pet banks." As the treasury surplus happened to be mounting, Congress, now in Democratic hands, got rid of it by spreading the money among the state governments, nominally in the form of loans, practically in the shape of gifts.

In 1836 the second United States Bank automatically came to the end of its checkered career and the country under the inspiration of the new democracy entered an epoch of "wild cat" finance. The very next year, a terrible business depression fell like a blight upon the land, bringing as usual more suffering to farmers and mechanics than to the "rich and well-born"; but this calamity was likewise attributed by the masses to the machinations of the money power rather than to the conduct of their hero, President Jackson. Nothing would induce them to retrace their steps. For three decades a union of the South and West prevented a restoration of the centralized banking system. Not until the planting statesmen withdrew from Congress and the storm of the Civil War swept minor gusts before it were the ravages wrought by Jackson repaired by the directors of affairs in Washington.

The economic policies and personal conduct of Jackson split wide the Republican party of Jefferson and put a sudden term to the era of good feeling. No President had ever exercised such high perogatives as Jackson or shown so little consideration for the feelings of those who came under executive displeasure. Besides keeping the entire body of minor civil servants in constant terror of reprimand and dismissal, he treated his own Cabinet with scant courtesy, while deciding vital questions himself or with the advice of his backstairs coterie. When one Secretary of the Treasury refused to remove the deposits from the Bank on executive order, Jackson summarily appointed another; when the second also declined to be a mere tool, he chose a third, who finally did his bidding with the alacrity of an errand boy. Angered by a protest lodged by the Senate against his arbitrary conduct, Jackson made his followers force through a measure expunging the hated resolution, one of the lieutenants in flushed exultation blotting the censure from the records. Unawed by the majesty of the Supreme Court, Jackson treated the decisions of Chief Justice Marshall with little respect; and when death eventually removed that distinguished judge from the bench, the President put in Marshall's place Roger B. Taney, an able and astute politician who was known to favor state banking.

In faithful accord with the law of antithesis, the personality and measures of Jackson summoned into being an angry, if motley, opposition. His assault on the Bank aroused the undying hatred of high finance. His approval of a tariff that meant ultimately a material reduction in the protective features set most of the manufacturers fiercely against him. His efforts to stir up "the humble members of society—farmers, mechanics, and laborers," to repeat his phrase—against the "rich and powerful" had worried thousands of prosperous people in the South, especially cautious planters who thought they had as much to fear from the leveling passions of small farmers in the back country as from the tariffs of New England mill owners. In South Carolina they had an additional reason for opposing Jackson for he had talked in a high and mighty fashion of suppressing "insurrection" and hanging "traitors."

Here then were the elements for a powerful political combination if some process of welding could be discovered. Doubtless Jackson's enemies owned the major portion of the working capital of the country. Certainly they commanded oratory and ingenuity; but, as yet united merely by common antipathy to the President and his party—by the timidity of property in the presence of unfathomable dangers—they presented no solid array for a political contest. Only statecraft of the highest order could amalgamate nullifiers and nationalists, protectionists and free traders, planters and manufacturers into a working association. Only skill in appealing to popular imagination could convince the mass of voters that the great hope could be realized at last.

Nevertheless the task was worth while for many reasons and Henry Clay of Kentucky seemed fated for leadership in the undertaking. All things considered, Clay had several kinds of availability: he was from the West and so could invade Jackson's home province; he was favorably known among the manufacturers and financiers of the East but, unlike Webster, was not charged with being the pet and pensioner of capitalists. Though a facile speaker, he had not hopelessly committed himself in his school days to the ponderous periods of Cicero; while he could at times soar to the empyrean, he was always able to talk to the public in the vernacular.

Taking the title abandoned by Jackson, opponents of that popular hero called themselves "National Republicans" and later "Whigs," for short, after the manner of the English adversaries of royal prerogative. In 1832, with Clay at their head, they tried to oust the President by employing all the approved methods of politics, including propaganda and social terrorism.

In an imposing phalanx, they marshaled most of the middle classes—friends of the national bank, advocates of sound money, lawyers, merchants, manufacturers, businessmen of the higher ranges, and college professors. Managers of the Bank subsidized the press by large payments for advertising. Mill owners threatened workmen with dismissal in case Jackson was elected. A packer in Cincinnati told the farmers that he would pay $2.50 a hundred for pork if Clay was victorious and a dollar less if his opponent, the Democratic President, was returned to power in Washington.

And purists attacked Jackson in their especial field. Since his system of theology was about as nebulous as his politics, they charged him with irreligion. They accused him of beginning a long journey from the Hermitage on a Sabbath and he only escaped the serious censure of the virtuous by showing that he really started on Monday. When he declined to proclaim a day of prayer for relief from the cholera, suggesting instead that under the Constitution it was a matter for the states to decide, Clay pounced upon him for his impiety and moved a resolution in the Senate to name the day for the appeal to God. During the campaign the voters were not allowed to forget that impiety and unsound finance went hand in hand. And still all the legions and all the artillery could not defeat the hero of New Orleans.

After ruling the country with an iron hand for eight years, supported by the acclaim of the masses, Jackson naturally regarded the choice of his successor as a part of his sovereign prerogative. Indeed at the opening of his first administration, he had made it known discreetly that he wanted his Secretary of State, Martin Van Buren of New York, to take his place when he left the White House. Obedient to his lightest wish, his kitchen companions bent their efforts to the task of securing the throne for the "crown prince" and their labors were successful.

In a well-selected convention, "fresh from the people," they nominated Van Buren as the party candidate for the presidential election of 1836. By this time the Jacksonians had discarded the safe old title of Republican, chosen by Jefferson, and had taken instead the flaunting label, "Democrat"—a word that once had grated as harshly on urbane ears as its constant companion, "anarchist." Subject to the law of familiarity, the insignia that had frightened grand gentlemen and fine ladies of the heroic days had become a household emblem; men who shrank from it with horror two decades before now wore it proudly on their shields.

Though they had in Van Buren a less formidable candidate to face, the Whigs, failing to unite on a single leader, went down to defeat. But just when everything seemed hopeless, the tide turned. The victorious President fell into a series of misfortunes that gave heart to his enemies. On the threshold of his administration, he encountered a disastrous business panic, the wild tumult of speculation and inflation ending in an explosion. While Jackson's war on high finance had doubtless hastened the inexorable, it was not the sole cause of the crash.

The fact was that one of the periodic cycles of capitalism was at hand and the party in power at Washington could offer no effective remedies, if any there were. On the contrary, it accelerated the ruinous process by repealing the law which provided for the distribution of surplus federal revenues among the state treasuries and by issuing the specie circular which directed federal officers to accept only gold and silver, save in certain cases, in payment for public lands. Having taken these precautions in the interest of its credit, the government simply allowed the winds to blow. Hundreds of banks failed; mills were shut down; work on canals and railways was stopped; thousands of laboring people were turned into the streets; federal revenues fell until a deficit supplanted a surplus; land sales dropped off; and speculation came to a standstill.

Throughout this panic President Van Buren maintained a kind of academic composure. As the leader of Jacksonian Democracy, he could do nothing that would please business men and financiers anyway; and his party had no constructive plan of its own. He, therefore, contented himself with urging the establishment of an independent treasury to receive and guard the funds of the federal government—a simple project of doubtful merit which Congress, after three years of discussion, finally adopted in 1840.

At that moment another presidential campaign was at hand. Whigs were making ready to restore Hamilton's system of economy; and Democrats to destroy the last vestiges of the "money power." Astute Whig leaders, counting heads, saw that they would have to be clever if they were to overcome the multitudinous Jacksonian host made up of farmers and mechanics with some of the planters in the vanguard. Accordingly they exercised the wisdom of serpents. They cast aside Clay, whose views on the Bank, tariff, and other economic questions were too well known and beat the Democrats at their own game, by themselves nominating a western farmer and military hero, General William Henry Harrison.

This man of Mars was, of course, no Napoleon comparable to the great Jackson of New Orleans, but he had beaten some Indians at the battle of Tippecanoe and had served with honor in the War of 1812. More than that, at the close of his military career, he had pleased western agrarians by settling down in a modest home in Ohio. To make his appeal perfect in the eyes of Whig managers, Harrison's political opinions were so hazy that no one could be alienated by them.

It was with an eye to such qualifications for the presidency that the shrewd Biddle, tutored by his experience with Jackson, gave sound direction to party managers in this style: "If Genl. Harrison is taken up as a candidate, it will be on account of the past. . . . Let him say not one single word about his principles, or his creed—let him say nothing— promise nothing. Let no Committee, no convention—no town meeting ever extract from him a single word about what he thinks now or will do hereafter. Let the use of pen and ink be wholly forbidden."

Conjuring with this spirit, the Whigs of 1840 refused to frame any platform of principles, and simply offered General Harrison to the country as a man of the people while they attacked Van Buren as an eastern aristocrat. In this fashion the tables were reversed: the old party of Tiberius Gracchus was trying to elect a patrician from New York, whereas the party of the rich and well-born was trying to elevate a Cincinnatus straight from the furrow.

Given these factors, the campaign of 1840 was naturally exuberant. Sobered by the possession of power and led by a man who loved good wine and old silver, symbols of aristocracy, Democrats softened their former raucous campaign cries. But the Whigs, made desperate by two defeats, took up the discarded tactics of their opponents. As a party they adopted no policies, avowed no doctrines. Carlyle's "magnificent" Webster assumed the fustian of the demagogue, announcing that he was ready to engage in a fist-fight with anyone who dubbed him an aristocrat, ex- pressing deep regret that he too had not been born in a log cabin, and rejoicing that his older brothers and sisters had begun their lives in such a humble abode. "If I am ever ashamed of it," he boasted, "may my name and the name of my posterity be blotted from the memory of mankind!" That fastidious New York lawyer, William H. Seward, rode ostentatiously about in an old green farm wagon making speeches at crossroads villages on the superlative merits of the hero of Tippecanoe. The rank and file erected in every town of importance log cabins from which hard cider was served in copious draughts to stimulate the enthusiasm of the voters.

Before gaping crowds, Whig orators berated Van Buren as a man addicted to high living and lordly manners, alleging that he even put cologne on his whiskers and was liable to die of the gout before the end of his term, if elected. They accused him of eating from gold plate and declared that he "laced up in corsets such as women in town wear and if possible tighter than the best of them."

Having summarily disposed of Van Buren, the showmen then presented to the enfranchised their own candidate, General Harrison, as a noble old Roman of the West who lived in a hut, worked with his own hands in the field and barn, and left his latchstring out hospitably for the wayfaring man. "We've tried your purse-proud lords who love in palaces to shine," they sang. "But we'll have a ploughman President of the Cincinnatus line."

Probably this buffoonery was distasteful to the staid and respectable Whigs of the East. In any event, since it was not as unplatable as a low tariff and an unsound currency, they swallowed the medicine of the campaign in the hope of better times after the election. What else could they do? Whatever their pains, the returns from the polls afforded them abundant consolation. Harrison won 234 electoral votes while Van Buren limped in with sixty.

After carrying the country in a dust storm, the Whig leaders soon revealed their inmost desires. If Harrison had not died shortly after his inauguration leaving his high office to the Vice President, John Tyler, they might have gone far on the way toward a restoration of the Hamilton system. At any rate, with the aid of protectionist Democrats speaking for special constituencies, they were able to push through the tariff act of 1842 raising the customs duties and destroying the compromise measure enacted nine years before. And, had no factional disputes intervened, they might have established a third United States Bank then and there.

Unfortunately for all designs veering in that direction, their two high captains, Tyler in the White House and Clay in the Senate, were looking beyond immediate results to their own possibilities in the coming election. The President, a Virginia man originally taken up by the Whigs to catch southern votes, knew very well how unpalatable were Hamilton's doctrines below the Potomac and he would only approve a national bank of restricted powers. On the other hand, Clay, long associated with financial interests in a practical way, deluded himself into believing that the country was ready for something more thorough. Neither one of the contestants, therefore, did his best to bring about an accommodation; a fight seemed better to them than a truce. So Tyler vetoed two bank bills in succession and Clay, turning back to the tactics of 1832, proposed to submit the issue to the voters at the polls.

As in the first instance, the solemn referendum of 1844 ended in the discomfiture of those who proposed it. Once more the shout of the

Democratic masses rose to heaven against "the money power." Its machinations, they alleged, were more tyrannical than ever, citing for proof the increase in tariff duties and the effort to revive the hated Bank. In addition they drew attention to an attempt made in Congress in 1843 to force upon the federal government the assumption of bonds repudiated by a number of states in the late general panic. Though this scheme was not successful, as everybody knew, it furnished to the rural mind conclusive evidence that eastern capitalists and English creditors were trying to make the whole nation pay debts which it had not contracted.

Furthermore, the Whigs were compelled to bear the brunt of a damaging attack on the score that their English sympathies were as strong as those of the Federalists half a century earlier. In 1842 Webster, as Secretary of State, they were reminded, had negotiated with Lord Ashburton, representing England, an agreement relative to the long-disputed boundary of Maine in which he surrendered to Great Britain a large section of land that, under the treaty of 1783 closing the war for independence, appeared to belong to the United States. In spite of the fact that this concession seemed to be the only alternative to war or continual quarreling, the American public was not at all happy with the outcome and Webster felt it necessary to sweeten the pill by spending some money out of the secret service funds of his department to carry on a favorable propaganda through the religious press of Maine. Though the treaty was eventually ratified, it was roundly condemned by discontented Democrats, and especially by the doughty old warrior, Benton, who called it "a shame and an injury"—"a solemn bamboozlement." When the use of public money in creating opinion for the support of the treaty became known through a congressional investigation, the wrath of the Democrats burst all bounds.

An accumulation of forces was certainly menacing the Whigs when the campaign of 1844 approached. Yet, determined to face the economic issues more firmly than in the previous contest, they nominated Clay— a threat which the Democrats answered by choosing as their candidate a friend and neighbor of Jackson, James K. Polk of Tennessee. In the referendum so clearly put the verdict of the voters was emphatic. The party of the Bank, sound money, and high protection was thoroughly routed, in a sweep as decisive as that of 1800 which ousted the Federalists from the national capital. Spokesmen of the planting aristocracy, now alarmed by slavery agitation and deeply concerned over the fate of Texas, were beginning to comprehend that they had more to hope from leadership in a democracy of farmers, mechanics, and laborers in general, than from coöperation with the elements that composed the Whig party in the North.

On the other hand, the Whigs themselves were made dimly aware that the balance of power was shifting into western hands; but it took more defeats to convince them that they could not destroy their foes with Hamilton's weapons alone. Not until 1860 were they able to make an effective union with the western farmers under the traditional name of Republican—the name which Jefferson had chosen in the early days of his party's history and Clay had approved when in 1832 he had christened the Federalist faction anew.

4

new sources and
new interpretations

As we have noted in chapter 1, students of contemporary political behavior—political scientists, sociologists, and psychologists—have elaborated several ways of analyzing popular voting systematically. They have
polled individual voters, collected detailed election returns, and correlated both kinds of data with other information, particularly demographic statistics describing the electorate. From this they have proceeded
to explain the outcome of any single election and to develop a number
of propositions about the general nature of electoral behavior.

Historians of Jacksonian politics have adapted these interdisciplinary
methods and findings to their own purposes. They have read widely in
the literature of contemporary electoral analysis for insight into the
range of factors potentially affecting political choice. They have developed from this a number of propositions about voting behavior that
they can test against their own evidence from the Jacksonian period.
Most of all, however, they have focused on improving their data. They
have carefully collected the election returns necessary to spell out exactly
where each party received its popular support. They have constructed
systematic time series of election results and pinpointed where and when
changes took place in the level of support for one or the other party.
Most important of all, they have related voting patterns to the characteristics of the population in order to determine the social bases of electoral
choice and political belief. In all of this their emphasis has been on moving away from their traditional reliance upon literary data and substitut-

ing precise measurement of actual behavior for informed but subjective and possibly wide-of-the-mark hunches.

For these purposes, we have had to collect a wide range of quantitative data, particularly the voting returns and socioeconomic statistics of the towns, urban wards, and counties participating in elections in the 1830s and 1840s. Unfortunately, there is a relative scarcity of historical data compared to what is available to contemporary analysts. In-depth interviewing of individual voters, the hallmark of contemporary electoral research, cannot be done. Nor is all of the useful quantitative data from the nineteenth century readily available. Much was never collected, more has disappeared. At best, the information is often difficult to locate. But there is enough hard statistical evidence at hand, particularly in census returns and in the reports of elections reprinted in newspapers, almanacs, and official documents, to enable us to make many of the measurements and correlations desired. In addition, some social data can be located in more traditional sources such as county and church histories, city directories, the occasional atlas, and a number of biographical lists. All of these play an important role in developing as comprehensive a picture as possible of a particular geographic unit or group of voters. (The material needed in this kind of systematic research is so massive, and requires so much searching out, that it has stimulated the development of large-scale data banks to collect and process the needed electoral and demographic information.)

This emphasis on interdisciplinary methods and conceptions and the collection of neglected data in order to pose new questions and resolve traditional problems has been very difficult to accomplish, but has had important results. The following pages present part of the picture of this interdisciplinary historical enterprise. The first section (Sources) includes examples of the range of quantitative data available to historians. In the "Interpretations" section are articles demonstrating how election statistics have been utilized and what social scientists think about the general nature of popular voting behavior. Finally, there are six essays presenting the results of these new attempts to understand electoral behavior and political ideology in the Jacksonian era.

A. SOURCES

Election returns

Having adequate quantities of election returns is the *sine qua non* for the quantitative analysis of American political history. Fortunately, there are a number of readily available sources for certain kinds of returns. Contemporary newspapers in every state reported the vote in each county soon after an election; the official results are often available in state historical depositories or government archives; and several almanacs published in the Jacksonian period reprinted the same data. The Inter University Consortium for Political Research at the University of

Michigan has collected and made available for research county-level returns for all elections since 1824 for specific offices (governor, congressman, and president). County-level returns such as these allow us to pinpoint a number of important matters: areas of strength for each party, the level of competition between them, and the location and extent of any changes in their voting strength between elections. In other words, the returns provide the kind of overview of voting across time that is the prerequisite for systematically determining who voted for whom and why.

But it requires more than county-level totals to answer the question, Who voted for whom, fully. Most of the time, the distribution of the vote between the parties was not the same in every subcounty electoral unit. Although more of the counties reported substantial numbers of voters for each party, the votes were rarely evenly distributed everywhere in each county. The selection included here (reporting the gubernatorial returns for New York State in 1834) provides a good picture of this condition. In Allegany County in 1834, the Whigs and Democrats each received close to 50 percent of the vote, but towns such as Almond, Andover, Birdsall, and Burns, among others, were overwhelmingly one-sided. Returns at this level are vital for our purposes, therefore, because they allow us to pinpoint for close investigation, as the county returns cannot, towns throughout a state with distinct partisan preferences. Furthermore, since most towns tended to be relatively socially homogeneous in population, whereas counties were much less so, each town's political choice can be related to its socioeconomic character as a means of measuring the importance of different demographic characteristics on particular voting patterns.

Unfortunately, an even better source, records of how each person in an area actually voted, are rarely available for the nineteenth century. There were a few voter lists compiled during the era identifying party preferences and voting habits of individuals, but not enough have survived to permit systematic investigation. We can, at best, only infer how individuals voted from the political character of the groups to which they belonged. This problem of the lack of data bedevils us at other levels too. Despite a relative wealth of such returns in some states, not all minor civil division returns still exist. States such as New York have relatively extensive records of returns, and even there not all can be located for all elections. Other states are more spotty in coverage. A few are so deficient as to make systematic analysis dependent on town-level returns impossible. Further, some of the returns, even when reported, are problems. There are contradictions in totals between newspaper reports and other sources which are not easily resolved. Minute election data, in other words, can be an elusive and frustrating source. Nevertheless, what does exist provides, to an important degree, the raw material for drawing the actual electoral map of the United States in the Jacksonian era.

5. *Election Returns reported by Towns and Wards, New York State, 1834. From Edwin Williams,* ed., Williams New York Annual Register for the Year 1836 (*New York, 1836*), *pp. 92–95.*

Towns in the state of New-York, with . . . the number of votes taken for governor at the election in November, 1834.

ALBANY COUNTY

Towns	Marcy	Seward
Albany City,		
1st ward	515	606
2d ward	442	504
3d ward	127	213
4th ward	536	499
5th ward	327	306
	1947	2128
Bern	352	368
Bethlehem	263	351
Coeymans	443	143
Guilderland	216	318
Knox	107	318
New Scotland	283	333
Rensselaerville	477	172
Watervliet	469	509
Westerlo	358	247
Tot., 10 Towns	4917	4888

ALLEGANY COUNTY

Towns	Marcy	Seward
Alfred	84	191
Allen	67	92
Almond	270	78
Amity	116	103
Andover	76	22
Angelica	149	108
Belfast	78	101
Birdsall	58	16
Bolivar	54	72
Burns	37	117
Caneadea	99	69
Centerville	81	151
Clarksville		
Cuba	116	130
Eagle	57	121
Friendship	207	110
Genesee	23	52
Grove	96	123
Haight	74	70
Hume	76	155
Independence	89	71
Nunda	99	185
Ossian	64	84
Pike	156	246
Portage	167	176
Rushford	131	96
Scio	119	28
West Almond*		
Tot., 28 Towns	2643	2767

BROOME COUNTY

Towns	Marcy	Seward
Barker	85	122
Chenango	338	412
Colesville	161	245
Conklin	92	128
Lisle	99	141
Nanticoke	33	27
Sandford	138	60
Triangle	137	135
Union	251	220
Vestal	76	99
Windsor	174	209
Tot., 11 Towns	1584	1798

CATTARAUGUS COUNTY

Towns	Marcy	Seward
Ashford	68	62
Burton	70	74
Conewango	112	77
Dayton		
Ellicottville	76	80
Farmersville	92	101
Franklinville	123	82
Freedom	56	168
Great Valley	64	57
Hinsdale	163	80
Leon	133	62
Little Valley	59	57
Lyndon	20	51
Machias	71	53
Mansfield	56	51
Napoli	113	122
New Albion	42	95
Olean	104	92
Otto	70	219
Perrysburgh	211	309
Persia		
Randolph	113	58
Yorkshire	68	104
Tot., 23 Towns	1884	2054

*Included in Almond.

Towns	Marcy	Seward
CAYUGA COUNTY		
Auburn	355	456
Aurelius	291	203
Brutus	191	186
Cato	273	105
Conquest	177	151
Fleming	136	112
Genoa	214	252
Ira	242	139
Ledyard	177	242
Locke	146	162
Mentz	451	293
Moravia	230	123
Niles	303	147
Owasco	110	90
Sempronius	149	74
Scipio	208	221
Sennet	193	164
Springport	147	183
Sterling	155	147
Summer Hill	108	157
Venice	227	222
Victory	214	123
Tot., 22 Towns	4697	3957
CHAUTAUQUE COUNTY		
Arkwright	71	131
Busti	97	263
Carroll	152	120
Charlotte	96	124
Chautauque	221	243
Cherry Creek	70	81
Clymer	51	39
Ellery	133	253
Ellicott	200	288
Ellington	122	199
French Creek	27	63
Gerry	70	161
Hanover	316	267
Harmony	121	352
Mina	77	55
Poland	56	125
Pomfret	186	503
Portland	109	226
Ripley	194	148
Sheridan	93	246
Sherman	39	85
Stockton	119	175
Villenova	98	138
Westfield	224	248
Tot., 24 Towns	2942	4533
CHENANGO COUNTY		
Bainbridge	292	259
Columbus	127	152

Towns	Marcy	Seward
Coventry	132	172
German	80	75
Greene	370	247
Guilford	293	228
Lincklaen	55	120
Macdonough	135	73
New Berlin	341	221
Norwich	481	353
Otselic	109	129
Oxford	354	228
Pharsalia	175	34
Pitcher	153	116
Plymouth	176	145
Preston	126	103
Sherburne	230	314
Smithville	184	117
Smyrna	114	254
Tot., 19 Towns	3932	3340
CLINTON COUNTY		
Beekmantown	197	89
Champlain	163	101
Chazy	212	192
Ellenburgh	51	48
Mooers	34	97
Peru	421	406
Plattsburgh	420	215
Saranac	37	53
Tot., 8 Towns	1535	1201
COLUMBIA COUNTY		
Hudson City,		
1st ward	269	300
2d ward	229	296
	498	596
Ancram	151	200
Austerlitz	204	224
Canaan	217	191
Chatham	433	240
Claverack	300	333
Clermont	147	84
Copake	153	172
Gallatin	124	208
Germantown	54	146
Ghent	225	248
Hillsdale	308	177
Kinderhook	371	217
Livingston	154	275
New Lebanon	276	153
Stockport	86	197
Stuyvesant	186	117
Taghkanick	253	86
Tot., 18 Towns	4150	3861

Towns	Marcy	Seward	Towns	Marcy	Seward
CORTLAND COUNTY			Washington	216	298
Cincinnatus	150	45	Tot., 18 Towns	4984	3971
Cortlandville	250	457			
Freetown	90	62	**ERIE COUNTY**		
Homer	150	486			
Marathon	89	98	Buffalo City		
Preble	143	114			
Scott	135	121		700	1038
Solon	275	94	Buffalo Town		
Truxton	283	374	Alden	84	272
Virgil	382	258	Amherst	52	299
Willet	75	54	Aurora	155	366
			Boston	64	231
Tot., 11 Towns	2022	2163	Clarence	60	363
			Colden	54	62
DELAWARE COUNTY			Collins	92	437
			Concord	85	339
Andes	75	165	Eden	82	148
Bovina	84	110	Evans	150	226
Colchester	133	96	Hamburgh	231	395
Davenport	220	11	Holland	82	105
Delhi	208	147	Lancaster	52	172
Franklin	367	23	Newstead	84	283
Hamden	140	47	Sardinia	142	94
Hancock	103	48	Wales	86	216
Harpersfield	158	133			
Kortright	266	87	Tot., 17 Towns	2254	5046
Masonville	120	108			
Meredith	153	70	**ESSEX COUNTY**		
Middletown	227	89			
Roxbury	365	158	Chesterfield	109	173
Stamford	161	176	Crownpoint	208	197
Sidney	200	49	Elizabethtown	67	111
Tompkins	287	59	Essex	130	142
Walton	185	114	Jay	73	188
			Keene	16	104
Tot., 18 Towns	3462	1690	Lewis	64	199
			Minerva	15	33
DUTCHESS COUNTY			Moriah	91	289
			Newcomb	0	12
Amonia	201	223	Schroon	243	71
Beekman	102	172	Ticonderoga	159	239
Clinton	266	105	Westport	151	171
Dover	270	142	Willsborough	99	93
Fishkill	886	473	Wilmington	49	86
Hyde Park	233	198			
La Grange	218	157	Tot., 15 Towns	1474	2113
Milan	229	118			
North East	168	119	**FRANKLIN COUNTY**		
Pawlings	140	174			
Pine Plains	160	150	Bangor	48	110
Pleasant Valley	249	150	Belmont	27	16
Poughkeepsie	675	605	Bombay	89	44
Red Hook	291	265	Brandon	25	48
Rhinebeck	236	337	Chateaugay	126	120
Stanford	272	160	Constable	25	82

Towns	Marcy	Seward
Dickinson	48	39
Duane	8	13
Fort Covington	109	119
Malone	128	289
Moira	103	52
Westville	54	55
Tot., 12 Towns	790	987

GENESEE COUNTY

Towns	Marcy	Seward
Alabama	94	162
Alexander	219	221
Attica	241	263
Batavia	254	521
Bennington	200	224
Bergen	102	176
Bethany	199	262
Byron	115	255
Castile	183	261
China	60	137
Covington	136	319
Darien	277	215
Elba	97	492
Gainesville	200	166
Java	129	142
Le Roy	172	586
Middlebury	218	244
Orangeville	57	227
Pembroke	133	237
Perry	135	417
Sheldon	119	239
Stafford	126	281
Warsaw	184	294
Wethersfield	119	161
Tot., 24 Towns	3769	6502

GREENE COUNTY

Towns	Marcy	Seward
Athens	201	232
Cairo	285	278
Catskill	425	518
Coxsackie	328	326
Durham	325	249
Greenville	242	83
Hunter	276	210
Lexington	451	69
New Baltimore	293	87
Prattsville	191	60
Windham	171	220
Tot., 11 Towns	3191	2392

HERKIMER COUNTY

Towns	Marcy	Seward
Columbia	259	64
Danube	160	140
Fairfield	214	171
Frankfort	217	154
German Flats	353	72
Herkimer	329	109
Litchfield	188	125
Little Falls	360	199
Manheim	189	115
Newport	219	153
Norway	113	128
Russia	231	171
Salisbury	236	128
Schuyler	133	164
Starks	110	169
Warren	246	105
West Brunswick	79	46
Winfield	205	145
Tot., 18 Towns	3846	2358

JEFFERSON COUNTY

Towns	Marcy	Seward
Adams	237	346
Alexander	282	150
Antwerp	198	235
Brownville	189	315
Champion	250	173
Clayton	234	241
Ellisburg	537	417
Henderson	188	235
Hounsfield	197	394
Le Ray	348	224
Lorraine	124	137
Lyme	322	229
Orleans	164	147
Pamelia	158	224
Philadelphia	135	141
Rodman	157	192
Rutland	247	192
Watertown	385	339
Wilna	206	101
Tot., 19 Towns	4558	4433

KINGS COUNTY

Towns	Marcy	Seward
Brooklyn City,		
1st ward	78	151
2d ward	322	227
3d ward	46	216
4th ward	401	278
5th ward	329	109
6th ward	102	88
7th ward	128	68
8th ward	68	21
9th ward	16	24
	1590	1182
Bushwick	213	97
Flatbush	67	78
Flatlands	47	43
Gravesend	31	51
New Utrecht	92	45
Tot., 6 Towns	2040	1493

Census records

The best source of demographic information about the areas for which we have voting returns are the various nineteenth-century censuses. Taken together, the federal decennial censuses and the few state censuses available provide a significant amount of information about occupation, amount and value of personal property, number and nature of churches in a community, and the national backgrounds of the people living in an area. The federal census contains the best economic materials we have. The example included here, from the sixth federal census in 1840, lists, for instance, the occupational distribution of each minor civil division in Virginia, as well as the number of slaves in each, giving us two indices of economic character that we can compare to voting habits. In another direction, the listing here of the number of adult white males by age cohorts is helpful in estimating the extent of voter turnout in elections.

Until 1850, the federal census did not supply ethnocultural information. But some state censuses did. New York's Census of 1845, part of which is included here, listed the country of birth of each member of a town's population as well as the churches in each unit, both crucial for testing the importance of noneconomic variables in voting.

The original manuscript entries, which listed each person individually, still survive and can be very helpful on those rare occasions when a voting list is available. But these manuscripts are particularly useful in providing social information about political and economic elites in communities as we seek to learn more about the relationship between wealth and political leadership.

Unfortunately, not all censuses contain all of the information we would like for the years reported. The historian must fit together what he can, conscious that there will be gaps in his information. Nor is the available information always reported in a form compatible with the election returns we have or the level of analysis we wish to make. Important demographic information may be accessible only at the state or county level, for example, while township data remains particularly elusive. The accuracy of the census may also be questioned, and with reason. We know that many nineteenth-century census takers had idiosyncratic enumerating habits which often led to undercounts and other errors. (See Peter R. Knights, "A Method for Estimating Census Under-Enumeration," *Historical Methods Newsletter,* III [December, 1969], 5–8.) In addition, the standards for estimating land value and other economic indices varied widely from one census taker to another.

The census, in other words, is a most helpful, if incomplete, source, always somewhat slippery and often treacherous for the unwary seeking to uncover the substance underlying voting behavior. Despite their limitations, however, these censuses are the best we have and an important part of the pattern of evidence we must put together to get a clear picture of nineteenth-century demographic patterns.

6. *Sixth Census or Enumeration of the Inhabitants of the United States . . . 1840. (Washington, 1841), pp. 204–205. Aggregate Amount of Each Description of Persons Within the Eastern District of Virginia.*

FREE WHITE PERSONS

Males

NAME OF COUNTY, &c.	Under 5	5 and under 10	10 and under 15	15 and under 20	20 and under 30	30 and under 40	40 and under 50	50 and under 60	60 and under 70	70 and under 80	80 and under 90	90 and under 100	100 and upwards
Accomack													
Accomack parish	392	373	316	214	426	273	173	122	58	28	2	....	....
St. George's parish	403	351	278	190	410	312	172	103	51	21	4	1	....
Total Accomack county	795	724	594	404	836	585	345	225	109	49	6	1	....
Albemarle													
Albemarle (in part)	496	344	291	260	512	246	187	134	82	47	10	....	....
St. Ann's parish	438	379	330	356	482	281	202	141	89	34	9	4	....
Total Albemarle county	934	723	621	616	994	527	389	275	171	81	19	4	....
Amelia	237	193	189	154	242	166	126	99	62	25	2	1	....
Amherst	525	453	376	368	599	353	248	183	102	57	12	2	1
Bedford													
Southern district	651	479	433	401	490	309	252	162	95	53	22	4	2
Northern district	388	305	240	183	406	358	153	94	70	35	10	4	1
Total Bedford county	1,039	784	673	584	896	667	405	256	165	88	32	8	3
Brunswick	451	355	300	257	374	268	196	128	82	32	10	....	....
Buckingham													
Northern district	254	227	192	169	277	180	153	94	44	30	12	2	....
Southern district	313	264	237	225	378	220	150	100	80	30	9	3	....
Total Buckingham county	567	491	429	394	655	400	303	194	124	60	21	5	....

Source 6 (cont.)

FREE WHITE PERSONS

NAME OF COUNTY, &c.	Under 5	5 and under 10	10 and under 15	15 and under 20	20 and under 30	30 and under 40	40 and under 50	50 and under 60	60 and under 70	70 and under 80	80 and under 90	90 and under 100	100 and upwards
					Females								
Accomack													
Accomack parish	367	326	278	262	436	328	230	139	69	29	4	1	...
St. George's parish	380	299	271	230	505	334	211	132	75	27	12	...	...
Total Accomack county	747	625	549	492	941	662	441	271	144	56	16	1	...
Albemarle													
Albemarle (in part)	414	346	310	305	487	242	193	114	80	40	17	3	...
St. Ann's parish	449	356	316	306	440	277	178	147	81	45	10	2	...
Total Albemarle county	863	702	626	611	927	519	371	261	161	85	27	5	...
Amelia	225	188	187	190	278	206	117	94	57	28	8	...	...
Amherst	488	417	412	388	536	351	246	141	89	55	18	5	1
Bedford													
Southern district	555	488	388	424	605	324	241	156	91	50	15	1	1
Northern district	365	303	255	251	334	227	141	93	57	35	12	3	1
Total Bedford county	920	791	643	675	939	551	382	249	148	85	27	4	2
Brunswick	419	311	293	276	453	324	183	148	71	30	11	...	...
Buckingham													
Northern district	276	204	232	208	316	176	125	86	56	31	9	2	2
Southern district	325	262	211	236	343	213	127	129	63	39	9	...	...
Total Buckingham county	601	466	443	444	659	389	252	215	119	70	18	2	2

FREE COLORED PERSONS

NAME OF COUNTY, &c.	Males						Females					
	Under 10	10 and under 24	24 and under 36	36 and under 55	55 and under 100	100 and upwards	Under 10	10 and under 24	24 and under 36	36 and under 55	55 and under 100	100 and upwards
Accomack												
Accomack parish	196	243	88	80	69	....	204	194	106	108	84	1
St. George's parish	241	191	101	80	67	....	226	212	153	97	107	....
Total Accomack county	437	434	189	160	136	....	430	406	259	205	191	1
Albemarle												
Albemarle (in part)	59	36	25	28	12	....	62	42	31	18	13	....
St. Ann's parish	41	39	26	21	9	1	39	37	37	18	9	....
Total Albemarle county	100	75	51	49	21	1	101	79	68	36	22	....
Amelia	31	29	25	13	4	....	40	36	20	17	7	1
Amherst	61	55	30	22	12	....	58	60	38	25	11	1
Bedford												
Southern district	15	12	8	7	9	....	12	6	5	5	2	....
Northern district	29	35	28	19	12	....	34	39	17	14	14	1
Total Bedford county	44	47	36	26	21	....	46	45	22	19	16	1
Brunswick	87	82	54	49	20	....	80	94	57	27	13	....
Buckingham												
Northern district	27	27	14	18	9	....	26	36	17	19	6	....
Southern district	37	49	20	15	15	....	30	37	24	18	5	....
Total Buckingham county	64	76	34	33	24	....	56	73	41	37	11	....

57

Source 6 (cont.)

SLAVES

NAME OF COUNTY, &c.	Males						Females						TOTAL
	Under 10	10 and under 24	24 and under 36	36 and under 55	55 and under 100	100 and upwards	Under 10	10 and under 24	24 and under 36	36 and under 55	55 and under 100	100 and upwards	
Accomack													
Accomack parish	213	245	116	66	42	....	203	227	129	88	41	1	7,590
St. George's parish	509	535	312	193	124	....	489	470	308	181	137	1	9,506
Total Accomack county	722	780	428	259	166		692	697	437	269	178	2	17,096
Albemarle													
Albemarle (in part)	1,046	861	483	391	154	....	1,091	856	459	327	154	....	11,308
St. Ann's parish	996	917	551	446	178	....	980	877	503	386	153	....	11,616
Total Albemarle county	2,042	1,778	1,034	837	332		2,071	1,733	962	713	307		22,924
Amelia	1,225	974	579	550	207	....	1,199	1,023	592	449	221	4	10,320
Amherst	1,014	831	490	391	177	....	987	901	446	378	162	....	12,576
Bedford													
Southern district	756	640	330	217	87	2	754	608	351	230	101	2	10,851
Northern district	840	718	519	333	111	1	815	677	400	255	116	1	9,352
Total Bedford county	1,596	1,358	849	550	198	3	1,569	1,285	751	485	217	3	20,203
Brunswick	1,580	1,301	702	653	244	....	1,530	1,258	758	527	250	2	14,346
Buckingham													
Northern district	874	746	528	453	162	2	809	767	390	336	123	....	8,746
Southern district	1,049	901	542	401	152	1	970	797	530	341	138	2	10,040
Total Buckingham county	1,923	1,647	1,070	854	314	3	1,779	1,564	920	677	261	2	18,786

NAME OF COUNTY, &c.	Mining	Agriculture	Commerce	Manufactures and trades	Navigation of the ocean	Navigation of canals, lakes, and rivers	Learned professions and engineers
Accomack							
Accomack parish	3	3,079	65	145	121	....	5
St. George's parish	....	2,518	42	255	30	73	41
Total Accomack county	3	5,597	107	400	151	73	46
Albemarle							
Albemarle (in part)	....	3,231	100	533	....	17	63
St. Ann's parish	1	3,214	68	371	1	89	36
Total Albemarle county	1	6,445	168	904	1	106	99
Amelia	....	3,339	....	463	....	15	31
Amherst	....	4,085	92	612	....	125	77
Bedford							
Southern district	....	3,081	18	173	....	....	10
Northern district	....	2,546	6	149	....	....	12
Total Bedford county	....	5,627	24	322	....	....	22
Brunswick	....	3,318	17	217	....	....	41
Buckingham							
Northern district	59	2,818	40	1,691	....	185	82
Southern district	....	2,944	....	432	15	143	....
Total Buckingham county	59	5,762	40	2,123	15	328	82

7. Census of the State of New York (1845). Albany County

NEW YORK CENSUS

TOWNS	Total population	No. of male persons in the county	No. of female persons in the county	No. of male persons in the county subject to militia duty	No. of persons in the county entitled to vote for all officers elective by the people	No. of aliens not naturalized in the county	No. of persons in the county who are paupers	No. of persons of color in the county not taxed	No. of persons of color in the county who are taxed	No. of persons of color in the county who are legal voters	No. of persons in the county born in the State of New York	No. of persons in the county born in any of the New-England States	No. of persons in the county born in any of the other States of the Union	No. of persons in the county born in Mexico or South America	No. of persons in the county born in Great Britain or its possessions
Albany,															
1st ward	3712	1845	1867	206	558	689	...	141	1	1	2048	82	20	...	1092
2d ward	3676	1813	1863	402	751	776	...	55	8	6	2268	234	59	1	1014
3d ward	5053	2450	2603	384	1043	710	1	108	4	...	3097	299	73	...	1225
4th ward	4759	2297	2462	492	1127	448	...	69	2	1	3100	365	86	...	1042
5th ward	3129	1473	1656	364	563	274	...	78	2	2	1862	223	124	33	894
6th ward	3661	1680	1981	437	723	548	...	32	1	1	2437	201	44	...	949
7th ward	3532	1774	1758	492	745	828	...	7	...	...	2200	175	25	2	1102
8th ward	4001	1943	2058	251	673	152	...	27	11	3	2624	66	28	2	1239
9th ward	5204	2631	2573	377	999	732	...	81	6	5	3457	269	51	2	1010
10th ward	4412	2137	2275	299	795	602	281	154	1	2	2911	207	64	4	1115
Bern	3667	1868	1799	226	783	22	...	5	...	...	3493	92	3	...	53
Bethlehem	3315	1750	1565	169	705	144	9	86	13	...	2758	54	8	...	185
Coeymans	2978	1505	1473	223	681	50	3	82	...	...	2813	49	5	...	87
Guilderland	2995	1501	1494	206	682	50	4	47	3	3	2559	46	7	1	80
Knox	2161	1079	1082	116	500	4	...	5	...	...	2005	52	5	...	6
New Scotland	3288	1687	1601	206	754	31	8	30	1	1	2923	15	11	...	60
Rensselaerville	3589	1821	1768	397	865	39	9	8	1	...	3112	155	6	...	97
Watervliet	11209	5672	5537	748	2264	1157	4	85	4	2	7372	888	148	...	2500
Westerlo	2927	1460	1467	244	667	2	2	7	...	...	2852	51	19	...	73
Total	77268	38386	38882	6339	15878	7258	321	1107	58	27	55891	3523	777	45	13823

NEW YORK CENSUS — CHURCHES OR PLACES OF WORSHIP

TOWNS	No. of persons in the county born in France	No. of persons in the county born in Germany	No. of persons in the county born in other parts of Europe	Baptist			
				No. of churches	Cost of churches	Cost of other improvements	Cost of real estate
Albany							
1st ward	9	392	8				
2d ward	8	80	12				
3d ward	13	70	15	1	6000	600	9500
4th ward	11	87	8	2	8250	2500	12250
5th ward	6	13	6	1	34000		
6th ward	10	16	2				
7th ward	1	27	2				
8th ward		4	10				
9th ward	13	363	190	1	10000		14000
10th ward	20	89	2	1	800		
Bern	1	33	3				
Bethlehem	10	47					
Coeymans	2	9	4				
Guilderland	1	9	1	1	1200		
Knox	1	12	1				
New Scotland		10	1				
Rensselaerville	3	8		2	2500	200	450
Watervliet	14	92	32	2	3500		1200
Westerlo		1		2	3200	425	80
Total	123	1362	297	13	69450	3725	37480

Source 7 (cont.)

CHURCHES OR PLACES OF WORSHIP

TOWNS	Episcopalian				Presbyterian			
	No. of churches	Cost of churches	Cost of other improvements	Cost of real estate	No. of churches	Cost of churches	Cost of other improvements	Cost of real estate
Albany								
1st ward	....	....	....	....	....	....	....	....
2d ward	1	1250	250	....	1	6000	500	2500
3d ward	....	....	....	....	....	....	....	....
4th ward	1	18000	2500	10000	1	18000	6650	7000
5th ward	1	40000	....	....	1	50000	....	....
6th ward	....	....	....	....	2	24000	....	6000
7th ward	....	....	....	....	....	....	....	....
8th ward	....	....	....	....	....	....	....	....
9th ward	....	....	....	....	....	....	....	....
10th ward	....	....	....	....	....	....	....	....
Bern	....	....	....	....	....	....	....	....
Bethlehem	....	....	....	....	1	2200	286	120
Coeymans	....	....	....	....	....	....	....	....
Guilderland	....	....	....	....	1	900	....	....
Knox	....	....	....	....	....	....	....	....
New Scotland	....	....	....	50	1	650	....	....
Rensselaerville	1	3200	100	....	1	3300	300	1200
Watervliet	2	4000	....	400	2	3800	200	1000
Westerlo	....	....	....	....	....	....	....	....
Total	6	66450	2850	10450	11	108850	7936	17820

CHURCHES OR PLACES OF WORSHIP

TOWNS	Congregational				Methodist			
	No. of churches	Cost of churches	Cost of other improvements	Cost of real estate	No. of churches	Cost of churches	Cost of other improvements	Cost of real estate
Albany								
1st ward	....	....	....	....	....	....	....	....
2d ward	....	....	....	....	1	6000	500	2500
3d ward	....	....	....	....	....	....	....	....
4th ward	....	....	....	....	1	13000	1800	6400
5th ward	1	7000	....	....	....	....	....	....
6th ward	....	....	....	....	2	63000	5300	5600
7th ward	....	....	....	....	....	....	....	....
8th ward	....	....	....	....	....	....	....	....
9th ward	....	....	....	....	2	7400	....	5800
10th ward	....	....	....	....	....	....	....	....
Bern	....	....	....	....	3	2275	100	50
Bethlehem	....	....	....	....	1	700	100	....
Coeymans	....	....	....	....	3	3900	375	250
Guilderland	....	....	....	....	....	....	....	....
Knox	....	....	....	....	2	1700	472	15
New Scotland	....	....	....	....	1	2000	25	80
Rensselaerville	....	....	....	....	2	3600	50	500
Watervliet	....	....	....	....	5	6058	2133	570
Westerlo	....	....	....	....	1	1250	250	25
Total	1	7000			24	110883	11105	21790

63

Source 7 (cont.)

CHURCHES OR PLACES OF WORSHIP

TOWNS	Roman Catholics				Dutch Reformed			
	No. of churches	Cost of churches	Cost of other improvements	Cost of real estate	No. of churches	Cost of churches	Cost of other improvements	Cost of real estate
Albany								
1st ward	....	....	....	....	....	....	....	....
2d ward	1	13500	3500	2000	1	8500	350	3000
3d ward	1	200	....	2450	....	....	....	....
4th ward	....	25000	....	....	1	30000	4000	22500
5th ward	1	....	....	....	....	....	....	....
6th ward	....	20000	....	....	1	35000	....	....
7th ward	1	....	....	2500	....	....	....	....
8th ward	....	....	....	....	....	....	....	....
9th ward	....	....	....	....	....	....	....	....
10th ward	....	....	....	....	....	....	....	....
Bern	....	....	....	....	3	5400	50	2400
Bethlehem	....	....	....	....	2	6300	1500	5100
Coeymans	....	....	....	....	2	4250	40	150
Guilderland	....	....	....	....	2	6000	600	....
Knox	....	....	....	....	1	1000	....	....
New Scotland	....	....	....	....	4	4200	....	50
Rensselaerville	....	....	....	....	....	....	....	....
Watervliet	1	5000	300	1500	4	27000	600	2800
Westerlo	....	....	....	....	2	3500	256	....
Total	5	63700	3800	8450	23	131150	7396	36000

CHURCHES OR PLACES OF WORSHIP

TOWNS	Universalist				Unitarian			
	No. of churches	Cost of churches	Cost of other improvements	Cost of real estate	No. of churches	Cost of churches	Cost of other improvements	Cost of real estate
Albany								
1st ward	……	……	……	……	……	……	……	……
2d ward	1	10000	……	……	……	……	……	……
3d ward	……	……	……	14000	……	……	……	……
4th ward	……	……	……	……	1	4500	5449	……
5th ward	……	……	……	……	……	……	……	……
6th ward	……	……	……	……	……	……	……	……
7th ward	……	……	……	……	……	……	……	……
8th ward	……	……	……	……	……	……	……	……
9th ward	……	……	……	……	……	……	……	……
10th ward	……	……	……	……	……	……	……	……
Bern	……	……	……	……	2	1355	300	19
Bethlehem	……	……	……	……	……	……	……	……
Coeymans	……	……	……	……	……	……	……	……
Guilderland	……	……	……	……	……	……	……	……
Knox	……	……	……	……	……	……	……	……
New Scotland	……	……	……	……	……	……	……	……
Rensselaerville	……	……	……	……	……	……	……	……
Watervliet	……	……	……	……	……	……	……	……
Westerlo	……	……	……	……	1	1100	……	……
Total	1	10000	……	14000	4	6955	5749	19

65

Source 7 (cont.)

CHURCHES OR PLACES OF WORSHIP

TOWNS	Jews			Quakers			
	No. of churches	Cost of churches	Cost of other improvements	No. of churches	Cost of churches	Cost of other improvements	Cost of real estate
Albany							
1st ward	...	...	...	...	...	...	...
2d ward	1	2000	200	...	...	...	...
3d ward	...	...	...	...	...	...	...
4th ward	...	...	...	1	3000	200	2200
5th ward	...	...	...	...	...	...	...
6th ward	...	...	...	...	...	...	...
7th ward	...	...	...	...	...	...	...
8th ward	...	...	...	...	...	...	...
9th ward	...	...	...	...	...	...	...
10th ward	...	...	...	1	200	...	20
Bern	...	...	...	...	...	...	...
Bethlehem	...	...	...	...	...	...	...
Coeymans	...	...	...	...	...	...	...
Guilderland	...	...	...	...	...	...	...
Knox	...	...	...	...	...	...	...
New Scotland	...	...	...	...	...	...	...
Rensselaerville	...	...	...	2	900	210	50
Watervliet	...	...	...	1	1000	100	100
Westerlo	...	...	...	...	...	...	...
Total	1	2000	200	5	5100	510	2370

Biographical lists

When we turn to study the political affiliation of economic elites in Jacksonian America or the wealth and other demographic characteristics of party leaders, there is more information on hand than there is about the masses of ordinary voters. In addition to the manuscript census entries, city directories, various kinds of biographical directories (official and otherwise), tax lists, and church records provide information about individual party affiliation, church membership, political and business careers, residence and wealth. Unfortunately, the problems of incompleteness and error still remain. Like the other material included here, biographical sources are incomplete, selective, and too often inaccurate in the information they report. Their quality forces the historian, once again, to be both wary of his sources and conscious of the difficulty of collecting systematic information about even the most prominent political groups.

The following selection, a few pages from John Lomas and Alfred S. Peace, *The Wealthy Men and Women of Brooklyn and Williamsburgh* (Brooklyn, 1847), pp. 7–13, is one example of the kinds of material available. A popular activity among newspapermen and others in the mid-nineteenth century was publishing lists of the wealthy men in their community, including some indication of the total wealth of each. Such a source, if complete and accurate, is invaluable because it allows us to compare individual wealth with partisan affiliation. Although many such lists were neither complete nor accurate, this particular compilation has been cited for the general accuracy of its wealth estimates. The list includes, in the words of the two authors, "a complete list of all whose estimated possessions (in real and personal property) amount to the sum of TEN THOUSAND DOLLARS AND UPWARDS." As a bonus the compilers included brief biographical sketches of "many meritorious and eminent persons"—usually Brooklyn's wealthiest citizens. The sketches are neither deep nor detailed but do include some information on place of birth, party affiliation, church membership, career, and occupation.

8. JOHN LOMAS AND ALFRED S. PEACE

The Wealthy Men and Women of Brooklyn and Williamsburgh (1847)

Abbot Francis H.	$25,000
Ackerman Catharine	10,000
Acosta John	25,000
Adair Henry	15,000
Adams Benjamin	20,000
Agar Edward	20,000

A native of New York. About twenty years since he obtained a situation in the Brooklyn Navy Yard as Purser's clerk; which, through strict attention to the duties of his office and his gentlemanly deportment, he still retains, enjoying the respect of all who know him.

Ainslie James, Williamsburgh	15,000
Allen William J.	20,000
Allen Moses	75,000
Anderson D.	20,000
Anderson P. B.	10,000
Anthony Edward	100,000
Appleton William H.	35,000
Archer George B.	15,000
Arnold Daniel H.	150,000
Atkins Joshua	25,000
Atkinson John A.	30,000
Attwater G. M.	40,000
Augur John B.	25,000
Austin Mrs. S. E.	75,000
Aymar Benjamin	15,000
Ayres Daniel	35,000
Ayres Ellis F.	15,000
Babad William	25,000
Bach Robert (estate of)	70,000
Backhouse Edward T.	15,000
Bacon Daniel P.	15,000
Bailey Elisha	30,000
Bailey Robert	10,000
Baird William	50,000

This gentleman, a native of Erin' Isle, commenced his career in Brooklyn as a humble laborer, and by economy, frugality, and untiring industry amassed sufficient means to enable him to commence business as a contractor on public roads. He soon manifested an aptitude and ability for such undertakings as to place him in the first rank of the profession, and has, by a series of fortunate operations, amassed his present large possessions. He is one of the leading democrats of the county, and has considerable influence as a politician.

Baisley Richard	10,000
Baisley Thomas	10,000

Baker John H.	35,000

This gentleman is the owner of a large pin manufactory in Raymond street, and resides in a magnificent house in Myrtle avenue. He has contributed largely to the prosperity of the eastern section of the city, is exceedingly popular with all classes of his fellow citizens, and, if ambitious of political distinction, may hereafter become the representative of this district in the national councils. He is, we believe, one of the most prominent leaders of the whig party in Kings county.

Baker Mills P., Williamsburgh	20,000
Ballard F. G.	25,000
Ballard Loomis	30,000
Banks Robert	15,000
Barker J. I.	15,000
Barnes H. W.	30,000
Barney Hiram	30,000
Barr John	12,000
Barritti Francis	12,000
Barstow Caleb	30,000
Barstow William	20,000
Bartow E. J. & G. A.	500,000

Few, if any, of our citizens are more distinguished for their munificence and liberality, than these enterprising and opulent merchants. Edgar J. has at his own expense, erected the "Church of the Holy Trinity," an edifice far surpassing in architectural grandeur and costliness of material and workmanship any similar structure in this city. It may appropriately be termed the Cathedral of Brooklyn, and will serve to perpetuate the name and munificence of its founder in ages yet to come. He is, we believe, in politics, a democrat, and was selected by that party as its chosen candidate for mayor; but he declined the honors offered him, notwithstanding that he would, beyond all reasonable doubt, have been elected. His heart and abundant means are ever open to the appeals of charity, and no one in this community has done more than he has towards relieving the necessities of the poor.

Bassett Isaac H.	50,000
Baxter John	10,000
Baxter Timothy	20,000
Baylis Abraham B.	20,000
Baylis Gilbert	10,000
Baylis Thomas	20,000

Beam John 10,000
Becar Noel 350,000
Bedell Benjamin W. 15,000
Bedell Daniell 10,000
Bedell Mott 50,000
Beers J. D. 10,000
Bell James 25,000
Bellamy Joseph 15,000
Bellamy Nancy 10,000
Bennett Cornelius, Jun. 10,000
Bennett Elisabeth 10,000
Bennett Wynant P. 15,000
Benson Alfred 30,000
Benson John 50,000
Bergen Cornelius P. 10,000
Bergen Garritt 25,000
Bergen John S. 15,000
Bergen Lefferts 20,000
Bergen Theodore 20,000
Bergen Tunis G. 50,000
Berry Peter J. 10,000
Berry Richard 25,000
Berry Richard, Williamsburgh 120,000
Berry Richard B., Williamsburgh 20,000
Bierwith Leopold 30,000
Bidwell Rev. Walter H. 140,000
Bill Charles E. 20,000
Birdsall Thomas W. 30,000
Blackburn Robbins 40,000
Blake Anson, Jun. 100,000

The immense and rapid growth of the southern section of the city is chiefly owing to the indomitable enterprize, perseverance, and public spirit of the father of this gentleman. The latter became unfortunate in business matters some years ago, arising from the panic which prostrated so many men of property, and the consequent fluctuations in value of real estate. He is now, however, in the full tide of successful experiment, and will soon, we doubt not, reach as high a position in wealth as his fortunate son, whose extensive business in New York has mainly contributed to his success.

Blake Stephen M. 30,000
Bloomfield Joel 15,000
Boerum Abraham 30,000
Boerum Jacob B. 20,000
Boerum Henry 20,000
Bogert James 200,000
Bogert Judith 150,000
Bokee David A. 40,000

Few persons in the community have obtained a more widely spread popularity than this gentleman; and his public career, as a member of the Common Council, has obtained for him the high estimation of all classes of society, and the friendly regard of a large majority of his political opponents. Possessed of great ability as a debater, and an uprightness and integrity impregnable to party considerations, he is eminently worthy of the highest station which the people of this district can confer upon him. Though a prominent sectarian in religious matters, he is liberal and tolerant to all others, and has unostentatiously contributed to many charitable institutions, besides being munificent in his donations to the distressed and poor.

Boorman James 35,000
Bouton Samuel 30,000
Bowne Samuel 500,000

Mr. B. is now the sole proprietor of the Main and Catharine street ferry, from which he derives a large income, which has lately been considerably augmented by the legacy of a deceased brother. He, like many other of the rich men of Brooklyn, is distinguished for his liberality to the unfortunate and destitute of his fellow creatures, and in any movement tending to advance the interests of this flourishing city, and the welfare of its population, is among the foremost and most generous contributors.

Boyd Ann F. 10,000
Boyd Martha 30,000
Boyle Edward (estate of) 15,000
Bradish Lucretia 10,000
Brewster D. A. 15,000
Brice John 40,000

This gentleman, now far advanced in years, commenced his career in this country about fifteen years ago as the proprietor of a small drug store in James street, opposite the Fulton Market, which has since become one of the most popular retail establishments of the kind in Brooklyn. The business done there is immense, and its founder some time since retired with a large fortune, leaving the profitable concern to his son Israel B. Brice.

Brice Israel B. 25,000

Succeeded his father John Brice in the drug business in James street, where he has acquired considerable property. He is universally celebrated for his superior business qualifications, his amenity of manners, his charities to the poor and needy, and a blameless life.

Brinckerhoff Isaac 10,000
Broadhead Fanny 15,000
Broadhead Jacob 35,000
Brodie J. W. 35,000
Bronson John 12,000
Brown Jacob 10,000
Brown Levi 15,000
Brown Thomas S. 10,000
Brown William H. E., Williamsburgh 20,000
Brouwer John 35,000
Brownson John 100,000
Bruen Matthias (estate of) 70,000

Source 8 *(cont.)*

Brush Conklin	60,000	Carll S. Seal	20,000
Brush Jarvis	25,000	Carman Nelson G.	15,000
Buckley Thomas	30,000		
Buckley Thomas G.	25,000		
Bulkley William F.	35,000		
Bunce Jane	10,000		
Bunce Julia	15,000		
Bumford Edward	10,000		
Burbank William (estate of)	25,000		
Burdett Joshua A., Williamsburgh	15,000		
Burdon Joseph W., Williamsburgh	15,000		
Burrill S. N.	20,000		
Burt Edwin C.	40,000		
Burt James	30,000		
Burtis Abraham	10,000		
Burtis Oliver D.	25,000		
Butler James G.	20,000	Carman Samuel (estate of)	15,000
		Carman Thomas	15,000
Cahoone William	10,000	Carpenter Jacob	15,000
Callaghan Charles	40,000	Carpenter Thomas	30,000
Cammeyer John E.	10,000	Carter Abigail	15,000
Campbell F. D.	15,000	Cartwright David G.	30,000
Carll Conklin	15,000	Cary William H.	100,000

Carman Nelson G. — Mr. C. has accumulated his property by the most persevering application to business as a butcher, and is yet quite a young man, with every prospect of adding very materially to his possessions. In acts of charity and kindness to the poor and afflicted he has, we understand, been instrumental in doing much good without parade, ostentation, or show. Such men, though not desiring it, deserve to have their good deeds recorded in this world, as well as noted down (as certainly they will be) in that better and happier sphere allotted to "all born of woman."

B. INTERPRETATIONS

9. | LEE BENSON
"Research Problems in American Political Historiography"

Lee Benson has led the methodological assault on traditional studies of Jacksonian era politics. The following essay, which he published in 1957, suggests the utility of substituting, in Geoffrey Barraclough's phrases, "exact verifiable data" for "inspired guesswork" in political research. Reprinted with permission of The Macmillan Company, from "Research Problems in American Political Historiography," by Lee Benson, in *Common Frontiers of the Social Sciences,* edited by Mirra Komarovsky, pp. 123–55, 182–83. Copyright © 1957 by The Free Press, a Corporation. [Footnotes omitted.]

GENERALIZED INTERPRETATION ANALYZED IN TERMS OF TIME, SPACE, AND RATE DIMENSIONS

The election of 1884 put a Democrat in the White House for the first time since the Civil War and various historical explanations have been offered for Grover Cleveland's hairbreadth victory over James Blaine. Not surprisingly, the closeness of the election has been used to reinforce the doctrines of that "fortuitous" school of history which minimizes the possibility of discovering causal patterns in human behavior. Since various "accidental" factors of that campaign usually have been pointed to as determinants of the final result, the conclusion could be drawn that sheer chance was responsible for Blaine's defeat. But Allan Nevins, in his Pulitzer Prize biography of Cleveland, attempted to reformulate the problem in such a manner as to place "accidents" and petty factors in perspective, and thereby dispose of the fortuitous explanation. Discussing the situation in New York, the one "close state" whose electoral votes could have decided the outcome in favor of either candidate, Nevins dismissed the charge that Democratic fraud cost Blaine the election:

The whole cry of fraud like the charges of mismanagement shortly [thereafter] brought against Chairman Elkins and Jones [Republican campaign managers], was essentially an effort to obscure the real cause of Blaine's failure. The vote cast in Republican districts for St. John [Prohibitionist]; the rain that kept rural Republicans at home; the loss of more than 2,000 Republican votes in Conkling's [Republican rival of Blaine] home, Oneida County; the Burchard alliteration [Rum, Romanism, and Rebellion]—these all counted. But the great central explanation of the defeat was simply that Blaine was morally suspect.

In effect, what Nevins did was to set down the *basic condition* under which accidental factors operated to cause Blaine's defeat. They "counted" only because Blaine was morally suspect, otherwise their effect would have been unimportant. Whether his interpretation is correct or not, it is not too much to say that Nevins persuasively disposed of the fortuitous explanation the moment he reformulated the problem. Clearly, rain in the rural districts, Republican desertions to minor parties, politically embarrassing oratorical gimmicks, were no more rampant than in the 1896 campaign, for example, when more basic issues were sharply drawn between the two parties and the Republican plurality in New York State was over 250,000. In all likelihood, under those circumstances similar campaign "accidents" would have had little influence in determining any but a small number of votes. In any event, the number of votes "accidentally" determined in 1884 hardly would have dented the Republican plurality of 1896.

Stated in other terms, the significant question posed by the 1884 election is not whether chance factors affected the small number of ballots which were enough to give the Democrats the winning electoral votes. Narrowly conceived, this may be a "correct" explanation of the 1884 election. Seen in meaningful perspective it is a gross distortion because chance factors are made out to be of major importance in accounting for voting behavior, whereas, at best, they affected a minute percentage of the total vote either in New York or the nation at large. The significant question is the very reverse of whether or not accidental developments determined a small number of votes. *Why was the outcome so close, why were chance factors of any significance in the election of 1884?*

To begin with, let us assume that Nevins' hypothesis is verifiable and restate it as presented in his two chapters dealing with the 1884 campaign:

The great central explanation of Blaine's defeat is that he was morally suspect because of unethical conduct in public office. At that particular time in American history *men all throughout the nation were in revolt against the entire system of government by special favor of which Blaine was simply the emblem. Under those conditions, the national contest became so close that a Democrat was elected president because of accidental factors.* But accidents determined the outcome only in the sense that the nomination of Blaine created a situation in which the election could turn on the relatively insignificant number of votes they directly influenced.

To support the hypothesis' claims that no issues were of major significance except the public integrity of the major party candidates, stress was given to the neat manner in which one of Cleveland's supporters summed up the "real issue" of the campaign:

We are told (he said) that Mr. Blaine has been delinquent in office but blameless in private life, while Mr. Cleveland has been a model of official integrity, but culpable in his personal relations [fathered an illegitimate child]. We should therefore elect Mr. Cleveland to the public office which he is so well qualified to fill, and remand Mr. Blaine to the private station which he is so admirably fitted to adorn.

In assessing the relative weight assigned to Blaine's integrity as a determinant of voting behavior no attempt is made here to interpret strictly the description, "real issue." A reasonable interpretation would be that in general, among groups and in areas where the Republican party percentage declined, Blaine's candidacy operated as a significant determinant of that change. It would not be expected to have acted with equal effect everywhere, but, according to our hypothesis, it must be shown to have acted generally, and to a greater extent than any other factor. To demonstrate the impact of Blaine's candidacy, therefore, it must be demonstrated that some measurable pattern of changed Republican strength actually exists. We must also specify the *group characteristics* or the *operative conditions* which can be shown to have been associated with Republican percentage declines resulting from Blaine's candidacy.

Questions of this order need to be posed: Did Blaine's candidacy merely result in a slight percentage decline in a few normally closely balanced states, or was there a nationwide Republican percentage decline of considerable proportions? Which, if any, distinguishable groups of voters were influenced by charges against his public integrity? Under what conditions, if any, did voters in specific areas become receptive to such charges? In other words, the hypothesis must make some explicit statement concerning who (i.e., voters by group or area, or both) cast less than normal Republican votes because of Blaine, *and why they did so and other voters did not.*

Both the generalized nature of the causal factor and the stress given it as the "real issue" in the campaign are sufficient to negate the possibility that it could have been operative only in one state, or a few states. If it were the real issue in the nation, why, for example, should Blaine's integrity have been a determinant of voting behavior only in New York State? To make such a claim, one would have to provide detailed, verifiable evidence that though it was the real issue everywhere, Blaine's questioned integrity was a significant voting determinant only in New York because of group characteristics or operative conditions, or some combination thereof, peculiar to that state. Moreover, it is not necessary to rely solely upon logical argument. Two full chapters are given to the 1884 campaign in the book from which the hypothesis is drawn and they make it abundantly clear that the "morally suspect" explanation is not confined to New York but is applicable to the nation at large. Those chapters maintain that the impact of Blaine's nomination was not only widespread but considerable. It is described as the single, most important factor causing marked Republican losses throughout the country. The extensive quotations strung together below are from different pages but are in context and provide an accurate summary:

For several reasons the campaign of 1884 will long be counted among the most memorable in American history. It is the only campaign in which the head of a great party has gone down to defeat because of charges impugning his integrity . . . [Blaine's] nomination [on June 6] was the signal for a revolt which took the most experienced observers by surprise, for in volume and intensity it surpassed the hopes of the Democrats and the fears of the Republicans . . . [Before Cleveland's nomination on July 11]. The campaign had already taken on the quality of a great moral crusade. The uprising of the independent voters to vindicate the principle that the presidency must forever be barred to any man of doubtful integrity had gained tremendous momentum, arousing a fervor such as tens of thousands had not felt since the Civil War. . . . The hour was ripe for precisely such a movement. The health of a nation requires, from time to time, a far-reaching moral movement to awaken men from old lethargies and fix their eyes upon some new city in the heavens. Ever since Appomattox the government had in great part been subject to the selfish materialism of the worst wing of the Republican party . . . [details of corruption] men were in revolt against the entire system of government by special favor of which Blaine was simply the emblem. They knew that he would not take bribes in the White House. But they also knew that by virtue of his record, his associates, and his coarseness of fibre, his election would give new encouragement to the crew of lobbyists, spoilsmen, and seekers after privilege. They wanted an honest man who stood in hostility to the whole discreditable and dangerous tradition.

At the Republican Convention the rebels had mustered but a corporal's guard. Before the week was over, it was a brigade; before June ended, an army . . . . It was impossible to conduct such a campaign except upon an emotional plane. Men who were intent upon a change in the very spirit of government could not be bound down to prosaic issues like the tariff and currency. Seldom has so little account been taken of platform or pledges, for as George W. Curtis truly said, "the platforms of the two parties are practically the same." . . . It was evident that the real issue was the public integrity and capacity of the two candidates, and that old questions of private conduct [Cleveland's social indiscretions] were essentially irrelevant.

What has been done here so far is to state in general terms the relative weight assigned to the causal factor, its widespread operation, and its considerable effect in changing voters' party support. It occasioned a revolt which "in volume and intensity . . . surpassed the hopes of the Democrats and the fears of the Republicans"; before June ended the rebels had mustered "an army," etc. But we have not identified *any particular groups* who were affected by Blaine's candidacy, nor *any particular conditions* which could distinguish voters in areas affected by the issue from voters in areas not affected by the issue. ("Independent voters" obviously does not provide such identification.) Though the relevant chapters give no clue in this regard, since the hypothesis is assumed to be verifiable, it becomes necessary to devise a procedure yielding some specific statement concerning voting behavior subject to systematic demonstration.

Precisely because statements of the following kind seem to be obvious and are therefore frequently overlooked, one of the things we must demonstrate is that considerable *changes* actually took place in voting behavior adverse to the Republicans. Men could not have been ripe for a political revolt precipitated by Blaine's nomination if, for example, the 1884 election returns showed little variation in the normal relative strength of the Republican and Democratic parties throughout the nation in general, and each state in particular. Thus, a logical way to begin to evaluate the hypothesis is to tackle the task of specifying *whom* the issue affected, and why, by employing systematic methods to learn what actually happened in the election of 1884, i.e., what spatial voting patterns can be distinguished in 1884, *in contrast to previous elections.*

The importance of
constructing time series

The two chapters discussing the 1884 campaign made little comparison between it and previous elections but did present statistics indicating that Cleveland won a very narrow victory over Blaine:

> His [Cleveland's] margin in New York was of less than 1200 votes, but it was decisive. He had carried every Southern state, together with Indiana, New Jersey, and Connecticut, and though his popular majority over Blaine was less than 25,000 in a total vote of more than ten million, he had 219 electoral votes to Blaine's 182.

Since the 1884 election was extremely close, *for a marked change to have taken place, the Republican vote in previous elections must have provided that party with a comfortable margin of victory.* If we could identify in geographic terms, i.e., states, counties, townships, etc., the areas where its vote declined perceptibly, we would be in a better position to identify the groups among whom vote-switching took place, and then attempt to demonstrate that Blaine's candidacy explained the switching. *But, conversely, if in fact no general pattern existed of marked Republican decline, the hypothesis would rest on an erroneous factual assumption.* In other words, attention is directed here to the necessity of demonstrating the accuracy and inclusiveness of the factual elements in the hypothesis before attempting to demonstrate the validity of its interpretative elements. And that it is possible for erroneous assumptions to be accorded status as accepted facts relative to the 1884 campaign is readily indicated.

Has the common assumption really been established that even in New York accidental features of the campaign "all counted" against Blaine? Though one can cite numerous *assertions* to this effect, to my knowledge no one has demonstrated that the much discussed "accidents" actually swung any votes from him. In fact, given the prevalence of anti-Catholic sentiments, it becomes a difficult problem even to think of how one would go about attempting to show that the Burchard incident *hurt or helped* Blaine. But perhaps the possible usefulness of systematic research methods for political history can be illustrated by examining another assertion concerning the impact of accidental factors upon voting behavior in 1884.

In the book from which the hypothesis is drawn, stress was given the idea that the 1884 Prohibition Party vote was a consequence of actions taken at the Republican nominating convention; there "the Republicans painfully humiliated the temperance forces." This humiliation was said to have been a definite factor in the events which led to the decision to run an erstwhile Republican, John P. St. John, on the Prohibition ticket; "The Republicans were to rue their indifference to him." Since in 1884 the Prohibition vote was about 150,000 for the nation and 25,000 in closely contested New York, it might appear that Republican arrogance did swing enough votes from Blaine to have been of some significance, given the central hypothesis that Blaine was "morally suspect."

But when one constructs *a time series for voting behavior,* the candidacy of St. John and the vote given him are both seen in a considerably different perspective. The temperance forces had been running presidential candidates since 1872 and continued to do so after 1884. *Even more important, though the 1884 Prohibition vote in New York was much larger than in the previous presidential election, it was slightly smaller than the party had polled in 1882 for Governor. That is, the Prohibition candidate for Governor received 25,783 votes in 1882. Two years later the party's presidential candidate received only 25,006 votes, although the total was 200,000 more than in 1882.* Further, in 1882, the Democratic gubernatorial candidate, Grover Cleveland, was given a majority of unprecedented proportions. In 1884, Grover Cleveland, the Democratic presidential candidate, carried New York by a scant 1,149 votes out of 1,167,189 cast.

That the Prohibition vote in the state had been growing after 1880 is shown in Table I. But in broad terms, the table also indicates that the Prohibition vote was relatively stable between 1882 and 1888, inclusive, whether it was cast in a state or national election.

TABLE I

New York State vote for president or highest state officer, 1880-1888

	REP.	DEM.	PROHIBITION	PROH. PERCENTAGE
1880	555,544	534,511	1,517	0.13
1881	416,915	403,893	4,445	0.53
1882	342,464	535,318	25,783	2.81
1883	446,108	427,525	18,816	2.08
1884	562,005	563,154	25,006	2.16
1885	490,331	501,465	30,867	2.98
1886	461,018	468,815	36,437	3.75
1887	452,811	469,888	41,850	4.00
1888	650,338	635,965	30,231	2.28

When the New York Prohibition vote is viewed in historical perspective, i.e., over time, it obviously cannot be taken as an accidental product of the 1884 campaign. In assigning weight to Republican defections to the Prohibitionists, it must be recognized that these defections, if they were *Republican* defections, on balance, occurred before Blaine's candidacy. In New York, and elsewhere, compared with 1882, sharp losses were suffered *not by the Republicans with Blaine but by the Democrats with Cleveland.* For in 1882 the Democrats had achieved a "political revolution" throughout the country which may be said to have marked the first major post-Civil War switch to them from the Republicans. And since the Prohibition vote in New York was practically constant in 1882 and 1884, an assessment of its impact upon Blaine's defeat focuses attention instead upon the sharp Democratic retrogression from 1882, and the extent to which the Republicans had recovered. Thus, the conclusion appears warranted that the hypothesis concerning the 1884 election which assumes that the Republican party underwent a general, marked decline, runs counter to the fact that with Blaine as a candidate the Republicans *gained ground* compared to the major election contests immediately preceding. One index of their recovery is the close vote in New York (and elsewhere) compared to the 1882 Democratic sweep; another is the Republican gain in Congress. The party composition of the House of Representatives demonstrates the shift.

TABLE II

Congressional election contests, 1876–1886

	1876	1878	1880	1882	1884	1886
Rep.	140	130	147	118	140	152
Dem.	153	149	135	197	183	169
Other	0	14	11	10	2	4

Republican Performance in 1884. Republican gains in 1884 with Blaine as a candidate do not in themselves indicate that he failed to hurt the party. Conceivably, certain events after 1882 could have improved the Republicans' position to such an extent that another candidate might have won. If this were the case, however, the historian would have to identify those events and demonstrate their political impact. For example, the argument might be advanced that a situation had developed analogous to the Republican recovery in 1880, which, the claim could be made, resulted from the end of depression in 1879 and the great burst of prosperity preceding the election. Just a reverse situation obtained, however, in 1884. After four years of high prosperity a recession did set in shortly before the 1882 elections, but it was not until the Spring of 1884 that the depression of the mid-eighties really developed. Since a Republican administration was in office, if it had any political effect at all, economic depression worked against, not in favor of Blaine. Under these circumstances, a "great moral crusade" which by June had enlisted "an army" against Blaine should not have resulted in a Republican political resurgence. Other events would have to be subjected to similar analysis if it were argued that they explained Republican recovery.

Even if the significant political developments of the four years between elections are ignored, the 1884 voting record shows little evidence of a nation-wide revolt against Blaine's candidacy. Despite the fact that in 1880 the Republican percentage of the total vote was higher than in any election between 1876 and 1892, inclusive, *Blaine had only 00.09 percent less of the total vote than James Garfield, the victorious Republican candidate of 1880,* and the Democratic increased share was only 00.28 percent!

TABLE III

Presidential elections, 1876–1892, percent of popular vote cast for Republican and Democratic candidates

	REPUBLICAN	DEMOCRAT
1876	47.87	50.86
1880	48.31	48.20
1884	48.22	48.48
1888	47.83	48.63
1892	42.96	45.90

Possibly the most remarkable feature of the election of 1884 was that in terms of net shift, compared to its predecessor, it showed *less* arithmetic percentage change than any other in American history. Actually, Blaine received about 400,000 more votes than Garfield. An additional 9,000 votes would have enabled him to match the latter's percentage exactly because the total vote was larger in 1884. It cannot therefore be demonstrated, as our hypothesis requires that it must, that Blaine's candidacy cut into the popular vote attained by the Republican party at preceding elections. His vote actually represented *increased* Republican strength as compared to 1876, and greater strength than in 1888 and 1892. An unchanged popular vote means that if the Republicans suffered losses in certain states due to Blaine's candidacy, these losses *were counterbalanced* by Republican gains. At best, a hypothesis which can only be applicable to Republican losses must be considered partial. But this line of reasoning can be carried further. If Republican gains and losses were of equal magnitude, and if in certain states no change occurred, the hypothesis making Blaine's candidacy the "great central explanation of the [Republican] defeat" must be *capable of explaining all three sets of voting data if, without explicit restricting conditions, its general explanation of any one set is to be considered potentially verifiable.*

In view of the remarkably small net shift in 1884 party strength as compared to 1880, no more justification exists for regarding Republican gains and constancy as deviant cases from a hypothesis based upon Blaine's *weakness* as a candidate than for regarding Republican losses as deviations from a hypothesis postulating Blaine *as a strong candidate.* Though numerous types of causal factors might have differential effects upon voting behavior among different groups or in different areas, the hypothesis under consideration does not offer one of that nature. Particularly since it makes no attempt to identify groups or areas more susceptible to charges against Blaine's integrity, the hypothesis in fact offers no explanation for the different types of voting behavior revealed in 1884 when the voting data is arranged systematically. For example, if sectional conflict were designated as the "real issue" of the 1884 campaign, and if each party were identified with a particular section, then in comparison with 1880 one would expect to find differential effects upon party strength consistent with the parties' sectional identification.

But if Blaine's nomination precipitated a widespread and considerable revolt against the Republican party in 1884, why should voting performance in 1884 have shown no net change in the parties' relative strength, as well as a markedly irregular pattern throughout the country when analyzed over time on a state level? Yet systematic analysis yields voting patterns of such irregularity as to prevent one from specifying the groups of voters, i.e., "Yankee stock," "voters in rural-agricultural or urban-industrial states," etc., *who* voted against the Republicans because of Blaine, and then attempting to explain *why* they did so. Because the hypothesis postulates that Blaine's nomination led both to widespread and considerable decline in Republican percentage strength, it is regarded here as demonstrably unverifiable. As shown below, it cannot satisfy the systematic voting data obtained when the time, space, and rate dimensions are employed.

Time, space, and rate of change

Though even a crude index such as net change over time is of considerable utility in testing a hypothesis concerning voting behavior, more intensive examination of the voting data suggests a standard procedure for handling the problem in terms of the three dimensions available to historians, i.e., time, space, and rate of change. The popular national vote showed less net change in 1884 than in any election before or since but it would be inaccurate to conclude that only an insignificant proportion of voters changed allegiances. Gains and losses might have been so closely balanced that a *gross turnover* of significant proportions could have occurred yet not be reflected in the *net turnover*. To study the extent to which voters switched allegiances, it is necessary to combine the time and space dimensions, i.e., break down the net turnover in the total *national vote* to the net turnover in the *individual state's vote*. If more precise data were desired concerning the gross turnover, the state totals would have to be broken down further and the units of analysis arranged in descending order, counties, towns, wards, election districts, or variations thereof. But for our purposes changes in the state totals are all that is necessary.

As indicated above, comparison of the Republican vote in 1880 and 1884 permits classification of state voting behavior in three distinct categories: states where the Republican party increased its percentage of the popular vote; states where its percentage decreased; states where its percentage remained constant. Constant is defined here as $\pm.99$, an increase is $+1.00$ and over, a decrease is at least -1.00. Like all definitions of categories the criteria are arbitrary. But only under unusual circumstances would they significantly distort the patterns of voting behavior because they operate identically in both directions, and there is room for movement in both directions. A larger number of categories would cut down the possibility and extent of distortions due to cluster around the criterion points, ±1.00, but would be less convenient to handle. Actually, the 1884 results are such that the amount of distortion due to specific criterion points is insignificant and can be ignored. (Slightly different results would be yielded if the criteria were $\pm.50$ or ±2.00, but the basic picture would not be altered.) Table IV is arranged in descending order of Republican improvement in 1884 compared to 1880; the second set of columns gives the improvement in 1888 compared to 1884.

The table shows that if only two categories are used, i.e., gains or losses, then in 1884 the Republicans gained in 18 states compared to *all parties* and lost in 20 states. Gains ranged from $+9.4$ (Virginia) to $+0.4$ (Arkansas); losses from -0.7 (Georgia) to -10.6 (South Carolina). Rather than a uniform trend below 1880, an arithmetic range of 20.0 existed between Republican performance in Virginia and South Carolina. The fact that a relatively smooth curve results when the improvement (positive and negative) in each state is plotted in graph form confirms the impression gained from the table that the 20.0 range does not

TABLE IV

Republican improvement, 1880–1884, and 1884–1888; arithmetic percentage change in popular vote by states

	1	2	3	4
State	*Rank*	*% Change 1880–1884*	*Rank*	*% Change 1884–1888*
Virginia	1	+9.4	15	+0.6
Nevada	2	+8.7	8	+1.5
Missouri	3	+8.3	22	−0.7
West Virginia	4	+6.7	6	+1.7
Mississippi	5	+6.5	37	−10.2
Louisiana	6	+5.4	38	−16.0
Texas	7	+4.7	30	−3.9
Maine	8	+3.9	5	+2.2
Tennessee	9	+3.5	25	−2.0
Colorado	10	+3.0	11	+1.2
Kentucky	11	+3.0	4	+2.2
Pennsylvania	12	+2.1	19	−0.2
California	13	+2.1	26	−2.4
Alabama	14	+1.5	34	−6.0
Florida	15	+1.2	36	−7.0
Oregon	16	+0.4	3	+3.7
Maryland	17	+0.4	9	+1.4
Arkansas	18	+0.4	27	−3.2
Georgia	19	−0.7	33	−5.5
Ohio	20	−0.7	24	−1.5
New Hampshire	21	−0.8	23	−0.8
Illinois	22	−0.9	21	−0.6
Indiana	23	−1.2	13	+0.9
New Jersey	24	−1.7	10	+1.2
North Carolina	25	−1.7	14	+0.8
New York	26	−2.1	12	+1.0
Kansas	27	−2.3	28	−3.4
Connecticut	28	−2.5	16	+0.4
Vermont	29	−3.4	2	+4.8
Wisconsin	30	−3.7	20	−0.6
Rhode Island	31	−4.2	31	−4.2
Michigan	32	−4.2	7	+1.6
Minnesota	33	−4.4	32	−4.7
Delaware	34	−4.5	17	+0.2
Iowa	35	−4.5	18	−0.1
Nebraska	36	−5.6	29	−3.8
Massachusetts	37	−10.1	1	+5.0
South Carolina	38	−10.6	35	−6.2

simply reflect changes in Virginia and South Carolina. But dividing the data into two categories tends to obscure the fact that at least three basic patterns of voting behavior can be observed in the 1884 election. (A more precise analysis would distinguish at least five categories; the

±1.00 criterion, and a ±5.00 criterion to subdivide further, gains and losses.)

Any hypothesis concerning the 1884 election must be consonant with the fact that 15 states recorded gains for the Republicans, 7 were constant, and in 16 states the GOP lost support either to Democrats, minor parties, or both. More than that, the hypothesis has to be consonant with the *group characteristics* and *operative conditions* of the individual states within each category, the magnitude of the shift in each case, and the *rate* of shift. The magnitude can be calculated from the state totals for 1880 and 1884 but the *rate* of shift requires at least one more datum point, the vote in 1888.

If statistics are available only for one election the historian's analysis is restricted to the space dimension; if two elections are known he can use both the time and space dimensions to indicate party gains and losses in different states; three elections enable him, in addition, to make some limited statement concerning the *rate* of change between 1880 and 1884 in different states. That is, one must have two sets of successive elections in order to have the basis of comparison necessary to establish a rate. An arithmetic increase of 10.0 from 1884 to 1888 might be steep if the increase from 1880 to 1884 were 1.0, it would be shallow if the increase had been 30.0 instead of 1.0. If we introduce the rate dimension, therefore, instead of three categories reflecting a direct comparison between 1880 and 1884, it is possible to classify voting behavior in at least eight distinct categories. Before describing these categories it might be well to discuss their utility for evaluations of a hypothesis such as the one under consideration.

The contention might reasonably be made that systematic demonstration of three different categories of irregular state voting behavior (gains, losses, constancy) definitely requires restatement of the hypothesis but does not invalidate it entirely, nor limit its potential verifiability to a certain number of states. Conceivably, Blaine's candidacy checked a sharply rising *long-term trend* of Republican strength in the 22 states which showed increases or were constant in 1884, and accelerated a trend away from the party in the 16 states where losses were recorded. If we could determine the trend in each state, and the rate of change in 1880–1884 compared to 1884–1888, a more precise and meaningful statement would be available concerning voting behavior. We could then judge Republican performance in 1884 in short-run historical perspective and better identify those states which could have been affected adversely by Blaine's candidacy.

For example, there would be little likelihood that a Republican *down-trend* state showing a steep Republican *increase* in 1884 reacted unfavorably to Blaine; a steep *decrease* in a Republican *up-trend* state might have been due to him. The most significant states, therefore, are those which display counter-trend movements in 1884, and the rate dimension enables us to identify them. Less significant are those states which display uniform trends (up or down) from 1880 to 1888. Nonetheless, even where the trend is uniform, the rate dimension enables us to distinguish further between Republican performance in 1884 and 1888.

Categories of voting behavior

Table IV contains all the information necessary to form eight categories of voting behavior. A state such as Virginia, represented by a plus sign in both the second and fourth columns, is one in which the Republican trend was upwards from 1880 to 1888. Kansas has minus signs in both columns and exemplifies a continual Republican downtrend. Mississippi has first a plus sign and then a minus sign indicating that the Republican vote in 1884 was *higher* than in both 1880 and 1888. Not only did the Republican 1884 performance improve over 1880, it was clearly *above* the trend for the three elections. Contrariwise, Massachusetts has first a minus sign and then a plus sign. The Republican vote was *less* than in both 1880 and 1888 and clearly *below* the trend.

So far a method has been described to establish four categories of states to evaluate Republican performance. Category I comprises states such as Virginia in which the Republican trend was continually upward. Category II, states such as Kansas where the Republican trend was continually down. Category III, with Mississippi the prototype, states where Republican performance was better than trend. Category IV, Massachusetts, where Republican performance was worse than trend. Applying this method to Table IV the 38 states participating in the three elections fall into these categories:

I (8 states)	II (11 states)	III (10 states)	IV (9 states)
Virginia	Kansas	Mississippi	Massachusetts
Colorado	Georgia	Alabama	Connecticut
Kentucky	Illinois	Arkansas	Delaware
Maine	Iowa	California	Indiana
Maryland	Minnesota	Florida	Michigan
Nevada	New Hampshire	Louisiana	New Jersey
Oregon	Nebraska	Missouri	New York
West Virginia	Ohio	Pennsylvania	North Carolina
	Rhode Island	Tennessee	Vermont
	South Carolina	Texas	
	Wisconsin		

Simply in terms of gain and loss, without the constancy criterion, these categories show that in 1884, Republican strength increased in 18 states (I and III), continued a down-trend in 11 more (II), and in 9 states declined counter to trend (IV). Thus, before the rate dimension is introduced, the trend data indicate *that only the 9 states in Category IV displayed adverse Republican voting patterns which might be attributed primarily to Blaine's candidacy.* For example, it would be illogical to offer this explanation in the case of a category II state such as Kansas where Republican strength declined *at every election after 1864 until 1896.*

TABLE V

Republican percentage of popular vote,
Kansas, 1864–1900

YEAR	PERCENTAGE	ARITHMETIC CHANGE
1860	–	–
1864	81.7	–
1868	68.8	–12.9
1872	67.0	–1.8
1876	63.2	–3.9
1880	60.4	–2.8
1884	58.1	–2.3
1888	54.8	–3.4
1892	46.7	–8.0
1896	47.5	+0.8
1900	52.6	+5.1

Not every state in category II shows a similar pattern of unbroken decline but with rare exceptions the Republican percentage in 1884 was *below* that recorded in all previous elections and *above* that recorded in all subsequent ones until 1896. And when the rate dimension is employed, as can be seen from the Kansas table (Table V) even more precise statements can be made. Though the Republican party continued to give ground in 1884 in Kansas, its rate of decline was *less* than in the two elections before and after.

The rate dimension now enables us to subdivide further the four categories and describe eight patterns of voting behavior in 1884. For example, the Republican gain in Virginia (Category I) from 1880 to 1884 was +9.4, much steeper than the +.6 recorded for 1884–1888. Had the Republicans continued to increase their strength at the same rate, the latter figure should also have been +9.4. Had their rate of increase in 1888 bettered that of 1884 it should have been at least +9.41. In Oregon, another Category I state, the Republican rate of increase did pick up in 1888, +.4 was followed by +3.7.

Similarly, it is possible to compare the rates of increase or decrease for the three other categories, and subdivide them accordingly. Diagrams A and B below represent a steep and shallow rate, respectively, in an up-trend state; C and D represent a steep and shallow rate in a favorable counter-trend state. Actually, D represents steeper than short-run trend gains in 1884 rather than what might be termed a true counter-trend movement. That is, the Republican percentage in 1888 is also higher than in 1880, although it is below that of 1884. In contrast, C represents an 1884 reversal of a short-run down-trend for 1888 is lower than 1880. Of these four patterns of voting behavior, only Diagram B could be offered as an example of a state in which the voting statistics show Republican improvement was possibly retarded by Blaine's candidacy. The other three represent more favorable than trend Republican voting in various degrees of *improvement*.

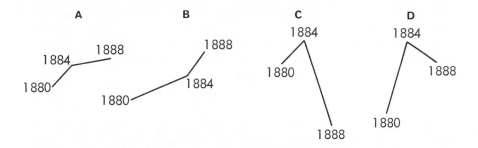

The four diagrams below represent the same patterns in down-trend states. Here G is the true counter-trend type, and F is a state such as Kansas where Blaine's candidacy might have slowed down the rate of Republican *decline*.

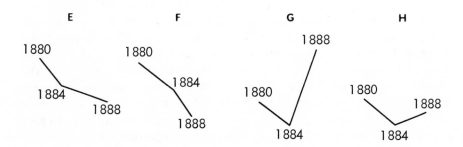

Evaluating Republican
performance in 1884

The information which can be obtained from analyzing the 1884 vote would increase with the number of datum points utilized to establish trends and rates. If the diagrams above were extended to include elections from 1860 to 1900 the short-run movements from 1880 to 1888 could be seen in terms of a long-run perspective, and interpretations of the 1884 election might be expected to fit not only the immediate events of the campaign but more fundamental patterns of American politics in the post-Civil War decades. According to the degree of precision desired, we could use more than three datum points, set up more than eight categories for all parties, and thereby obtain a clearer description of American voting patterns. Particularly if the analysis were carried down to the county level, where in the states the number of units occasionally runs in the hundreds and for the country at large, in the thousands, an increased number of categories would facilitate accurate thinking about the results of any one election. We would then know what we are attempting to explain, and, presumably, be in a better position to do so.

A uniform distribution of units in the various categories would indicate one pattern of national voting behavior; a sharply skewed distribution would have another meaning entirely. For our purposes such detailed diagrams are unnecessary and their results can be summed up in this fashion: With few exceptions the Republican party's state percentages declined preceptibly after 1872 in comparison with the average percentage of elections from 1860 to 1872 inclusive, and the process was not reversed until 1896. The exceptions are states in which recovery began one or two elections before 1896. In every state the party more or less declined after 1872.

Seen in long-run perspective and broken down into meaningful categories, Republican performance in 1884 obviously takes on a different aspect than the one usually given it. But even the information gained from analyzing the three elections, 1880–1888, is of considerable aid in evaluating the hypothesis under consideration. *It demonstrates that no factual basis exists for a possible assumption that Blaine's candidacy checked the rate of Republican increase and accelerated the rate of decline throughout the country.* Had this assumption been true the number of states in category G, unfavorable counter-trend, should have been large, and the number in C, favorable counter-trend, should have been small. The reverse pattern is found; there were six states in category C, and only one in G. Moreover, there were three times as many states in category A (steeper increase) than in category B (shallower increase), but categories E and F were equal in number. The 38 states break down as follows:

A	B	C	D
Virginia	Maryland	Mississippi	Missouri
Colorado	Oregon	Alabama	Pennsylvania
Kentucky		Arkansas	Tennessee
Maine		California	Texas
Nevada		Florida	
West Virginia		Louisiana	

E	F	G	H
Illinois	Kansas	Vermont	Connecticut
Iowa	Georgia		Delaware
Nebraska	Minnesota		Indiana
South Carolina	Ohio		Massachusetts
Wisconsin	Rhode Island		Michigan
			New Jersey
			New York
			North Carolina

New Hampshire (−.79 and −.79)

What emerges from a systematic analysis of the statistical data available on state voting behavior, therefore, does not support the hypothesis that Blaine's candidacy was "the great central explanation" of the Republican party's defeat in 1884. (Affirmative results which emerge from this analysis will be discussed in another section.) *Its arithmetic net loss in the national total vote was only 00.09 percent. The party had been declining since 1872. In a considerable number of states its performance was better than the short-time trend and in six states it clearly reversed an unfavorable trend.* At best, only in certain states (G and H) could the party be said to have done worse than might have been expected from the trend of presidential elections. *And this takes no account of the stunning defeats suffered by the Republicans in 1882 and other adverse political developments after 1880 for which Blaine cannot be held responsible,* nor the fact that both major parties were under increasing attack after 1872. Thus, in both New York and New Jersey where the Republican party declined slightly from 1880 and recovered slightly in 1888, Democratic strength also diminished in 1884. Moreover, if one examines in detail the political situation in the other seven states in categories G and H, additional possible explanations for Republican losses suggest themselves.

In Massachusetts, for example, where the party's percentage of the popular vote was 10.1 below its 1880 percentage, the decline might be explained by the vote polled for ex-Governor Ben Butler on a combined Anti-monopoly and Greenback ticket. Examination of the Massachusetts annual voting statistics from 1876 to 1884 indicates that when Butler ran for state office on a Greenback fusion ticket with the Democrats, as he did in 1878, 1879, 1882, and 1883, significant inroads were made into Republican strength. Thus, in 1880 he was not a candidate and the Republican presidential percentage was 58.5. Nor was he a gubernatorial candidate in 1881, and the GOP vote increased to 61.3 percent. But in 1882 Butler won the race for governor on a fusion ticket and Republican strength plummeted to 46 percent. He lost his bid for re-election in 1883 to a Republican but only by a small margin, and in 1884 his presidential campaign gave him 8.1 percent of the Massachusetts vote. Though Blaine's percentage was 10.1 lower than that attained by Garfield in 1880 and 9.1 lower than Hayes in 1876, the Democratic party with Cleveland as its candidate only registered an increase of 0.7 over 1880 and was 1.7 less than the vote given Tilden in 1876. In other words, the marked decrease in Republican strength was not accompanied by anything like a corresponding increase in Democratic strength.

TABLE VI

Massachusetts popular vote; party percentages for president or governor, 1876-1884

YEAR	OFFICE	REP.	DEM.	GREENBACK
1876	Pres.	58.0	42.0	–
1877	Gov.	49.5	39.7	1.9
1878	Gov.	52.6	4.0*	42.7*
1879	Gov.	50.4	4.1*	44.8*
1880	Pres.	58.5	39.6	1.6
1881	Gov.	61.3	34.6	3.1
1882	Gov.	46.8	52.2**	**
1883	Gov.	51.3	48.1**	**
1884	Pres.	48.4	40.3	8.1

*Democratic party offered candidates but bulk of party fused with Nationals (Greenbackers) to support Ben Butler.
**Fusion of Democrats and Greenbackers to support Butler.

The statistics in Table VI are not offered to "prove" that Butler's candidacy explains the Republican decline in Massachusetts. They are cited to indicate that even in a category H state such as Massachusetts little basis exists for the *automatic* assumption that Blaine was solely responsible for the decline. In similar fashion, having once identified the states in categories G and H, it is possible to show that other explanations than the one given by our hypothesis may account for Republican losses.

Surely the fact that in 1882 Cleveland had scored the greatest victory in New York Democratic annals is worth consideration in explaining the slight Republican decline in that state during a political era when native sons were expected to attract votes. (Actually, the Democrats also declined slightly in Cleveland's home state, New York; their arithmetic percentage decrease was 0.1. Contrariwise, in Maine, the home state of Blaine, the Republican arithmetic increase was 3.9, the Democratic decrease was 6.0, and minor party increases made up the difference. If the real issue had been the public integrity of the two candidates, among people who presumably knew them best, Blaine had been given a vote of increased confidence, Cleveland had not.)

Even if other possible explanations are ignored, however, the procedures carried out above of reformulating our hypothesis and analyzing the pertinent voting data systematically have demonstrated that it is at best applicable to a small number of states. Logically, therefore, the hypothesis also must be required to state, and shown to be consistent with, the conditions which produced the different voting patterns described in the eight categories, A to H; a requirement which it cannot satisfy. Of more importance, however, is the logical requirement that it also state the conditions which made the personal characteristics of the Republican and Democratic presidential candidates the "real issue" of the campaign!

Just as Nevins acutely observed that accidental factors such as "Rum, Romanism, and Rebellion" were only significant under specific circumstances (assuming now that they were), analysis of the 1884 campaign indicates that the candidates became *the "real issue" only because certain conditions then prevailed in the country.* Again the 1896 election can be used as a reference point. After several years of deep depression and growing social conflict it is almost inconceivable that hypothetical indiscretions by Bryan and dubious transactions by McKinley could have replaced "free silver" and sectional antagonism as the primary issues in 1896. A comprehensive hypothesis concerning the 1884 campaign, or any other, must not only identify the causal factors which explain the systematic data, it must also answer the more fundamental question of why those specific causal factors were operative. If this contention is accepted, then the need becomes obvious to develop at least a crude body of theory concerning American presidential elections—a task, however, to which this study will only call attention but prudently will not attempt to undertake.

The 1884 election reconsidered

Having been employed above to evaluate Nevins' hypothesis as unverifiable, the systematic data presented can also be employed to designate another impressionistic explanation of the 1884 election as *potentially verifiable.* This explanation also puts the fortuitous interpretation into proper perspective by answering the significant question posed by the campaign. The question: Is it possible to identify the basic conditions which explain why the candidates' personal characteristics dominated the 1884 campaign? Historians, it is contended here, would answer that question with impressive unanimity. There simply were no significant issues which distinguished the national Republican and Democratic parties in 1884, nor indeed, at a minimum, between 1877 and the early 1890's. Nevins clearly should subscribe at least to the first part of that proposition, for he quoted George W. Curtis approvingly, "the platforms of the two parties [in 1884] are practically the same," and himself affirmed that "Seldom has so little account been taken of platform or pledges . . ." His explanation was that Blaine's candidacy precipitated such a state of affairs. But after all, with virtually identical platforms, with both parties animated by the same philosophy and controlled by essentially the same groups, what else could Democrats and Republicans stage an election "contest" around other than Cleveland's private, and Blaine's public, indiscretions?

To borrow Harry Carman's and Harold Syrett's neat phrase, the period between the end of Reconstruction and the emergence of Populism can be described as "the politics of dead center." Under such circumstances the election of Cleveland or Blaine simply was fraught with insignificance, except, of course, to the politicians involved, their entourages, and the "special interests" which expected to benefit if "their" candidate won. It was hardly an accident that Republican gains and losses were nearly equal, that no new patterns emerged and that a Republican net decline of 00.09 from 1880 in the percentage of the popular vote was barely overbalanced by a Democratic increase of 0.28. Reinforcing this point is the fact that the net turnover from 1884 to 1888 was the second smallest in American history. Republicans won the election although they recorded a −0.39 arithmetic percentage change, and Democrats lost though they improved their showing with a +0.15. (Gross turnover was even more restricted than in 1880–1884.)

Obviously, the voting data cited above do not prove the "politics of dead center" explanation. But they do indicate how systematic methods can be used to evaluate conflicting hypotheses derived from impressionistic research. Moreover, it seems reasonable to assert, by demonstrating the factual error in the "moral crusade" interpretation the systematic voting data have pointed up the methodological dangers of judging history from the documents, records, and publications of contemporary elite groups. (Here the term "elite group" embraces the political, economic, social, and cultural leaders of a given period in a broad sense; it does not refer to "social position" in the conventional usage.)

Impressionistic research is particularly vulnerable to the dangers of unintentional distortion and one-sidedness because, to a striking degree, source materials reflecting elite groups' views and experiences are the ones most frequently preserved and readily accessible to later scholars. Perhaps the "Mugwumps" who led the "moral crusade" genuinely believed that Cleveland's election was imperative if American political institutions were to be preserved. (The genuineness of their moral crusade is debatable.) Perhaps they also were convinced that they embodied and reflected the nation's will and wisdom. (This point is more easily conceded—that is, their conviction as distinct from the fact.) But in the 1884 election, the voting returns appear to demonstrate that they can hardly be said to have represented anyone but themselves.

In New York County, for example, where the "crusade" attained its greatest publicity and commanded its most powerful press support, the Republican party percentage was almost identical in 1880, 1884, and 1888. The Democratic party percentage in 1884 was actually 1.4 *less* than in 1880, and 1.6 *less* than in 1888.

Less intriguing than cryptic entries in carefully preserved private journals, less colorful than professional politicians' speeches or the public rhetoric of articulate leaders, *systematic voting statistics are more reliable indicators of popular attitudes and beliefs.* This is not to argue that impressionistic source materials such as the records and writings of elite groups in a given period are valueless. On the contrary, they are indispensable and can provide the historian with valuable insights into the whole range of contemporary politics. Nonetheless, the records of elite groups which happen to be preserved and accessible do not constitute an adequate basis for the description and interpretation of an election outcome. Their representative quality and accurate depiction of reality can best be evaluated when they are employed in conjunction with systematic data. Another key proposition of this study holds that such data give the historian a solid foundation upon which to stand in working through those documents fortunate enough to withstand the hazards of time, and the whims of mice and men.

GENERALIZED INTERPRETATION ANALYZED IN TERMS OF THE HISTORIAN'S SPACE DIMENSION

The space dimension becomes particularly valuable to a historian whenever a substantially new phenomenon occurs, or when the available data preceding or following the phenomenon under study is too fragmentary for adequate comparison. In those situations, though it can be put to limited uses, historians are largely deprived of their basic methodological tool, the recording and analysis of phenomena as they occurred over time. If the requisite data are available, it is possible to analyze phenomena in terms of subsequent developments or of other phenomena which preceded it, no matter how fragmentary the data. But the value of the time dimension is considerably diminished as a result. To paraphrase artillery gunners, when the "target" is not bracketed between "before" and "after," its significance is difficult to gauge. More than ever, it becomes necessary to utilize the space dimension fully in attempting to understand and explain the phenomenon at issue.

The space dimension is not only valuable in dealing with "new" developments; as the case study in the previous section was designed to demonstrate, it is far more effective when combined with the other historical dimensions. But whether used alone or in conjunction with time and rate, spatial recording and analysis of data has two essential characteristics of particular interest to political historians; above all to American historians who must deal with a federal system placing a high premium on geography.

Plotted in spatial terms, a party's voting support, for example, can be recognized and described as widespread or restricted, random or regular in pattern, concentrated or spotty. Such determinations are extremely useful in describing *what happened,* and they are also good ways to begin the difficult task of learning *who voted for it to happen.* Once voting data are plotted spatially in units such as wards, townships, counties, states, etc., all other data which might help to answer the question, and capable of representation in the same form, can be similarly plotted. In effect, data pertaining to various kinds of designated voting groups are superimposed on voting performance data arranged in ecological unit order.

Consciously or otherwise, the two characteristics of the space dimension sketched above are almost invariably used by political historians, indeed, by political pundits of any kind or lack of qualification. For example, if the present farm price support issue becomes a topic of conversation, one "instinctively" thinks of particular geographic areas where it might be a significant voting determinant, and of particular voting groups in those areas who might be affected (corn-hog farmers, wheat farmers, dairy farmers, and the like).

Precisely because it is so conveniently and casually used, the space dimension lends itself to marked confusion and error in impressionistic research. A phenomenon which appears to be common and widespread may actually be rigidly restricted or erratically spotty. And voting performance apparently associated with a particular occupational group in a given area may actually cut across class lines and be far more accurately associated with religious affiliation. No claim is made here which even implies that systematic research methods and data eliminate all error and solve all problems connected with the space dimension's use. It is contended, however, that they can substantially increase its effectiveness and reliability when employed in political historiography. The case study in this section is designed to illustrate these claims in practice, as well as amplify the points made above.

The election of 1824

The election of 1824 is of considerable interest to historians because it marked the break-up of the one-party rule developing after Jefferson's victory in 1800, because it was the first in which a country-wide popular vote was cast, and because Andrew Jackson, though unsuccessful in his bid for the presidency, was thereby established in national politics on a firm footing. Placing stress upon the latter point, Arthur Schlesinger, Jr. stated in his Pulitzer Prize work: "His immense popular vote in 1824 came from his military fame and from the widespread conviction of his integrity." The sentence clearly offers an explicit explanation of voting behavior throughout the country in 1824 and will be analyzed in those terms.

At first sight Schlesinger's explanation might appear to be of the type which cannot be verified but only argued about. The causal factors, i.e., Jackson's military fame and widespread conviction of his integrity, are of such a highly generalized nature as to make it difficult to measure their impact and separate them out from other possible determinants of voting behavior. Stated in terms of the original formulation, the explanation would force historians to rely upon impressionistic data, and scholars of equal competence might reasonably be expected to offer contradictory albeit plausible estimates of its validity. How, for example, could one even begin to attempt to determine whether an *undifferentiated* number of men voted for Jackson because they were impressed with his heroism and integrity or because he was, as an alternative hypothesis has it, a representative of the frontier? Without fairly precise delineation of the *kind* of men who voted *both for and against Jackson,* explanations of why a certain number of men voted for him are not subject to systematic tests of their potential verifiability.

But it is possible to reformulate Schlesinger's original statement and thereby render the hypothesis more susceptible to verification. The factual elements in the hypothesis are that a widespread conviction existed of Jackson's integrity, that his military fame was at least equally widespread (by implication), and that his popular vote was "immense." Thus, the common denominator in the factual elements of the formulation is their "widespread" incidence. Neither the size of the vote for Jackson nor the influence of his fame and integrity upon voting behavior is described in local or sectional terms but in terms of the nation as a whole. The relationship between fact and interpretation is clear when the implications are made more explicit. Stated in other words, Schlesinger's hypothesis is that a large if unspecified proportion of the "masses" throughout the country were impressed by Jackson's military fame, were convinced of his integrity, and, primarily for those reasons, voted for him in the 1824 election. That such formulation does not distort his position is evident, it would seem, from this quotation:

In the republic's early years, martial reputation had counted little for future political success. But the broadening of the suffrage, the thrill of surging nationalism and the declining glamour of the old ruling class created a favorable atmosphere for new idols, and the War of 1812 promptly produced the military hero. The old aristocracy resented such vulgar and *parvenu* prestige, and a man with Jackson's credentials was almost forced into the opposition. Moreover, while the newly enfranchised and chauvinistic masses regarded the military hero with wild enthusiasm, to the old aristocracy, raised on classical analogies, no figure could seem more dangerous to the republic.

Particularly when put in those terms, the assertion seems warranted that Schlesinger's thesis has to satisfy at least two stipulations: Jackson obtained *a large proportion of the "masses'" vote; his support was not restricted to specific states and sections but was national in scope.* When the thesis is restated it is more subject to verification and calls for analytical emphasis to be placed upon the historian's space dimension. The presidential contest in 1824 was the first in which the American people directly participated to a measurable extent, or as H. J. Ford has put it, the first to mark "the beginning of a concentration of popular interest on the presidential election." No comparable statistics of the popular vote are available before 1824 and in that election the national vote stood:

Jackson	153,544
Adams	108,740
Clay	47,136
Crawford	46,618
	356,038

These statistics make it possible to translate the vague factual description, "immense vote," with its connotation of extremely widespread support, into an explicit statement that Jackson received approximately 43 percent of the popular vote, his nearest rival 31 percent, and his two other rivals, 13 percent each. (No statistics were presented by Schlesinger for either the popular or the electoral vote on a state or national basis.) Once the verbal description is translated into even such gross quantitative terms as the national totals and percentages, once the problem is not to explain why an "immense," or "overwhelming," or "very large" proportion of the American people wanted Jackson to be president, but why 43 percent of the "small" (defined below) number of people who actually cast ballots voted for him, the problem becomes easier to handle.

Who voted for Jackson?

Since Jackson received less than 50 percent of the vote, the statistics appear to rule out the likelihood that all throughout the country the majority of the "chauvinistic masses" who voted cast ballots for Jackson, unless it can actually be demonstrated that his support was more or less uniformly distributed along tight class lines. This follows since the "masses" must logically be expected to outnumber the other classes or the term "masses" is not revelant to the election of 1824. If Jackson's support was very heavy in some areas and very light in others, in some places both the masses and the other classes voted preponderantly for him, and in other places both groups voted preponderantly against him. This conclusion would have to follow unless two conditions obtained; a different proportion of voters are to be designated as belonging to the "masses" and "other classes" in different areas, and both groups displayed uniform voting behavior throughout the country.

To my knowledge no evidence has ever been offered that in 1824 significantly different proportions of the masses voted in the different states where popular suffrage obtained; moreover, breaking down the returns by states demonstrates anything but a uniform distribution. It suggests that if Jackson's widespread military fame and reputed integrity actually do explain his lead in the popular vote, then these generalized factors operated in a remarkably selective manner which demand both explicit statement and further specification. For he carried but eight of the eighteen states in which popular votes were cast, only in six did he get 50 percent or better, and as Table VII shows, Jackson's margin over his nearest rival was 2 to 1 or better only in Alabama, Tennessee, and Pennsylvania.

The approximately 50,000 *plurality* given him in the last two states more than accounts for his lead over John Q. Adams in the nation-wide vote, a fact which should be central to any interpretation of the 1824 election results and of Jackson's popular lead. That is, roughly 42 percent of Jackson's entire vote came from three states which cast only 23 percent of the national vote. In these three states he got about 80 percent of the vote, whereas he had only 43 percent of the national total, and 32 percent in the other 15 states.

TABLE VII

Popular vote, 1824 — states carried by Jackson

STATE	JACKSON	%	ADAMS	%	CRAW-FORD	%	CLAY	%	TOTAL
Tennessee	20,197	97.5	216	1.0	312	1.5	–	–	20,725
Pennsylvania	36,100	76.2	5,440	11.5	4,206	8.9	1,609	3.4	47,355
Alabama	9,443	69.4	2,416	17.8	1,680	12.3	67	0.5	13,606
Mississippi	3,234	64.1	1,694	33.6	119	2.4	–	–	5,047
North Carolina	20,415*	56.7	–	–	15,621	43.3	–	–	36,036
New Jersey	10,985	51.6	9,110	42.8	1,196	5.6	–	–	21,291
Indiana	7,343	46.6	3,095	19.6	–	–	5,315	33.7	15,753
Illinois	1,901	40.4	1,542	32.7	219	4.7	1,047	22.2	4,709

*"Peoples Ticket," or anti-"Caucus" vote

Several pertinent facts concerning the election in general, and the strong Jackson states in particular, further indicate the partial nature at best of an explanation which attributes his support primarily, if not exclusively, to "his military fame and . . . the widespread conviction of his integrity." That approximately 350,000 votes in all were cast, out of a population of nearly 11,000,000, indicates how small a percentage of the "chauvinistic masses" actually voted. (The comparable figures for 1828 were 1,150,000 votes, 12,250,000 people.) And to quote Stanwood's standard work on American presidential elections, the figures given above credit to Jackson:

. . . a great many votes which, like the 20,000 in North Carolina, were cast for no candidate in particular, but in opposition to the caucus ticket generally [opposition to nomination by a Congressional party caucus of Crawford as the "regular," albeit unofficial, candidate], and of which it was estimated at the time that 5,000 were given by friends of Adams; and other votes which, in some Northern states, were cast against Adams generally, without being for any particular candidate.

A major source of distortion relative to the popular vote is that the statistics do not include six states where the Legislatures made the choice. In three of the states Jackson received none of the electoral votes; in New York, the most populous state in the Union, he received one out of 36; he took 3 out of 5 in Louisiana, and all 11 in South Carolina. Hence as Jackson received but 15 of the 71 electoral votes of these states, pending a detailed study, the presumption seems reasonable that their popular vote would have substantially decreased his percentage of the national total. Such reasoning is speculative, yet to indicate how little is really known about the popular sentiment in 1824, Stanwood observed that: "there were real contests in very few of the States, so that the partisans of neither [sic] candidate were fully represented at the polls." Thus, Massachusetts, home state of John Q. Adams, where Jackson did not get a single vote, cast more than 66,000 ballots for governor in 1823 and only 37,000 in the presidential election a year later.

Viewed in light of the above considerations, the conclusion seems warranted that Schlesinger's hypothesis regarding the extent and reasons for Jackson's vote in 1824 is not consonant with the election statistics. *The factors denoted by him as voting determinants throughout the country could have been operative only in certain localities, states, and sections; they could not have had the unrestricted nationwide impact demanded by his hypothesis.*

Conditions favorable to Jackson

When attention is turned to the three states in which Jackson was strongest, the historian's obligation to specify the conditions under which causal factors actually function becomes more obvious. In states where Jackson secured few votes, or only a minor percentage of the total vote, either his fame and integrity were unknown and publicized (subject to investigation if deemed important), or far more likely, they were ineffective as determinants of voting behavior. On the other hand, it is possible that these alleged causal factors were operative in Tennessee, Alabama, and Pennsylvania. Schlesinger's hypothesis then could be restated to set forth the conditions under which Jackson's military fame and integrity determined voting behavior and those which yielded opposite results. By way of illustration, among other conditions which it might be necessary to take into account: Tennessee was Jackson's home when such a factor was extremely important, particularly in a western state seeking national influence (he ran about 40 to 1 in Tennessee). Neighboring Alabama was a frontier area strongly responsive to the victor of the Creek War of 1813–1814 which opened it to settlement. Jackson was of Scotch-Irish descent when marked conflict existed between the New England "Yankee" element, strongly based on the seaboard, and the Scotch-Irish and German elements west of the Alleghenies. Probably associated with these ethnic loyalties and conflicts as a determinant of political behavior—here research using manuscript sources would be indispensable to verify the assumption—is the fact that as early as 1821 the leading politicians of Pennsylvania had decided to run Jackson as a candidate. Local, sectional, and ethnic influences aided his rivals as well, but this only underscores the point that *the significance of the voting statistics is not apparent if only the national totals are considered in isolation and the basic conditions affecting voting patterns in various areas are left unspecified.*

The main point of the discussion has been that the greater the precision achieved in breaking down voting statistics over space, the greater the possibility of fixing the conditions under which a given explanation can be valid. Hypotheses take on more precision, and a greater possibility of verification, if the factual stipulations which they must logically be expected to satisfy are carefully thought out and then demonstrated rather than assumed.

In frontier Tennessee the vote for Jackson was "immense"; in neighboring Kentucky, the home of Henry Clay, Jackson was badly beaten (roughly 17,000 to 6,000). Obviously, in Kentucky military fame and reputed integrity were not key determinants of voting behavior. But it is possible, and, for purposes of illustration, it will be assumed here as fact, that in a number of Kentucky counties Jackson did run ahead of Clay. A comprehensive explanation of the 1824 election would have to explain such phenomena, or at least it should state explicitly that it does not satisfy certain systematic findings.

If the deviant cases not satisfied by the explanation were of the magnitude indicated above—a number of Jackson counties in a strong Clay state—then it would be logical to expect the historian to deal explicitly with questions of this nature: What conditions, if any, differentiated the Jackson counties from those voting for the native son, Henry Clay? Was Jackson's fame greater, and belief in his integrity more firm, in certain counties than in others? If opposite voting patterns occurred in counties where detailed investigation leads one to conclude that his fame and integrity were uniform, what other conditions were different? Given Schlesinger's primary causal factors, why should these different conditions have operated to bring about different patterns of voting behavior?

The last question, the "why" question, would be the interpretative element in formulating that part of the hypothesis covering the deviant cases; the previous "what" questions are in the category of factual description. Factual questions yield information analogous to the natural scientist's statement of the conditions under which water boils at a certain temperature, but they fail to explain why the phenomenon occurs under those conditions. To take a hypothetical case: We might factually demonstrate that in all counties where over 50 percent of the entire population was Scotch-Irish, over 50 percent of the popular vote went to Jackson. To explain why this result occurs in such counties is a job of another order and explicit recognition of the distinction between fact and interpretation favors progress towards its solution.

The following possibility is suggested to bring out the potential dangers of generalized explanations which do not attempt to specify the conditions necessary for them to be verifiable. A careful analysis of the areas of Jacksonian strength and weakness, in order to state the conditions under which his military fame and reputed integrity operated as determining factors, might lead to the unanticipated conclusion that they were of relatively minor importance everywhere. It might be observed that Jackson was strong only in areas having certain characteristics: frontier areas not settled by New England migrants and no "native son" candidate; areas dominated by Scotch-Irish and German voters; agrarian areas dependent upon certain staple crops; and so forth. It might also be observed that in a number of areas where detailed investigation demonstrated little or no perceptible differences in awareness of Jackson's heroism or stress upon his integrity, his proportion of the vote *varied widely* depending upon the extent to which the area possessed the characteristics denominated above.

If Schlesinger's explanation could be valid only in areas having specific characteristics in common, and does not hold true when these characteristics are absent, it would be more logical to try to explain the vote for Jackson in terms of these specific characteristics rather than general causes which did not in fact operate generally. No implication is intended that any of these developments took place in fact. The point is that the procedure of attempting to specify the conditions under which a given set of causal factors operate might yield systematic findings not consonant with the hypothesis. These findings might then lead to reformulation of the hypothesis, or to construction of a series of new hypotheses more consonant with the data. In turn these hypotheses would be subject to additional testing through the re-analysis of existing data and the collection of additional data necessary to their verification. . . .

EPILOGUE

Until this point the study has essentially dealt with the problems of learning what happened, where and when it happened, and who did it. In a sense, although filled with technical difficulties and demanding arduous research, these phases of inquiry are relatively the easiest in terms of satisfactory resolution. They call for a high order of intellectual clarity and articulation but the major difficulties they present might really be viewed as mechanical and administrative, requiring efficient organization and adequate forces rather than highly skilled, intelligent, imaginative historical research.

When attempts are made to answer questions involving the why and how of American political behavior, a considerably more complex field is entered. Granted that we were able to describe what happened accurately, and who voted for it to happen, we still would not know why they voted as they did, and how their beliefs came to be formed. In other words, what are the opinion-making and opinion-manipulating devices and institutions utilized at various times to persuade various groups that they should vote for a particular party or individual, for particular reasons? How effective are these several instrumentalities in achieving such persuasion, and under what conditions? To what extent does tradition condition voter beliefs; to what extent are voter beliefs the specific result of purposive action by specific individuals, groups or institutions; to what extent are these beliefs by-products of ostensibly nonpolitical groups, activities, social processes, and institutional patterns; to what extent are these beliefs consciously or unconsciously acquired or inculcated?

Obviously, questions involving the why and how of political behavior are extremely difficult to answer for so heterogeneous and dynamic a country as the United States. It cannot be overstressed that establishing the objective correlations indicated above does not automatically solve these questions. On the contrary, *they merely allow these questions to be put forth in meaningful form.* That is, questions can then be derived from known facts, not erroneous or metaphysical impressions, and the answers to the questions can be tested to conform with all known facts. Moreover, attempts to answer these questions may reveal that insufficient correlations have been established and lead to efforts to establish additional correlations.

But if one essays beyond simple description, correlations can only point the way for historical research, they cannot take its place. One may be able to establish beyond reasonable doubt, for example, that for given time periods German–Americans tend to conform to the dominant patterns of their community without knowing why they do so, how they came to be persuaded, and under what persuasion they ceased to do so. Correlations thus can be thought of on two levels, descriptive and interpretative; they are adequate for the first but merely suggestive for the second.

This study is not designed to deal with the complicated problems involved in the attainment of genuinely objective historical interpretations of systematic, well-described, known data; that is, interpretations which can be described accurately as consistent with scientific procedures. Yet it seems reasonable to maintain that before we can have such interpretations, or even argue logically whether they are possible under any circumstances, *we must have known data in manageable form.* Lacking sufficient data of this character, statements on the subject, both *pro* and *con,* really are incapable of resolution. No implication of mechanical separation is intended here. Self-evidently, the processes do not take place independently of each other, nor would it be desirable that they do so. Nonetheless, at the present stage of controversy and development, known data of the type called for above and techniques to handle them would seem to be a prerequisite if historiographic advances are to be made, and if arguments relative to "scientific history" are not to remain at the mercy of the rapid changes of intellectual climate so characteristic of the twentieth century.

10. | DONALD STOKES
Voting

Research into "the why and how of political behavior" in contemporary America has aided the political historian by expanding his knowledge of the possible range of influences affecting individual voter decisions. Donald Stokes, one of the leading students of contemporary electoral behavior, here sums up the state of our current knowledge. "Voting" by Donald Stokes. Reprinted with permission of the Publisher from the *International Encyclopedia of the Social Sciences,* David L. Sills, Editor. Volume 16, pages 391–394. Copyright © 1968 by Crowell Collier and Macmillan, Inc.

Empirical studies of voting quickly shattered the naive view of the elector as unbiased juror reaching a fresh verdict in each election. Research showed that, on the contrary, many electors had very long-established partisan attachments, "standing decisions" in V. O. Key's phrase, which deeply influenced their perception of contemporary candidates, issues, and political events. The tendency for these dispositions to color the partisan voter's response to new elements of politics lessens the amplitude of change in the electorate as a whole and tends to increase the stability of party systems. What is more, although the relationship is a complex one, data from several nations suggests that because political interest and information tend to increase with strength of partisanship, the less informed, less interested elector may be the one more likely to change his vote and to bring about a change of government.

Studies of both adult electors and children have shown that partisan ties often extend back deep into childhood, with the family as the main agency of political socialization. Greenstein has found the frequency of party identification among a sample of schoolchildren in one New England city to be as great as in the youngest age group of the American adult population. Adult studies relying on recall of early partisanship have repeatedly shown that large majorities of electors continue to hold the party allegiances of their parents. These findings are far from unambiguous, however, since parents give their children a social location in terms of class and other factors which have partisan significance in adult life, quite apart from the child's exposure to political values in the home. The relative importance of family, school, friendship groups, and other influences in the early years of the political life cycle is increasingly the focus of research. Such work is by no means confined to the development of partisanship; many types of affective and cognitive orientations to politics have come under review (Hess & Easton 1960; Hyman 1959).

In general, the longer a party allegiance is held, the stronger it becomes. Measures of the strength of party identification have repeatedly been found to increase with age. The relative plasticity of party ties in younger voters partly accounts for the phenomenon of political "generations"—differences in the direction of partisanship among age cohorts. Voters entering the electorate in a period which is strongly favorable to one party are likely to hold the same party allegiance in later years; thus, the great depression's generation of American voters held a Democratic partisanship and the first post-war generation of British voters kept a party allegiance to Labour.

Political systems vary in the amount of short-term electoral change. In some systems, such as the Norwegian, where party loyalties are tightly bound to a social structure which itself changes little, there is slight variation of party preference between elections, although the variation still may be enough to bring a change of government. In other systems, such as the American, in which the ties of party identification to social-structural factors are looser, substantial short-term change may occur even in the absence of change in the electorate's underlying party loyalties. Understanding the interplay of basic partisan predispositions and short-run party preferences can help in the analysis of immediate forces on the electorate, preventing mistakes of interpretation which can be made if enduring dispositions are not taken into account.

CLASS AND GROUP INFLUENCES

In many cases early learning of political attitudes within the family involves the perception of political values appropriate to the family's social identity. Thus, a working-class child may perceive that his parents are Labour *because* of their class or a Negro child may perceive that his parents are Democratic *because* of their race. In fact, a wide range of class, regional, ethnic, racial, religious, and other identifications may be involved in long-term partisan commitments and short-term movements of political opinion.

The ways in which these identifications are related to party will vary greatly. In general terms, we may speak of three types of relationship—interest-related, symbolic, and subcultural, or normative. Where the relationship involves some interest, those identified with a given group accord support to a party out of a sense of some benefit actually or potentially accruing to the group. A well-defined example of such a tie is the appeal of rival parties to social classes whose interests are seen as opposed. The "democratic class struggle," in S. M. Lipset's phrase, has probably been the most obtrusive basis of partisanship in Western political systems, and parliamentary revisions of Marxist thought, the most widely accepted explanation of group voting. Empirical studies have cast doubt on the idea that class consciousness, in any full Marxist sense, plays much of a role in the thinking of mass publics; yet the tie between class and party still may be *interest-related* for the person who sees a party as favoring his class, even if he does not consider any other class or party particularly hostile.

Other examples of interest-related group voting are plentiful enough. A series of sectional interests have influenced the alignments of American electoral history, and regional or sectional interests have competed with class as the basis of party alignments in a number of Western nations. Sectional interests may be primarily economic, as they were in the struggles over American tariff policy for more than a century. But they may also reflect important ethnic, racial, or religious interests, as in the long sectional conflict leading to the withdrawal of Ireland from the United Kingdom.

The interests of a group may attach individually to its members or they may attach more to the group as a collective whole, conferring primarily psychological benefits on members or identifiers. But some ties between group and party which have demonstrable effects on voting lie so far outside the concept of interest as to constitute a symbolic relationship. This was true, for example, of the massive influences on American voting behavior of the two candidates of Roman Catholics for the presidency. There is no evidence that either Protestant or Roman Catholic voters expected major policy changes affecting religion if John Kennedy were elected president; their reaction to his candidacy had to do rather with the symbolism of a Catholic assuming the presidency. The processes by which voters are bound to political leaders on the basis of class, racial, ethnic, or even geographic identifications are very similar.

A good deal of class or group voting, however, must be ascribed to the acceptance of *subcultural norms.* Party attachments, particularly long-established ones, may simply pass into the content of a given subculture and be maintained in much the same way as differences of dress, speech, or childrearing are maintained between classes, regions, and racial groups. Because conformance to normative expectations is involved here, some writers have connected this type of behavior to the concept of role. Participation, as well as party attitudes, may involve conformity of this kind, and turnout differences between men and women have been treated in terms of culturally defined roles.

Any of these types of group effects, but especially symbolic or normative influence, will depend on the strength of the individual's attachment to the group; the stronger his identification, the more likely he is to behave politically in accord with the group. The psychological identifications involved here may be quite unrelated to formal membership, although the relationship of "objective" criteria to "subjective" identifications, explored most extensively in the case of social class is itself an important area of inquiry. Once it is distinguished from formal membership, the concept of identification can include the *negative* identifications of those who may be hostile to a class or group. Thus, the endorsement of trade unions may be the kiss of death for a political candidate seeking office in an area which is strongly hostile to unions.

Face-to-face ("primary") groups may play an important role in making effective the standards of a wider ("secondary") group, particularly when group effects involve the acceptance of political norms. Berelson and his associates have indeed argued that this is the principal means by which group differences are preserved and that the sharpening of secondary-group differences during an election campaign is the natural consequence of the convergence of opinion within the network of face-to-face groups which forms within a class or other social group. The relationship between primary-group and secondary-group influence is a complex one. The face-to-face group may, for example, determine the receptiveness of the individual to the political standards of the wider group; a worker may owe his attitude toward the trade union to his workmates and be accessible to union political influence only if his co-workers identify positively with the union.

Variation in the strength of individual identification, in the closeness of the symbolic ties or interests which connect group to party, in the clarity of a group's political standards—all of these can produce differences of group effects over time or between political systems. Comparative measurement has been most satisfactory in the case of social class. Alford has compared class voting across five nations of the Anglo–American culture area, offering a range of explanations for the sharp differences found. Converse has compared the extent of class voting in America over a 12-year period, proposing that the condition of the economy is a fundamental determinant of the level of class "polarization."

POLITICAL INFORMATION AND PUBLIC ISSUES

Compared with traditional democratic beliefs, the findings of modern voting research present a sobering account of the information actually possessed by the electorate. Many electors are, of course, well informed, but the gradient of knowledge is so steep that very large parts of the public are, indeed, ignorant of very elementary political facts—such as, in the American case, the identity of the party holding a majority of seats in Congress.

The limits to the public's information force substantial revision of the liberal democratic view of the role of issues in electoral choice. However reasonable it may have seemed in an era of restricted franchise to think of electors as perceiving the decisions of government in much the same terms as they were seen by the decision makers themselves, such a view is almost wholly fanciful when applied to mass electorates. Contemporary studies which have probed the public's knowledge of detailed issues leave little doubt that this knowledge is typically slight.

Sometimes the conclusion drawn from such evidence is that issues play no real part in electoral choice, a view which is easily reinforced by evidence that most party loyalties go back far beyond the political issues of the day. This conclusion must be sharply qualified, however, if "issues" is understood to mean something more than the immediate, detailed policy questions confronting government. Many more people, including many long-term partisans, can be shown to have some sort of conception of what the parties or other elites contending for power have done in the past and would be likely to do in the future, and these conceptions are of demonstrable importance for electoral choice. That is to say, the diffuse images of the parties have discernible issue elements, and these help sustain the party loyalties of the relatively committed and help sway the party choices of the less committed.

The cognitive structure of these issue beliefs is still relatively unexplored. It is clear, however, that the parties' *images* can differ without the parties actually taking divergent *positions* as to what government should do. Some of the great issues of electoral politics do involve a marked difference of view both at the elite and mass levels about what ought to be done; America's entry into the League of Nations presumably was such a *position* issue. But many issues of electoral importance do not involve such a difference of belief either between the contending party elites or between the parties' mass supporters. In these cases the parties gain or lose support to the extent that they are associated in the public's mind with a condition or goal which is valued positively or negatively by the entire electorate. In modern times economic prosperity has been a clear example of such a *valence*, or *image*, issue: all of the parties and the entire electorate typically want it, but there may be widely diverging views as to how likely the parties are to achieve it.

A concern with cognitive and motivational elements of the public's response to issues has broadened the relevance of voting research to the study of a larger political order. Electoral research has an obvious role to play in formulating and testing theories of the party system, such as the models of party competition adumbrated by Hotelling, Smithies, and Downs on the analogy of economic competition in spatial markets. Equally, an understanding of the public's response to issues can clarify the normative and descriptive issues of democratic theory, as Janowitz and Marvick have argued in their elaboration of the thought of Schumpeter. Clarifying the nature and extent of popular influence in government will require a knowledge of more than what is in the voter's mind. But all theories of democracy must contain propositions about the public's response to the actions of government and the proposed actions of those who contend for electoral support. Assessing the adequacy of such propositions is widely recognized as a task for future electoral studies.

11. | RICHARD P. McCORMICK
     | *New Perspectives on Jacksonian Politics*

Richard McCormick's quantitative research into the development of political parties in the 1820s and 1830s led him to question a number of our usual views of the origins of democratic politics. In the following, from the *American Historical Review*, LXV (January, 1960), 288–301, he argues that popular participation in elections was often high before the Jacksonian era, was not materially affected by Jackson's campaigns, and that a mass surge to the polls in presidential elections did not actually occur until after Jackson had left office. Reprinted with permission of Richard P. McCormick. [Footnotes omitted.]

The historical phenomenon that we have come to call Jacksonian democracy has long engaged the attention of American political historians, and never more insistently than in the past decade. From the time of Parton and Bancroft to the present day scholars have recognized that a profoundly significant change took place in the climate of politics simultaneously with the appearance of Andrew Jackson on the presidential scene. They have sensed that a full understanding of the nature of that change might enable them to dissolve some of the mysteries that envelop the operation of the American democratic process. With such a challenging goal before them they have pursued their investigations with uncommon intensity and with a keen awareness of the contemporary relevance of their findings.

A cursory view of the vast body of historical writing on this subject suggests that scholars in the field have been largely preoccupied with attempts to define the content of Jacksonian democracy and identify the influence that shaped it. What did Jacksonian democracy represent, and what groups, classes, or sections gave it its distinctive character? The answers that have been given to these central questions have been—to put it succinctly—bewildering in their variety. The discriminating student, seeking the essential core of Jacksonianism, may make a choice among urban workingmen, southern planters, venturous conservatives, farm-bred nouveaux riches, western frontiersmen, frustrated entrepreneurs, or yeoman farmers. Various as are these interpretations of the motivating elements that constituted the true Jacksonians, the characterizations of the programmatic features of Jacksonian democracy are correspondingly diverse. Probably the reasonable observer will content himself with the conclusion that many influences were at work and that latitudinarianism prevailed among the Jacksonian faithful.

In contrast with the controversy that persists over these aspects of Jacksonian democracy, there has been little dissent from the judgment that "the 1830's saw the triumph in American politics of that democracy which has remained pre-eminently the distinguishing feature of our society." The consensus would seem to be that with the emergence of Jackson, the political pulse of the nation quickened. The electorate, long dormant or excluded from the polls by suffrage barriers, now became fired with unprecedented political excitement. The result was a bursting forth of democratic energies, evidenced by a marked upward surge in voting. Beard in his colorful fashion gave expression to the common viewpoint when he asserted that "the roaring flood of the new democracy was . . . [by 1824] foaming perilously near the crest. . . ." Schlesinger, with his allusion to the "immense popular vote" received by Jackson in 1824, creates a similar image. The Old Hero's victory in 1828 has been hailed as the consequence of a "mighty democratic uprising."

That a "new democracy, ignorant, impulsive, irrational" entered the arena of politics in the Jackson era has become one of the few unchallenged "facts" in an otherwise controversial field. Differences of opinion occur only when attempts are made to account for the remarkable increase in the size of the active electorate. The commonest explanations have emphasized the assertion by the common man of his newly won political privileges, the democratic influences that arose out of the western frontier, or the magnetic attractiveness of Jackson as a candidate capable of appealing with singular effectiveness to the backwoods hunter, the plain farmer, the urban workingman, and the southern planter.

Probably because the image of a "mighty democratic uprising" has been so universally agreed upon, there has been virtually no effort made to describe precisely the dimensions of the "uprising." Inquiry into this aspect of Jacksonian democracy has been discouraged by a common misconception regarding voter behavior before 1824. As the authors of one of our most recent and best textbooks put it: "In the years from the beginning of the government to 1824, a period for which we have no reliable election statistics, only small numbers of citizens seemed to have bothered to go to the polls." Actually, abundant data on pre-1824 elections is available, and it indicates a far higher rate of voting than has been realized. Only by taking this data into consideration can voting behavior after 1824 be placed in proper perspective.

The question of whether there was indeed a "mighty democratic uprising" during the Jackson era is certainly crucial in any analysis of the political character of Jacksonian democracy. More broadly, however, we need to know the degree to which potential voters participated in elections before, during, and after the period of Jackson's presidency as well as the conditions that apparently influenced the rate of voting. Only when such factors have been analyzed can we arrive at firm conclusions with respect to the dimensions of the political changes that we associate with Jacksonian democracy. Obviously in studying voter participation we are dealing with but one aspect of a large problem, and the limitations imposed by such a restrictive focus should be apparent.

In measuring the magnitude of the vote in the Jackson elections it is hardly significant to use the total popular vote cast throughout the nation. A comparison of the total vote cast in 1812, for example, when in eight of the seventeen states electors were chosen by the legislature, with the vote in 1832, when every state except South Carolina chose its electors by popular vote, has limited meaning. Neither is it revealing to compare the total vote in 1824 with that in 1832 without taking into consideration the population increase during the interval. The shift from the legislative choice of electors to their election by popular vote, together with the steady population growth, obviously swelled the presidential vote. But the problem to be investigated is whether the Jackson elections brought voters to the polls in such enlarged or unprecedented proportions as to indicate that a "new democracy" had burst upon the political scene.

The most practicable method for measuring the degree to which voters participated in elections over a period of time is to relate the number of votes cast to the number of potential voters. Although there is no way of calculating precisely how many eligible voters there were in any state at a given time, the evidence at hand demonstrates that with the exception of Rhode Island, Virginia, and Louisiana the potential electorate after 1824 was roughly equivalent to the adult white male population. A meaningful way of expressing the rate of voter participation, then, is to state it in terms of the percentage of the adult white males actually voting. This index can be employed to measure the variations that occurred in voter participation over a period of time and in both national and state elections. Consequently a basis is provided for comparing the rate of voting in the Jackson elections with other presidential elections before and after his regime as well as with state elections.

Using this approach it is possible, first of all, to ascertain whether or not voter participation rose markedly in the three presidential elections in which Jackson was a candidate. Did voter participation in these elections so far exceed the peak participation in the pre-1824 elections as to suggest that a mighty democratic uprising was taking place? The accompanying data (Table I) provides an answer to this basic question.

In the 1824 election not a single one of the eighteen states in which the electors were chosen by popular vote attained the percentage of voter participation that had been reached before 1824. Prior to that critical election, fifteen of those eighteen states had recorded votes in excess of 50 percent of their adult white male population, but in 1824 only two states—Maryland and Alabama—exceeded this modest mark. The average rate of voter participation in the election was 26.5 percent. This hardly fits the image of the "roaring flood of the new democracy . . . foaming perilously near the crest. . . ."

There would seem to be persuasive evidence that in 1828 the common man flocked to the polls in unprecedented numbers, for the proportion of adult white males voting soared to 56.3 percent, more than double the 1824 figure. But this outpouring shrinks in magnitude when we observe that in only six of the twenty-two states involved were new highs in voter participation established. In three of these—Maryland, Virginia, and Louisiana—the recorded gain was inconsiderable, and in a fourth—New York—the bulk of the increase might be attributed to changes that had been made in suffrage qualifications as recently as 1821 and 1826. Six states went over the 70 percent mark, whereas ten had bettered that performance before 1824. Instead of a "mighty democratic uprising" there was in 1828 a voter turnout that approached—but in only a few instances matched or exceeded—the maximum levels that had been attained before the Jackson era.

The advance that was registered in 1828 did not carry forward to 1832. Despite the fact that Jackson was probably at the peak of his personal popularity, that he was engaged in a campaign that was presumably to decide issues of great magnitude, and that in the opinion of some

TABLE I

Percentages of adult white males voting in elections

State	HIGHEST KNOWN % AWM VOTING BEFORE 1824		PRESIDENTIAL ELECTIONS					
State	Year	% AWM	1824	1828	1832	1836	1840	1844
Maine	1812ᵍ	62.0	18.9	42.7	66.2*	37.4	82.2	67.5
New Hampshire	1814ᵍ	80.8	16.8	76.5	74.2	38.2	86.4*	65.6
Vermont	1812ᵍ	79.9	–	55.8	50.0	52.5	74.0	65.7
Massachusetts	1812ᵍ	67.4	29.1	25.7	39.3	45.1	66.4	59.3
Rhode Island	1812ᵍ	49.4	12.4	18.0	22.4	24.1	33.2	39.8
Connecticut	1819ˡ	54.4	14.9	27.1	45.9	52.3	75.7*	76.1
New York	1810ᵍ	41.5	–	70.4*	72.1	60.2	77.7	73.6
New Jersey	1808ᵖ	71.8	31.1	70.9	69.0	69.3	80.4*	81.6
Pennsylvania	1808ᵍ	71.5	19.6	56.6	52.7	53.1	77.4*	75.5
Delaware	1804ᵍ	81.9	–	–	67.0	69.4	82.8*	85.0
Maryland	1820ˡ	69.0	53.7	76.2*	55.6	67.5	84.6	80.3
Virginia	1800ᵖ	25.9	11.5	27.6*	30.8	35.1	54.6	54.5
North Carolina	1823ᶜ	70.0#	42.2	56.8	31.7	52.9	83.1*	79.1
Georgia	1812ᶜ	62.3	–	35.9	33.0	64.9*	88.9	94.0
Kentucky	1820ᵍ	74.4	25.3	70.7	73.9	61.1	74.3	80.3
Tennessee	1817ᵍ	80.0	26.8	49.8	28.8	55.2	89.6*	89.6
Louisiana	1812ᵍ	34.2	–	36.3*	24.4	19.2	39.4	44.7
Alabama	1819ᵍ	96.7	52.1	53.6	33.3	65.0	89.8	82.7
Mississippi	1823ᵍ	79.8	41.6	56.6	32.8	62.8	88.2*	89.7
Ohio	1822ᵍ	46.5	34.8	75.8*	73.8	75.5	84.5	83.6
Indiana	1822ᵍ	52.4	37.5	68.3*	61.8	70.1	86.0	84.9
Illinois	1822ᵍ	55.8	24.2	51.9	45.6	43.7	85.9*	76.3
Missouri	1820ᵍ	71.9	20.1	54.3	40.8	35.6	74.0*	74.7
Arkansas		–	–	–	–	35.0	86.4	68.8
Michigan		–	–	–	–	35.7	84.9	79.3
National Average			26.5	56.3	54.9	55.2	78.0	74.9

*Exceeded pre-1824 high   #Estimate based on incomplete returns
ᵍGubernatorial election   ᶜCongressional election
ᵖPresidential election   ˡElection of legislature

authorities a "well-developed two party system on a national scale" had been established, there was a slight decline in voter participation. The average for the twenty-three states participating in the presidential contest was 54.9 percent. In fifteen states a smaller percentage of the adult white males went to the polls in 1832 than in 1828. Only five states bettered their pre-1824 highs. Again the conclusion would be that it was essentially the pre-1824 electorate—diminished in most states and augmented in a few—that voted in 1832. Thus, after three Jackson elections, sixteen states had not achieved the proportions of voter participation that they had reached before 1824. The "new democracy" had not yet made its appearance.

A comparison of the Jackson elections with earlier presidential contests is of some interest. Such comparisons have little validity before 1808 because few states chose electors by popular vote, and for certain of those states the complete returns are not available. In 1816 and 1820 there was so little opposition to Monroe that the voter interest was negligible. The most relevant elections, therefore, are those of 1808 and 1812. The accompanying table (Table II) gives the percentages of adult white males voting in 1808 and 1812 in those states for which full returns could be found, together with the comparable percentages for the elections of 1824 and 1828. In 1824 only one state—Ohio—surpassed the highs established in either 1808 or 1812. Four more joined this list in 1828—Virginia, Maryland, Pennsylvania, and New Hampshire—although the margin in the last case was so small as to be inconsequential. The most significant conclusion to be drawn from this admittedly limited and unrepresentative data is that in those states where there was a vigorous two-party contest in 1808 and 1812 the vote was relatively high. Conversely, where there was little or no contest in 1824 or 1828, the vote was low.

TABLE II

Percentages of adult white males voting in presidential elections

STATE	1808	1812	1824	1828
Maine	Legis.	50.0	18.9	42.7
New Hampshire	62.1	75.4	16.8	76.5
Massachusetts	Legis.	51.4	29.1	25.7
Rhode Island	37.4	37.7	12.4	18.0
New Jersey	71.8	Legis.	31.1	70.9
Pennsylvania	34.7	45.5	19.6	56.6
Maryland	48.4	56.5	53.7	76.2
Virginia	17.7	17.8	11.5	27.6
Ohio	12.8	20.0	34.8	75.8

Note: No complete returns of the popular vote cast for electors in Kentucky or Tennessee in 1808 and 1812 and in North Carolina in 1808 could be located.

When an examination is made of voting in other than presidential elections prior to 1824, the inaccuracy of the impression that "only small numbers of citizens" went to the polls becomes apparent. Because of the almost automatic succession of the members of the "Virginia dynasty" and the early deterioration of the national two-party system that had seemed to be developing around 1800, presidential elections did not arouse voter interest as much as did those for governor, state legislators, or even members of Congress. In such elections at the state level the "common man" was stimulated by local factors to cast his vote, and he frequently responded in higher proportions than he did to the later stimulus provided by Jackson.

The average voter participation for all the states in 1828 was 56.3 percent. Before 1824 fifteen of the twenty-two states had surpassed that percentage. Among other things, this means that the 1828 election failed to bring to the polls the proportion of the electorate that had voted on occasion in previous elections. There was, in other words, a high potential vote that was frequently realized in state elections but which did not materialize in presidential elections. The unsupported assumption that the common man was either apathetic or debarred from voting by suffrage barriers before 1824 is untenable in the light of this evidence.

In state after state (see Table I) gubernatorial elections attracted 70 percent or more of the adult white males to the polls. Among the notable highs recorded were Delaware with 81.9 percent in 1804, New Hampshire with 80.8 percent in 1814, Tennessee with 80.0 percent in 1817, Vermont with 79.9 percent in 1812, Mississippi with 79.8 percent in 1823, and Alabama with a highly improbable 96.7 percent in its first gubernatorial contest in 1819. There is reason to believe that in some states, at least, the voter participation in the election of state legislators was even higher than in gubernatorial elections. Because of the virtual impossibility of securing county-by-county or district-by-district returns for such elections, this hypothesis is difficult to verify.

Down to this point the voter turnout in the Jackson elections has been compared with that in elections held prior to 1824. Now it becomes appropriate to inquire whether during the period 1824 through 1832 voters turned out in greater proportions for the three presidential contests than they did for the contemporary state elections. If, indeed, this "new democracy" bore some special relationship to Andrew Jackson or to his policies, it might be anticipated that interest in the elections in which he was the central figure would stimulate greater voter participation than gubernatorial contests, in which he was at most a remote factor.

Actually, the election returns show fairly conclusively that throughout the eight-year period the electorate continued to participate more extensively in state elections than in those involving the presidency. Between 1824 and 1832 there were fifty regular gubernatorial elections in the states that chose their electors by popular vote. In only sixteen of these fifty instances did the vote for president surpass the corresponding vote for governor. In Rhode Island, Delaware, Tennessee, Kentucky, Illinois, Mississippi, Missouri, and Georgia the vote for governor consistently exceeded that for President. Only in Connecticut was the reverse true. Viewed from this perspective, too, the remarkable feature of the vote in the Jackson elections is not its immensity but rather its smallness.

Finally, the Jackson elections may be compared with subsequent presidential elections. Once Jackson had retired to the Hermitage, and figures of less dramatic proportions took up the contest for the presidency, did voter participation rise or fall? This question can be answered by observing the percentage of adult white males who voted in each state in the presidential elections of 1836 through 1844 (Table I). Voter participation in the 1836 election remained near the level that had been established in 1828 and 1832, with 55.2 percent of the adult white males voting. Only five states registered percentages in excess of their pre-1824 highs. But in 1840 the "new democracy" made its appearance with explosive suddenness.

In a surge to the polls that has rarely, if ever, been exceeded in any presidential election, four out of five (78.0 percent) of the adult white males cast their votes for Harrison or Van Buren. This new electorate was greater than that of the Jackson period by more than 40 percent. In all but five states—Vermont, Massachusetts, Rhode Island, Kentucky, and Alabama—the peaks of voter participation reached before 1824 were passed. Fourteen of the twenty-five states involved set record highs for voting that were not to be broken throughout the remainder of the ante bellum period. Now, at last, the common man—or at least the man who previously had not been sufficiently aroused to vote in presidential elections—cast his weight into the political balance. This "Tippecanoe democracy," if such a label is permissible, was of a different order of magnitude from the Jacksonian democracy. The elections in which Jackson figured brought to the polls only those men who were accustomed to voting in state or national elections, except in a very few states. The Tippecanoe canvass witnessed an extraordinary expansion of the size of the presidential electorate far beyond previous dimensions. It was in 1840, then, that the "roaring flood of the new democracy" reached its crest. And it engulfed the Jacksonians.

The flood receded only slightly in 1844, when 74.9 percent of the estimated potential electorate went to the polls. Indeed, nine states attained their record highs for the period. In 1848 and 1852 there was a general downward trend in voter participation, followed by a modest upswing in 1856 and 1860. But the level of voter activity remained well above that of the Jackson elections. The conclusion to be drawn is that the "mighty democratic uprising" came after the period of Jackson's presidency.

Now that the quantitative dimensions of Jacksonian democracy as a political phenomenon have been delineated and brought into some appropriate perspective, certain questions still remain to be answered. Granted that the Jacksonian electorate—as revealed by the comparisons that have been set forth—was not really very large, how account for the fact that voter participation doubled between the elections of 1824 and 1828? It is true that the total vote soared from around 359,000 to 1,155,-400 and that the percentage of voter participation more than doubled. Traditionally, students of the Jackson period have been impressed by this steep increase in voting and by way of explanation have identified the causal factors as the reduction of suffrage qualifications, the democratic influence of the West, or the personal magnetism of Jackson. The validity of each of these hypotheses needs to be reexamined.

In no one of the states in which electors were chosen by popular vote was any significant change made in suffrage qualifications between 1824 and 1828. Subsequently, severe restrictions were maintained in Rhode Island until 1842, when some liberalization was effected, and in Virginia down to 1850. In Louisiana, where the payment of a tax was a requirement, the character of the state tax system apparently operated to restrict the suffrage at least as late as 1845. Thus with the three exceptions noted, the elimination of suffrage barriers was hardly a factor in producing an enlarged electorate during the Jackson and post-Jackson periods. Furthermore, all but a few states had extended the privilege of voting either to all male taxpayers or to all adult male citizens by 1810. After Connecticut eliminated its property qualification in 1818, Massachusetts in 1821, and New York in 1821 and 1826, only Rhode Island, Virginia, and Louisiana were left on the list of "restrictionist" states. Neither Jackson's victory nor the increased vote in 1828 can be attributed to the presence at the polls of a newly enfranchised mass of voters.

Similarly, it does not appear that the western states led the way in voter participation. Prior to 1824, for example, Ohio, Indiana, and Illinois had never brought to the polls as much as 60 percent of their adult white males. Most of the eastern states had surpassed that level by considerable margins. In the election of 1828 six states registered votes in excess of 70 percent of their adult white male populations. They were in order of rank: New Hampshire, Maryland, Ohio, New Jersey, Kentucky, and New York. The six leaders in 1832 were: New Hampshire, Kentucky, Ohio, New York, New Jersey, and Delaware. It will be obvious that the West, however that region may be defined, was not leading the "mighty democratic uprising." Western influences, then, do not explain the increased vote in 1828.

There remains to be considered the factor of Jackson's personal popularity. Did Jackson, the popular hero, attract voters to the polls in unprecedented proportions? The comparisons that have already been made between the Jackson elections and other elections—state and national—before, during, and after his presidency would suggest a negative answer to the question. Granted that a majority of the voters in 1828 favored Jackson, it is not evident that his partisans stormed the polls any more enthusiastically than did the Adams men. Of the six highest states in voter participation in 1828, three favored Adams and three were for Jackson, which could be interpreted to mean that the convinced Adams supporters turned out no less zealously for their man than did the ardent Jacksonians. When Van Buren replaced Jackson in 1836, the voting average increased slightly over 1832. And, as has been demonstrated, the real manifestation of the "new democracy" came not in 1828 but in 1840.

The most satisfactory explanation for the increase in voter participation between 1824 and 1828 is a simple and obvious one. During the long reign of the Virginia dynasty, interest in presidential elections dwindled. In 1816 and 1820 there had been no contest. The somewhat fortuitous termination of the Virginia succession in 1824 and the failure of the congressional caucus to solve the problem of leadership succession threw the choice of a President upon the electorate. But popular interest was dampened by the confusion of choice presented by the multiplicity of candidates, by the disintegration of the old national parties, by the fact that in most states one or another of the candidates was so overwhelmingly popular as to forestall any semblance of a contest, and possibly by the realization that the election would ultimately be decided by the House of Representatives. By 1828 the situation had altered. There were but two candidates in the field, each of whom had substantial sectional backing. A clear-cut contest impended, and the voters became sufficiently aroused to go to the polls in moderate numbers.

One final question remains. Why was the vote in the Jackson elections relatively low when compared with previous and contemporary state elections and with presidential votes after 1840? The answer, in brief, is that in most states either Jackson or his opponent had such a one-sided advantage that the result was a foregone conclusion. Consequently there was little incentive for the voters to go to the polls.

This factor can be evaluated in fairly specific quantitative terms. If the percentage of the total vote secured by each candidate in each state in the election of 1828 is calculated, the difference between the percentages can be used as an index of the closeness, or one-sidedness, of the contest. In Illinois, for example, Jackson received 67 percent of the total vote and Adams, 33; the difference—thirty-four points—represents the margin between the candidates. The average difference between the candidates, taking all the states together, was thirty-six points. Expressed another way this would mean that in the average state the winning candidate received more than twice the vote of the loser. Actually, this was the case in thirteen of the twenty-two states (see Table III). Such a wide margin virtually placed these states in the "no contest" category.

A remarkably close correlation existed between the size of the voter turnout and the relative closeness of the contest. The six states previously listed as having the greatest voter participation in 1828 were among the seven states with the smallest margin of difference between the candidates. The exception was Louisiana, where restrictions on the suffrage curtailed the vote. Even in this instance, however, it is significant that voter participation in Louisiana reached a record high. In those states, then, where there was a close balance of political forces the vote was large, and conversely, where the contest was very one sided, the vote was low.

Most of the states in 1828 were so strongly partial to one or another of the candidates that they can best be characterized as one-party states. Adams encountered little opposition in New England, except in New Hampshire, and Jackson met with hardly any resistance in the South.

TABLE III

Differential between percentages of total vote obtained by major presidential candidates, 1828–1844

STATE	1828	1832	1836	1840	1844
Maine	20	10	20	1	13
New Hampshire	7	13	50	11	19
Vermont	50	10	20	29	18
Massachusetts	66	30	9	16	12
Rhode Island	50	14	6	23	20
Connecticut	50	20	1	11	5
New York	2	4	9	4	1
New Jersey	4	1	1	4	1
Pennsylvania	33	16	4	1	2
Delaware	–	2	6	10	3
Maryland	2	1	7	8	5
Virginia	38	50	13	1	6
North Carolina	47	70	6	15	5
Georgia	94	100	4	12	4
Kentucky	1	9	6	29	8
Tennessee	90	90	16	11	1
Louisiana	6	38	3	19	3
Alabama	80	100	11	9	18
Mississippi	60	77	2	7	13
Ohio	3	3	4	9	2
Indiana	13	34	12	12	2
Illinois	34	37	10	2	12
Missouri	41	32	21	14	17
Arkansas	–	–	28	13	26
Michigan	–	–	9	4	6
Average Differential	36	36	11	11	9

It was chiefly in the middle states and the older West that the real battle was waged. With the removal of Adams from the scene after 1828, New England became less of a one-party section, but the South remained extremely one sided. Consequently it is not surprising that voter participation in 1832 failed even to match that of 1828.

Here, certainly, is a factor of crucial importance in explaining the dimensions of the voter turnout in the Jackson elections. National parties were still in a rudimentary condition and were highly unbalanced from state to state. Indeed, a two-party system scarcely could be said to exist in more than half of the states until after 1832. Where opposing parties had been formed to contest the election, the vote was large, but where no parties, or only one, took the field, the vote was low. By 1840, fairly well-balanced parties had been organized in virtually every state. In only three states did the margin between Harrison and Van Buren exceed twenty points, and the average for all the states was only eleven points. The result was generally high voter participation.

When Jacksonian democracy is viewed from the perspectives employed in this analysis, its political dimensions in so far as they relate to the behavior of the electorate can be described with some precision. None of the Jackson elections involved a "mighty democratic uprising" in the sense that voters were drawn to the polls in unprecedented proportions. When compared with the peak participation recorded for each state before 1824, or with contemporaneous gubernatorial elections, or most particularly with the vast outpouring of the electorate in 1840, voter participation in the Jackson elections was unimpressive. The key to the relatively low presidential vote would seem to be the extreme political imbalance that existed in most states as between the Jacksonians and their opponents. Associated with this imbalance was the immature development of national political parties. Indeed, it can be highly misleading to think in terms of national parties in connection with the Jackson elections. As balanced, organized parties subsequently made their appearance from state to state, and voters were stimulated by the prospect of a genuine contest, a marked rise in voter participation occurred. Such conditions did not prevail generally across the nation until 1840, and then at last the "mighty democratic uprising" took place.

12.	RICHARD P. McCORMICK *"Suffrage Classes and Party Alignments:* *A Study in Voter Behavior"*

In this second study, reprinted from the *Mississippi Valley Historical Review* (now the *Journal of American History*), XLVI (December, 1959), 397–410, McCormick continues his assault on traditional assumptions about Jacksonian era politics. His systematic comparison of election returns with economic class data in two states strongly suggests that lower class voters, far from supporting Jackson's cause in overwhelming numbers, divided their votes relatively evenly between the two major parties. Reprinted by permission of the *Journal of American History* and Richard McCormick. [Footnotes omitted.]

The traditional ingredients of American political history have been personalities, classes, sections, parties, and issues. The voter, except in so far as he has been regarded as an element of a class or a section, has received relatively little attention. More recently, because of dwindling confidence in the efficacy of the hypotheses of Beard and Turner, we are less sure of our ability to conceive of the electorate in terms of classes and sections. Consequently, we are impelled to re-examine the entire field of voter behavior in order to obtain new understandings of the role of the electorate in the democratic process. In attacking one aspect of this large problem, this study deals with certain limited but critical questions related to the composition and behavior of the electorate in the early national period. More specifically, it is an analysis of the degree to which certain types of property qualifications restricted the size of the electorate and of the relationship of the economic status of voters to their party affiliation.

It is generally understood that in the decades before the Civil War property qualifications for voting existed in most states. What is not known with any degree of precision is the extent to which these barriers excluded adult males from the polls. Neither is it clear what effect extension of the franchise to lower economic segments of the population had on the relative strength of competing political parties. Equally clouded is the larger question of whether the electorate tended to divide between the major parties along lines of economic cleavage. It is doubtful whether these questions can be answered with assurance for most states, because the nature of the evidence is often such as to preclude methodical inquiry. There are, however, two states that provide highly favorable conditions for analyses of the type proposed, and for that reason they have been selected as the basis for this study.

These states—North Carolina and New York—have been chosen, then, not because they are necessarily typical, but because they afford more reliable and relevant data than can be secured for other states. Both states were unusual in that they had, for varying periods, dual property qualifications for voting. That is, voters having the minimum qualifications could vote for limited categories of officials, whereas those meeting higher qualifications were eligible to vote for all elective officials. This feature, together with others that will be considered, makes it possible to measure not only the restrictive effect of certain property qualifications but also the party affiliations of the different classes of electors.

It is convenient to examine first the experience of North Carolina. Its constitution of 1776 created a dual suffrage system. Only adult freemen possessed of fifty acres of land within the county in which they voted could vote for a member of the state senate. But all freemen—including the fifty-acre freeholders—who had paid county or state taxes were eligible to vote for members of the house of commons. After 1835, when the office of governor became elective by popular vote, the lesser franchise requirement was extended to apply also in gubernatorial elections. Not until 1856 was this dual arrangement replaced by general taxpayer suffrage. For eighty years, then, the fifty-acre freeholders can be distinguished as a separate electoral class in North Carolina. In any state election within that period it is possible to analyze the ratio of fifty-acre electors to those voters meeting only the taxpayer qualification. The party preferences of the two suffrage groups can also be determined. For the most reliable results, however, it is desirable to select a period when party lines were distinct and strong and when something approaching a maximum vote was registered. These conditions maintained between 1836 and 1856.

During those years the Whig and Democratic parties contested on a nearly even basis in North Carolina, with the Whigs dominant by a slight margin down to 1848. Voter participation was high, averaging 77 percent of the adult white male population. By comparing the size of the vote cast county-by-county for governor with the comparable vote for state senators, it is possible to measure the proportion of the total electorate that could not meet the fifty-acre requirement (See Table I). Then, by examining the distribution of each class of the electorate between the two major parties it can be determined whether economic status influenced party affiliation.

Table I indicates that approximately one-half of the total electorate lacked the amount of property required to vote for state senators. In 1840, for example, 57,460 votes were cast for governor and 31,241 for senator in the forty-six counties for which returns were available. Thus 45.6 percent of the voters lacked the fifty-acre freehold required of senatorial electors. The fact that a vote equivalent to 83 percent of the total adult white male population of the state was polled for governor in 1840 would suggest that the requirement that voters must have paid a state or county tax was not a serious limitation on the franchise. Even in states where unrestricted manhood suffrage existed, voter participation did not ordinarily exceed the 80 percent level. The conclusions regarding the proportion of taxpayers excluded from voting for senator is based on a sample ranging from 38.3 percent to 71.7 percent of the total state vote, and some degree of error could result from this lack of a complete enumeration. But the proportions are sufficiently consistent

TABLE I

Size of electoral classes in North Carolina, 1835-1856 [a]

YEAR	NUMBER OF COUNTIES IN SAMPLE	VOTE FOR SENATORS	VOTE FOR GOVERNOR	SENATE VOTE AS % OF VOTE FOR GOVERNOR	GOVERNOR VOTE AS % OF ADULT WHITE MALES
1835–36	26 of 64	18,532	33,066	56.0	67.1
1840	46 of 68	31,241	57,460	54.4	83.0
1844	22 of 73	15,209	31,481	48.3	78.7
1856	46 of 82	30,205	62,915	48.0	79.3

[a]The only available source of returns of elections of members of the state senate are the contemporary newspapers, and their coverage was not complete. The elections that I cite were chosen mainly because returns were found for a fairly large number of counties in various parts of the state. Because the returns for the 1836 senatorial elections were inadequate, I have used the returns for the 1835 election and have compared them with the 1836 gubernatorial returns. For the other three elections, the voting for governor and senators took place at the same time. Voting was by paper ballot and elections were held biennially in August. All returns are from the Raleigh *North Carolina Standard*, and can be found in the several issues following each election.

from election to election to indicate that the true figure would not be far from 50 percent. This reasoning is confirmed by the observations of the editor of the Raleigh *Standard* in 1848 that there were "between thirty and forty thousand freehold voters" in the state, and that the total electorate was "about eighty thousand."

TABLE II

Size of electoral classes in Wake County, North Carolina [a]

YEAR	VOTE FOR SENATOR	VOTE FOR GOVERNOR	SENATE VOTE AS % OF VOTE FOR GOVERNOR
1838	946	1,857	50.9
1840	1,006	2,187	46.0
1842	1,020	2,138	47.7
1844	1,083	2,344	46.2
1846	992	2,161	45.9
1848	1,023	2,284	44.8

[a]The vote figures are from the Raleigh *North Carolina Standard* in August of each election year.

The precise relationship of fifty-acre freeholders to taxpayers varied somewhat from county to county, although a one-to-one ratio prevailed in a remarkably high number of instances. Detailed studies could readily be made to determine whether the proportion of freehold voters was greater in some sections than in others, and such an analysis would be relevant to any intensive investigation of the North Carolina political environment. Table II indicates the pattern in Wake County, in which Raleigh was situated. The ratio between the two electorates was quite stable, and it was fairly close to the state-wide average.

Because of the dual suffrage system, it is an easy matter to compare the party affiliations of the fifty-acre freeholders with those of the lower electoral class. How wide an economic margin separated the two politico-economic classes is a matter for conjecture—or further research—but it would seem reasonable to assume that there was an appreciable distinction in status. The question, then, is whether the fifty-acre freeholders, as an upper-level economic group, differed markedly in their party affiliations from the remainder of the electorate.

Table III presents the results of a study of three state elections. In the first two columns are given the party distribution of votes cast for senator and for governor in the counties that comprised the sample. Column three gives the assumed vote of the non-freehold electors for governor and has been obtained by subtracting the senatorial vote of each party from the gubernatorial vote. The next three columns show

TABLE III

Distribution of party affiliation by electoral classes in North Carolina[a]

YEAR	PARTY	VOTE FOR SENATORS	VOTE FOR GOVERNOR	NON-FREEHOLD VOTERS	% BY PARTY SENATORS VOTE	% BY PARTY GOVERNORS VOTE	% BY PARTY NON-FREEHOLD VOTE
1840	Whig	16,760	30,594	13,834	53.7	53.2	52.7
	Dem.	14,481	26,866	12,385	46.3	46.8	47.3
1844	Whig	8,053	16,430	8,377	52.9	52.2	51.4
	Dem.	7,156	15,051	7,895	47.1	47.8	48.6
1856	Whig	13,231	27,035	13,804	43.8	43.0	42.2
	Dem.	16,974	35,880	18,906	56.2	57.0	57.8

[a]The votes have been compiled from the returns in the Raleigh *North Carolina Standard*.

the percentage distribution of the party vote cast by the senatorial electors, by the total electorate, and by the non-freeholders, respectively.

In each of the three elections the fifty-acre freehold voters were divided between Whigs and Democrats in almost exactly the same proportions as those who met only the taxpaying qualification. In 1840, for example, 53.7 percent of the freehold electors were Whigs, as were 52.7 percent of the less qualified electors. In none of the elections was there as much as a two percent difference in the party distribution of the two classes of voters. Indeed, the similarity of the party affiliations of the two groups was so nearly identical as to be astonishing. The fifty-acre freeholder class was from one to two percentage points more strongly Whig than the less privileged voters, a differential so small as to be inconsiderable. Thus, whether or not a man owned fifty acres or more of land seemingly had little or no influence on his party affiliation. Or, to express it differently, the economic distinction implicit in the dual suffrage system had no substantial significance as a factor in determining party alignments in these North Carolina elections.

The similarity of party distribution within the two classes of electors existed in almost every county; it is not the fabrication of an averaging process. In the 1840 election the same party that obtained a majority of votes in the senatorial election also received a majority in the gubernatorial contest in forty-three of the forty-six counties. In each of the three exception cases the vote was extremely close, and local circumstances may well have produced a majority for one party in the election of a senator and for the other in the gubernatorial election. What this means, of course, is that if the election of a governor had been determined by the fifty-acre freeholders alone, the same candidate would have been elected with almost precisely the same percentage of the total vote.

The implications of this analysis are both intriguing and suggestive. If it was true that in North Carolina the restriction of the suffrage to fifty-acre freeholders would have produced the same results as extending the franchise to all taxpayers, what happened in other states when the suffrage was broadened? Is there convincing evidence that when lower economic strata of the population were given the vote there resulted some measurable change in party alignments? Did the new voters, presumably homogeneous in their economic status, tend to move as a group into one of the two major parties?

Certain more or less ideal conditions must exist before this question can be answered with assurance for any state. There should be a marked reduction in suffrage qualifications occurring at a time when party lines were distinct and stable and when voter participation was at a sufficiently high level that the effect of the change in suffrage could be measured. The first condition is found in a number of states, but not usually in association with the two others. Most of the lowering of suffrage barriers in the United States took place before 1824 in a period when party alignments were unstable, weak, or nonexistent. After 1824 Rhode Island, Louisiana, Mississippi, and Virginia broadened the franchise, but in the first three states the increase in the proportion of adult white males voting was so small as to be inconsiderable. In Virginia the liberalization was accomplished in two steps, in 1830 and 1850, which rather lessened the impact of the change.

Probably the state which most nearly fulfills the specified conditions is New York. Moreover, because that state also had a dual suffrage system, it lends itself to analyses similar to those made for North Carolina. Under the New York constitution of 1777, only those men who owned freeholds valued at £100 were eligible to vote for governor, lieutenant-governor, and state senator. Those who had freeholds worth £20, or who rented tenements with a yearly value of forty shillings and paid public taxes, could vote for assemblymen and members of Congress. This dual system ended when a new constitution, effective February 28, 1822, conferred franchise privileges on all adult male citizens who paid county or state taxes, performed (or were exempted from) militia duty, or labored on the public highways. In 1826 all property and taxpaying requirements for voting in New York were eliminated.

There is no difficulty in determining how many electors were in each of the two suffrage classes. New York conducted censuses of electors at least once in every seven years between 1790 and 1821, and from these records the restrictive effect of the various suffrage qualifications can be computed and tabulated.

TABLE IV

Size of electoral classes in New York, 1801–1835[a]

YEAR	ADULT WHITE MALES	TOTAL ELECTORS	TOTAL ELECTORS AS % OF ADULT WHITE MALES	£100 ELECTORS	£100 ELECTORS AS % OF ADULT WHITE MALES	ELECTORS OTHER	OTHER ELECTORS AS % OF ADULT WHITE MALES
1801	125,000	85,907	68.7	52,058	41.6	33,849	27.1
1807	170,000	121,289	71.3	71,159	41.8	50,130	29.5
1814	239,000	151,846	63.5	87,491	36.6	64,355	26.9
1821	299,500	202,510	67.6	100,490	33.5	102,020	34.1
1822	312,700	259,387	82.9	–	–	–	–
1825	352,300	296,132	84.0	–	–	–	–
1835	467,000	422,034	90.3	–	–	–	–

[a]New York (State), Secretary of State, *Census of the State of New York for 1855* (Albany, 1857), ix-x, xli-xliii. The 1855 census contains a compendium of all preceding electoral censuses, giving the number of electors in each category by counties. This remarkably detailed information has been surprisingly neglected by students of voter behavior. Several other states, among them Ohio, Louisiana, Kentucky, and Tennessee, also conducted censuses of electors, but none was comparable in excellence to those of New York.

The data in this table indicate that prior to 1822 roughly two-thirds of the adult white male population could vote. The £100 freeholders averaged about 38 percent of the adult white male population. Between one-quarter and one-third of the adult white males possessed only the lower of the two suffrage qualifications and were therefore unable to vote for governor, lieutenant-governor, and senator. Approximately one-third of the adult males lacked the qualifications to vote in any elections before 1822. As a result of the constitutional change in the suffrage in 1822, the total electorate rose sharply to include 83 percent of the adult white males. Most important is the fact that the number of those eligible to vote for governor rose from 100,490 to 259,387, an increase of almost 160 percent. The elimination of the taxpaying requirement after 1825 had a relatively slight effect on the size of the electorate. In general terms, the economic-electoral classes within the population of New York in 1821 can be described as follows: the top third enjoyed full franchise privileges; the middle third had limited privileges; and the bottom third was disfranchised.

We can, as in the case of North Carolina, inquire whether the two suffrage classes in New York differed in party alignment. The election held in April, 1816, at which time a governor and members of Congress —as well as legislators—were chosen, saw the Federalists making their final full-scale effort against the Republicans. Because complete returns by counties for both the gubernatorial and congressional contests are available, it is possible to use these votes to determine the party alignments within the two suffrage classes (See Table V). The governor was elected by the £100 freeholders alone; the total electorate was eligible to vote for members of Congress.

TABLE V

Distribution of party affiliation by electoral classes in New York, 1816[a]

PARTY	VOTE FOR GOVERNOR	% BY PARTY	VOTE FOR CONGRESS	% BY PARTY	NON-FREEHOLD VOTERS CONGRESS	% BY PARTY
Republican	45,412	54.0	67,757	54.9	22,345	57.0
Federalist	38,647	46.0	55,514	45.1	16,867	43.0

[a]The returns for both the gubernatorial and congressional elections, which were held at the same time, are from the Albany *Advertiser*, June 15, 1816. The results of the congressional election were used because those returns were complete and those for the assembly districts were not. The estimates of the numbers of non-freehold voters participating in the congressional elections has been computed with the same procedure that was used in the North Carolina analysis.

Table V would seem to show that the non-freehold voters were only slightly more biased toward the Republican party than were the elite electors. Two circumstances, however, make interpretations of these data hazardous. If the voting figures are taken at face value, they indicate that 93 percent of those eligible to vote for governor actually went to the polls. This percentage is so suspiciously high as to suggest that many who lacked the £100 freehold may have voted in the gubernatorial election. Again, the figures imply that only 48 percent of the eligible non-freehold electors cast their ballots. If this was indeed the case, the question arises as to whether such a low turnout constitutes a realistic sample. The safest conclusion to be drawn is that the presence at the polls of the non-freehold electors—as evidenced in the congressional vote—did not significantly alter the party alignments manifested in the gubernatorial election.

The final problem to be examined is the effect of a marked broadening of the electorate on party alignments in New York. The liberalization of the suffrage in 1822 increased the number of those eligible to vote for governor from approximately 33 percent of the adult white males to 84 percent. The two parties in New York at this period were the Republicans and the Clintonians—the candidate of the latter for the governorship in 1820, 1824, and 1826 being De Witt Clinton. In 1820, prior to the expansion of the electorate, Clinton received 50.9 percent of the total gubernatorial vote of 93,437. In 1824, when lowered suffrage requirements resulted in a total vote of 190,545, his percentage was 54.3. In 1826 he polled 50.9 percent of the 195,920 votes cast. There is every reason to assume that the increased vote came from those electoral classes that previously had either lacked the vote entirely or had been ineligible to vote for governor.

According to the most recent authoritative survey of New York history, Clinton was regarded by the conservative forces as their champion; and the "liberal elements, whose strength was augmented by the widened suffrage, followed the leadership of the Albany Regency." Yet the foregoing analysis of the voting in New York demonstrates that the only observable effect of the extension of the suffrage was a very slight increase in Clinton's majority. Certainly the New York experience offers no support for the belief that even a drastic enlargement of the electorate resulted in any measurable change in party alignments. On the contrary, it gives added weight to the view that economic status as defined in suffrage restrictions had little or no influence on the party affiliations of voters. The new voters, drawn from an economic level that had previously been barred from the polls, apparently divided fairly evenly in party preferences between the Republicans and the Clintonians.

Perhaps Erastus Root was right when, speaking in the New York constitutional convention in 1821 in defense of manhood suffrage, he rejected the notion that the propertyless must be held in check because their interests were antagonistic to those of men of substance. "We have," declared Root, "no different estates, having different interests, necessary to be guarded from encroachments by the watchful eye of jealousy. We are all of the same estate—all commoners."

This analysis of suffrage conditions and voter behavior in North

Carolina and New York suggests several conclusions and raises some questions that merit further investigation. It is quite clear that in both of these states property qualifications effectively limited the size of the electorate. In North Carolina nearly one-half of those who went to the polls to vote for governor were unable to vote for state senators because they lacked the requisite fifty-acre freehold. In New York prior to 1821 approximately one-third of the adult white males were totally excluded from voting and another third was not qualified to vote for governor.

In both states the abandonment of property tests led to a sharp and immediate rise in the number of votes cast for those offices that had previously been elective by voters possessed of special qualifications. In New York, however, it seems quite probable that the constitutional restrictions were not rigidly enforced, with the result that a sizable number of inadequately qualified voters participated in gubernatorial elections. Moreover, when the suffrage was liberalized, the newly enfranchised voters manifested considerable apathy toward the exercise of their newly gained privilege.

Studies of other states—most notably New Jersey and Massachusetts—have tended to minimize the importance of property requirements as a factor limiting the size of the electorate. Obviously, for the period studied, this was not the case in New York or North Carolina. The point is that the experience of each state must be carefully investigated before any sweeping generalizations are made. The particular definitions of the suffrage qualifications must be examined, as well as the practical arrangements that existed for enforcement of the legal or constitutional requirements.

Although North Carolina and New York are not cited as "typical," they were two important—and even representative—states. Consequently, the conclusion that the upper economic-electoral class in each state divided between the major parties in almost the same proportions as the lower economic-electoral class raises significant questions about the general validity of economic-class interpretations of political behavior. Of course, the fact that parties did not reflect lines of economic cleavage in the periods under investigation does not necessarily imply that in other periods the same condition maintained. Here, again, is a field for further study.

It does not appear that the liberalization of the franchise had any measurable effect on the relative strength of the contending parties in either of the states investigated. To put it even more bluntly, when the common man was enfranchised in New York after 1821, he did not upset the political balance by throwing his weight heavily on the side of one party. Either he did not vote, or he showed as much preference for one party as for the other. If the broadening of the franchise did result in a major realignment of parties in any other state, that fact, I believe, has yet to be demonstrated.

The behavior of the voters of the lower electoral class in both North Carolina and New York indicates that there was little reason for the more substantial voters to fear the consequences of entrusting the masses with the franchise. How important was this fear factor, actually, in delaying the general movement toward white manhood suffrage in other states? Conversely, how vociferous were those who lacked the franchise in demanding voting privileges? Neither of these questions has been studied sufficiently in individual states to permit any firm general conclusions.

Finally, preoccupation with such matters as franchise restrictions and the influences shaping a voter's party preference should not result in neglect of the equally relevant problem of what stimulated voters to go to the polls. In North Carolina nearly all of the eligibles participated in elections. In New York a considerable fraction—around one-third in 1824—did not choose to vote. Such large variations in the rate of voter participation from state to state require explanation. It may well be that the factor most responsible for increasing the size of the actual electorate after 1824, for example, was not the elimination of suffrage barriers but rather the surge to the polls of voters who previously had not been sufficiently stimulated to cast their ballots. The voter, then, must be added to the traditional ingredients of American political history. Studies of his behavior hold some promise of adding a new dimension to our perception of the nature of our democracy.

13. | LEE BENSON
| *"Ethnocultural Groups and Political Parties"*

The power of the systematic use of quantitative evidence in political history is not primarily in the questioning of traditional interpretations. Rather, as Lee Benson demonstrated in his seminal book, *The Concept of Jacksonian Democracy: New York as a Test Case* (Princeton, 1961), it lies in our increased ability to develop precise answers as to why men behaved as they did at the polls. In the following, Chapter 8 of his book, he reports the results of his investigation of the relationship between election returns in New York in the 1840s and a number of possible influences on voting behavior including economic class and occupation, size and location of residence, religious and ethnocultural identification, and previous voting behavior. "Ethnocultural Groups and Political Parties," in Lee Benson, *The Concept of Jacksonian Democracy: New York as a Test Case* (copyright © 1961 by Princeton

University Press; Princeton Paperback, 1970), pp. 165–85 inclusive. Reprinted by permission of Princeton University Press. [Footnotes omitted.]

The present study rejects the economic determinist interpretation that Frederick J. Turner and Charles A. Beard impressed upon American political historiography. It also rejects the proposition that American political differences are random in character, that they reflect not group patterns, but the clashing ideas held by individual voters about the "community interest." And it rejects the proposition that socioeconomic cleavages are the obvious place to begin a study of American voting behavior. A counterproposition is advanced here: that at least since the 1820s, when manhood suffrage became widespread, ethnic and religious differences have tended to be *relatively* the most important sources of political differences. No attempt is made to "prove" that sweeping proposition, but this chapter and the following will try to show that it holds for New York in 1844. (Since the United States is highly heterogeneous, and has high social mobility, I assume that men tend to retain and be more influenced by their ethnic and religious group membership than by their membership in economic classes or groups.)

To anyone familiar with the literature, it will come as no surprise to read that the Democrats were the party of the immigrants and of the Catholics, the Whigs of the native Protestants, particularly those of New England stock. Unfortunately, that statement is almost as inaccurate and misleading as it is unoriginal. Collection and analysis of the relevant data reveal that the sharpest political cleavages occurred, not between immigrants and Yankees, *but between different groups of immigrants.*

By 1844, New York's population was remarkably heterogeneous. Thus before the relationships between ethnocultural group and voting behavior could be ascertained, it was necessary to work out a detailed classification system. The term *ethnocultural* is used in preference to ethnic, because the latter term lumps together men who came from the same "stock" but who, like the English in New England and New York, had developed considerably divergent cultures in the New World. Classifying men according to their membership in ethnocultural groups, however, enables us to uncover significantly different voting behavior patterns —patterns that are hidden or obscured when men are grouped according to ethnic attributes only.

Brevity was sacrificed to clarity when it came to labeling the two main categories of the classification system: "Groups in United States by 1790" (hereafter called "natives"); "Groups arriving in significant numbers after 1790" (hereafter called "immigrants"). Both the natives and the immigrants are subdivided, but our present concern is with the latter groups. For convenience, they are labeled "New British" and "New non-British." The former consisted of the Northern or Protestant "Irish," the Welsh, Scots, and English. Among others, the New non-British included the Southern or Catholic Irish, the Germans, French, and French-Canadians. (The "Irish" religious divisions actually corresponded closely with ethnic divisions, but the traditional terms of Protestant and Catholic Irish will be used hereafter.)

1. HOW DID THE IMMIGRANTS VOTE?

If the Democratic Party really had been the party of the immigrants, the ethnocultural groups identified above should have voted more or less alike. But they did not. Except for the Negroes, the New British were by far the strongest Whigs of any group in New York, the New non-British by far the strongest Democrats.

A. Protestant Irish and Welsh

Numerically the smallest of the New British groups, the Protestant Irish and the Welsh were probably the most homogeneous politically. Because the Protestant Irish failed to constitute a distinct, significant group in rural towns or urban wards, it is necessary to rely primarily upon contemporary observations for estimates of their party affiliation. Although precise estimates obviously cannot be verified, because contemporary observers agreed so unanimously, it seems safe to say that about 90 percent of the Protestant Irish voted Whig. (As is true of all such estimates presented below, that figure is not intended to be taken literally. Assigning groups a specific percentage enables us to indicate their *relative* party support.) The *Tribune* claimed "almost every Protestant Irishman" for the Whigs, the *New York Plebeian* (Democratic), the *Evening Post* (Democratic), and the *Freeman's Journal* (official Catholic organ) emphasized the "nativist," "anti-Catholic" proclivities that led the members of the group to vote against the Democrats.

According to the *Plebeian,* "every Orangeman" in the city voted American Republican in the 1844 mayoralty election, when the Whigs deserted their own nominees and voted for that party. Commenting upon this election and the 1844 anti-Catholic Irish riots in Philadelphia, the *Freeman's Journal* argued that "the most active, although not the most prominent of the Native Americans in New York, and probably in Philadelphia also, have been Irish Orangemen. They alone have been capable of furnishing the antisocial views with which our young *Natives* have been inoculated." The *Post* agreed that the "Orangemen" stood in the forefront of the "nativist" movement and, in effect, it wrote them off for the Democrats. Actually, as early as 1832 a Catholic Irish paper in

Albany, which was devoted to the Republican (that is, Jacksonian) cause, claimed that any "Orange Irish" who may once have been attached to that party were now "apostates." There seems to be no reason to doubt that claim or to believe that it was less accurate after 1832, particularly not in 1844 when the Whigs coalesced with the American Republicans in several counties and the Democrats identified themselves mores closely than ever with the Catholic Irish.

Although the Welsh had outposts throughout the state, they were most heavily concentrated in Oneida County. The first Welsh families came to the Oneida hills in 1795, and by 1808 they had formed a significant element in the population of the area. The high Whig vote in the predominantly Welsh agricultural town of Remsen bears out the *Tribune's* claim that "hardly one of them [was] a Loco-Foco." Remsen was the lowest ranking Democratic town in the county, and in 1844, when the median Democratic unit registered 50.8 percent, Remsen gave that party only 32.8 percent; in 1840, 25.6 percent. Since many voters in Remsen belonged to groups that did not strongly support the Whigs (including some Catholic Irish), the *Tribune* apparently was not exaggerating Welsh anti-Democratic sentiment. A reasonable estimate seems to be that about 90 percent of them *usually* cast Whig ballots (that is, unless abolitionist candidates were running).

B. English and the Scots

It is not possible to estimate precisely the number of voters of English and Scots descent, but they almost certainly constituted a much larger proportion of the electorate than the other two New British groups. The *Tribune* claimed nearly all the Scots and a "large portion" of the English for its party. Significantly, the *Evening Post* conceded the accuracy of that claim in a campaign editorial which argued that nativism would cost the Whigs many votes: "There is a large number of naturalized citizens in the interior counties of the state, and in all the western states, mostly English or Scotch by birth, who have hitherto [1844] voted with the Whigs. Not being gregarious in their manner of settlement, like the Irish and Germans, they do not pass for so large a portion of our population as they are found upon enquiry to make."

The *Post* erred in one respect, for the Scots were markedly "gregarious in their manner of settlement," and formed a respectable proportion of the population in counties as far apart as Washington, Fulton, Delaware, and Livingston. "Scots" towns comprised the lowest Democratic units in three of those counties and the second lowest (33.7 percent) in Fulton; the Scots were also well represented in the lowest (Johnstown, a manufacturing area). Putnam was the lowest ranking Democratic town (18.5

percent) in Washington as well as in the state. In 1844 it was overwhelmingly a community of Scots, as was York in Livingston, where the Democrats received only 23.0 percent of the total vote. Perhaps the clearest indication of the group's voting pattern is this; not a single town in which the Scots were clustered gave the Democrats a majority, *even in the strongest Democratic counties.*

Delaware County, for example, was a longtime Democratic stronghold. Yet the towns in which the Scots formed either a majority or a large minority of the population were the highest-ranking Whig units in the county. Hamden gave the Whigs 68.2 percent of its vote, followed closely by Andes which gave them 67.5 percent. Even Bovina, with 59.1 percent, was a "strong anti-Democratic" town. Such figures in traditionally Democratic Delaware County support the observations of the *Tribune* and *Evening Post* and justify the estimate that, like the Protestant Irish and the Welsh, about 90 percent of the Scots voted Whig.

The *Post* noted that the English were not "gregarious," and it has been possible to locate only two towns in which they formed a significant proportion of the population. Stockport in Columbia County and Stafford in Genesee were both "very strong Whig" communities. But they had voted much the same way before the English came and might well have continued to do so whether or not they contained any sizeable number of English "adopted citizens." As noted previously, Stockport was a manufacturing town; and Stafford had been an antimasonic stronghold prior to the arrival of immigrants from Devonshire. But it is at least suggestive that both towns were even more strongly Whig after sufficient time had elapsed for the English to make their presence felt. In Stockport, the Whigs received 69.6 percent of the vote in 1834, and 76.8 percent in 1844. In Stafford they received 69.0 percent and 70.1 percent, respectively. Thus there is no reason to doubt the *Post's* and *Tribune's* description of the English as Whig sympathizers. Moreover, other contemporary observers agreed that they shared the antipathy to the Catholic Irish that was characteristic of all the New British groups, and that they voted their antipathies. Nevertheless, there are nuances in *Tribune* editorials that suggest the English were *relatively* less homogeneous politically than the Protestant Irish, Welsh, and Scots. Since the *Tribune* editorials indicate that workers of "Radical" (Chartist) background tended to support the Democrats, it seems safer to estimate that only [*sic*] about 75 percent of the English voted Whig.

C. Catholic Irish

Though precise figures are not available, by 1844 the Catholic Irish undoubtedly formed the single largest immigrant group in New

York. Contemporary observations suggest that about 95 percent of the Catholic Irish who participated in the 1844 election cast Democratic ballots. But that group had not always formed so solid a bloc. During the late 1830s, enough Catholic Irish supported the Whigs to raise the expectations of men like Weed, Seward, and Greeley. Their expectations were badly blighted in 1840, however, when even Seward conceded that "the Irishmen . . . voted against us generally, and far more generally than heretofore." Desertions increased after 1840, and by November 1844 the *Albany Evening Journal* was printing letters that claimed, for example, that out of about 100 Catholic Irish voters in the city of Hudson, all were "against us except 2 or 3." (Whether the Catholic Irish voted along ethnocultural or religious lines will be discussed later.) .

Affiliation of the *urban* Catholic Irish to the Democratic Party has long been noted, although little attention has been given to changes in their voting behavior over time. What has tended to be overlooked is that the Catholic Irish voted Democratic in New York State, whether they lived in urban or rural communities, whether they were day laborers or freehold farmers—in short, their voting pattern represented an ethnocultural or religious group, not a place or class, phenomenon.

Most Catholic Irish lived in cities and large villages, but by 1844 many could be found in rural areas scattered throughout the state. Wherever they constituted a substantial proportion of the population, they voted as a bloc and made their presence felt politically. For example, in Franklin County "Irish [Catholic] settlers began to swarm into Bombay about 1825 . . . Mr. Hogan, the younger [the town's landowner], is said to have received these [settlers] with great kindliness, and to have located them upon what was then regarded as the very best lands in the town, which location came to be known as the 'Irish ridge.' " As the local historian noted, thanks to the solid Irish attachment to the Democrats, Bombay was a "strong Democratic" town in a traditionally Whig county.

Similarly, in 1844 in the Antimasonic and Whig county of Wyoming in western New York, the only town that gave the Democrats enough support to place it in a category above "neutral" was Java (58.6 percent). After the advance guard of Catholic Irish arrived in 1829, its farmlands began to attract many others. By 1844 substantial numbers of Irish Catholics must have lived there, for by 1855 the *Freeman's Journal* was proudly claiming that in Java and the adjoining town of China, "*there are one thousand Catholic families engaged in farming,* most of whom have already paid for their land." Though concentrated in Java, enough of those families lived in China to make it another high-ranking Democratic town.

Few agricultural towns contained as heavy concentrations of Catholic

Irish as Bombay and Java. But the *Evening Journal* and the *Tribune* emphasized that the Catholic Irish were sufficiently numerous to aid the Democrats materially in about half the counties of the state. Thus, once it is recognized that the Catholic Irish voted overwhelmingly Democratic wherever they lived and whatever their occupation, it follows that their voting behavior cannot be attributed to conditions peculiar to urban areas or to particular occupations.

D. Germans

Of the New non-British groups, the second largest, the Germans, were also strongly attached to the Democratic Party. Unlike the others, however, they divided into three distinct religious segments, Catholics, Protestants, and "Rationalists," or free thinkers. A credible source estimates that nearly one half the German settlers in New York State before the Civil War were Catholics; the remainder were divided among the Protestants and Rationalists.

Pending an intensive study, firm statements are unwarranted, but the available data suggest that the Protestant Germans, particularly the Prussian Lutherans, voted less strongly Democratic than the other two groups. Yet in the 1840s this difference in German voting behavior was apparently only a matter of degree, and Democratic papers claimed the Germans almost exclusively for their party. In Syracuse, for example, during the 1844 campaign, the *Argus* reported that "no Dutchman [*sic*] could be found to carry Gen. Granger's Banners, at the recent coon [Whig] celebration." Even before the nativist issue developed intensity, the Whigs conceded that the "great majority" of German voters were arrayed against them. From the *Tribune*'s admission—and it appealed strongly for German support—as well as from other evidence, it seems clear that they voted Democratic irrespective of religious affiliation. Nonetheless, the Catholic Germans probably voted most Democratic, the Protestants probably least Democratic.

A highly "gregarious" group, the Germans are easily detected in the rural areas. In Croghan, Lewis County, they appear to have constituted a larger proportion of the population than in any other New York town. Croghan was the highest ranking Democratic unit in the county (83.2 percent), and the second highest in the state. As part of its campaign to get the vote of "adopted citizens," the *Albany Argus* highlighted the presence of naturalized German citizens from Croghan at the Democrat's main rally in Lewis County. They were assigned a prominent place in the parade and their float's banner emphasized a favorite party theme: "The Naturalized Citizens of Croghan—Have Not We the same rights as Natives?"

Croghan, with its large proportion of Germans, was an extremely "poor" town in a Democratic county; Tonawanda (in Erie) and Irondequoit (in Monroe), each with large numbers of Germans, were "prosperous" agricultural towns in Whig counties. Both were the highest-ranking Democratic units in their counties, giving sizeable majorities to the party (65.6 percent and 58.6 percent, respectively), even though Erie and Monroe were longtime Antimasonic and Whig strongholds. With the exception of two towns settled by Prussian Lutherans, all towns in New York containing significant numbers of Germans were found to be high-ranking Democratic units. The estimate that approximately 80 percent of the Germans voted Democratic is based upon my analysis of the statistical data and the impressionistic evidence of contemporary observers, for example, "The victory of the Loco-Focos is not that of *Americans* but a triumph of *Irishmen* and *Germans* over *Americans*."

E. Catholic French

Though few in number and concentrated largely in New York City, the Catholic French also contributed to the 1844 Democratic victory. Under the headline, "A New Foreign Ally Brought Into the Field," the *American Republican* added the French to the Catholic Irish and German "foreign battalions," long mustered under Tammany banners. According to the *Express*, an ardently nativist Whig paper, the French as a group "since time immemorial," had abstained from political participation. But "this year they have wakened," the paper observed; and its tone suggested that the awakening would not bring joy to Whig politicians. Unwilling to concede the French to the Locofocos before election, the *Express* included them afterwards in its angry denunciation of "the avalanche of Germans, Irish, Swiss, Prussians, French, Russians, and Poles" that had rolled over the Whigs on election day. The *Herald,* an independent paper, also presented evidence sustaining the view that the French voted *en masse* for the Democrats in 1844.

Perhaps the most significant aspect of the solid French support for the Democrats relates to their socioeconomic status. In his illuminating study of New York immigrant life, Robert Ernst has noted that, unlike the Irish and the Germans, "there were few laborers or shanty dwellers among them [the French]." Also unlike those groups, a relatively sizeable percentage of the French were merchants, some of whom "grew rich from the increasing trade between New York, Le Havre and Paris." Since they probably voted as solidly Democratic as the Catholic Irish, and since their socioeconomic status was much higher than the latter's, French voting behavior strengthens the claim that in 1844 the New non-British acted along ethnocultural (and religious) rather than economic group lines.

F. French Canadians

The smallest of the New non-British groups, and the latest to arrive in the United States (after 1837), the French Canadians were highly concentrated in a few Northern Tier counties. Their small number and late arrival makes it difficult to estimate their 1844 party allegiance from statistical data. But the *Tribune* in effect conceded them to the Democrats. An impressionistic estimate that they voted along the lines of the Catholic Irish (95 percent Democratic) is probably not far off the mark. The 1852 data support that estimate, since by then enough time had elapsed for the voting statistics to reflect their presence. Clinton, where they were more highly concentrated than anywhere else in the state, gave the Democrats 74.1 percent of its vote and thereby became the party's banner unit in the county. (By 1860 the French Canadians comprised an even higher proportion of the electorate in Clinton, and the Democrats received 85 per cent of the town vote in that strong Republican county.) Similarly, Chateaugay in Franklin County was another French Canadian center, and its Democratic vote (72.7 percent) in 1852 was even higher than Bombay's (60.1 percent), where many Catholic Irish lived.

G. Summary

As noted above, the purpose of estimating group percentages is to suggest the relative rather than actual support given the major parties by different groups. The group estimates appear to be roughly accurate, at least, and they discredit the claim that the Democratic Party was the party of the immigrants. That claim may be literally accurate, but it is thoroughly misleading. The New non-British strongly supported the Democratic Party; the New British just as strongly opposed it. Because the former considerably outnumbered the latter in the state, it is undoubtedly true that many more "adopted citizens" voted Democratic than Whig. But that statistic is a demographic accident. Had migration been larger from New British areas than from New non-British, it seems reasonable to assume that the reverse situation would have developed in the state—as, in fact, it did in many localities.

2. HOW DID THE NATIVES VOTE?

Shifting attention to differences in voting behavior *between immigrant groups and native groups,* we find a significant phenomenon that will be noted here and commented upon in later chapters. Although all immigrant groups voted as solid blocs, the natives divided *relatively* closely between the two major parties (except for two small groups identified below).

A. Yankees

Contrary to the traditional view that voters of New England descent voted strongly Whig, the estimate here is that for the state as a whole they split about 55 percent Whig, 45 percent Democratic. (This estimate counts Liberty Party voters according to their previous affiliations.) That the generic term "Yankee" refers to men who derived from heterogeneous social and cultural backgrounds is suggested by this finding: unlike every immigrant group, and to a greater extent than any other native group, the Yankees varied widely in their voting behavior in different parts of the state and in different towns within the same county.

The small Whig margin among the Yankees actually derived from the original Anti-masonic strength in western New York. That extensive region constituted a "colony from New England," and the party that dominated it politically contained necessarily a large proportion of Yankees. But in many New York counties where the Antimasonic movement had failed to penetrate or had produced a counterreaction, the Democrats received strong Yankee support.

Since Yankees constituted about 65 percent of the state's electorate, it follows logically that they must have been closely divided in their party allegiance. Had the Whigs received much more than 55 percent of that group's vote, their opponents would invariably have been beaten badly on the state level, unless all other groups cast solid Democratic ballots. But logical deduction need not be relied on; "New England" counties and towns are easily located.

For example, the county of Suffolk, directly across Long Island Sound from Connecticut, was "completely Yankee in population." Traditionally a Democratic stronghold, in 1844 it ranked as the third-highest Democratic county and gave the party 57.8 percent of its total vote. Within the county, however, the descendants of Connecticut Yankees differed widely in political allegiance. Easthampton, an "unusually prosperous" agricultural town ($883), was the banner Democratic unit with 75.7 percent of the vote; Southhampton, a "very prosperous" agricultural, whaling, and fishing town ($632) was the lowest-ranking Democratic unit with 34.0 percent. (The voting record of the latter nicely illustrates the proposition stated in Chapter VII about the conditions under which economic interests are most likely to influence political behavior. A local Democratic newspaper explained its party's poor showing in Southhampton by citing the specific attractions that Whig policies held for its substantial nonagricultural interests.)

Much the same situation obtained in Delaware County (southeastern New York) as in Suffolk on eastern Long Island. Except for the Scots (and some Dutch in a couple of towns), Delaware was overwhelmingly Yankee. And yet, despite the solid Scots support for the Whigs, Delaware was the sixth-highest Democratic county in the state (57.3 percent). Again, striking variations in Yankee voting patterns appear on the town level. For example, Franklin, unmistakably a transplanted Connecticut community, gave the Democrats 72.9 percent of its total vote. Stamford, just as clearly an outpost of Fairfield County, Connecticut, gave them only 44.9 percent. Contrary to what the economic determinist interpretation of voting behavior would lead one to expect, both Franklin ($441) and Stamford ($473) were "prosperous" agricultural towns.

To an even greater extent than Delaware, Otsego County in central New York was settled by Yankees. The historian of that area noted, as late as the Civil War, that "the vast majority of the inhabitants traced their ancestry to New England." Yet "wool-growing" Otsego was traditionally Democratic and gave that party 54.5 percent of its vote in 1844. Moving up to the North Country, we find that Warren and St. Lawrence were other Yankee counties that traditionally voted Democratic. The former trailed Delaware closely in the party's honor roll with 55.1 percent, the latter ranked just above Otsego with 54.7 percent. And even in western New York many New England towns voted strongly Democratic. Prattsburg in Steuben County serves as a good example, since its settlers "were peculiarly a homogeneous population." Its pioneers were nearly all of Congregational background and "originally from Connecticut, of the best Puritan stock." In this "prosperous" agricultural town, the Democrats received 61.3 percent of the total vote.

Other examples would only belabor the point. The data, I believe, warrant these conclusions: 1) In no county did Yankee voting behavior resemble the bloc pattern characteristic of all immigrant groups. 2) In some counties the Yankees voted strongly Whig. 3) In other counties they divided more or less evenly. 4) In still others they voted strongly Democratic. Contrary to traditional assumptions, the group's voting behavior shows no significant class differences. Put another way, unless one knew *where* well-to-do or poor Yankees lived, or knew certain other information noted below, one would have little basis for predicting party affiliations. Yankee voting in New York during the 1830s and 1840s was heterogeneous, suggesting that so wide a variety of factors over time and space had influenced them that easy generalizations are exceedingly dangerous.

B. Negroes and Huguenots

Aside from the Yankees, I estimate that only two native groups cast Whig majorities in New York, the Negroes and the Huguenots (Protestant French). Unlike all other natives, members of each of these small groups had experienced or were experiencing "persecution," and each voted as a solid bloc.

Because of the property restrictions upon Negro suffrage which the Van Buren faction had written into the 1821 State Constitution, only about one thousand "persons of color" were eligible to vote in 1844. An analysis of the parties' opposing positions during the 1840's on the proposed constitutional amendment removing Negro suffrage restrictions strongly confirms Dixon Ryan Fox's conclusion that Negroes voted solidly Whig. To estimate that they supported the Whigs as solidly as the Catholic Irish supported the Democrats (95 percent) does not appear to be an overstatement.

Like the Negroes, the Huguenots were among the earliest inhabitants of New York province. An estimate based upon the best available study indicates that they comprised about three percent of the state's population in 1790. By 1844, however, as a result of the influx of native and foreign migrants to New York, they probably comprised less than one percent of the electorate and cast about 4,000 votes. Though it seems reasonably certain that they strongly supported the Whigs, the estimated figure of 75 percent is frankly impressionistic. Clusters of Huguenots lived in Ulster, Richmond, Westchester, New York and Kings counties, but only in the town of New Paltz, Ulster County, did they form a substantial part of the population. Unfortunately for our purposes, that town also contained many Dutch—a group that tended to vote Democratic. It is difficult, therefore, to draw any credible inferences from the 52.3 percent the Whigs received in New Paltz. Contemporary references to enthusiastic Huguenot participation in the 1844 anti-Catholic campaign suggest, however, that the 75 percent Whig figure is not too inaccurate an estimate of their group voting pattern.

The *American Republican* carried frequent and glowing reports concerning "the progress of Americanism" in the "old Huguenot county of Ulster." Both New Paltz and Hurley (another Huguenot center) were "all right" and ready to do their part at the polls. An editorial hailing the group's contribution to the success of an "immense" Fourth of July party rally in Ulster is revealing. "That county may be considered as the Huguenot county of the State. It is filled with a class of people who appreciate all the blessings of liberty, and are sensitively alive to anything that threatens danger to the Protestant faith." Although resolutions passed at the July rally denounced the Whigs as well as the Democrats for "truckling to papal interests," the *Tribune* later revealed that before the campaign was over the Whigs and American Republicans had practically merged in Ulster. Nonetheless, a not insignificant proportion of Huguenots must have voted Democratic or that party's vote would have been lower in New Paltz.

C. Other "Yorkers"

The Huguenots comprise one of four native groups classified here as "Yorkers," the descendants of men who came directly to the province of New York rather than migrated to it after first settling in New England, New Jersey, or elsewhere. The Dutch, the Palatine Germans, and the "Old British" complete the list. This latter group is really a composite and includes the English, Welsh, Scots, and Scotch-Irish living in New York by 1790. Long residence in the country as well as behavior patterns and traditions associated with Revolutionary and early national struggles differentiated them from the post-1790 "New British."

Like the Huguenots, the other Yorker groups were largely clustered in eastern portions of the state that had been settled before the Revolution, particularly in the Hudson, Mohawk and Schoharie valleys. But, contrary to the Huguenot pattern, I estimate that roughly 60 percent of the Dutch, Palatines, and Old British voted Democratic. (Only a study that examined the evidence microscopically could isolate their separate voting patterns.) The estimate, 60 percent, is supported by the comfortable Democratic majorities in most Yorker counties and communities. Thus they comprised either a majority or a substantial minority of the population in the *highest-ranking Democratic towns in 14 counties; they comprised either a majority or a substantial minority of the population in the lowest ranking Democratic towns in only two counties.*

Dutch, Palatine, and Old British majorities for the Democrats powerfully discredit the traditional assumption that the Whigs represented primarily the prosperous farmers living on better soils or along good transportation routes. Having arrived early, the Yorker families had decades, often centuries, to pick out the best sites, accumulate wealth (and status), and pass it along to descendants. This is not to imply that all Yorkers in 1844 were well-to-do. But as a group, their early arrival had given them relatively high places on the economic scale. For example, as a local historian observed, long devotion to agriculture by the Dutch in Rockland County had paid off handsomely. "Wealth brought with it grand and comfortable homes. Money begat money. 'Money saved is money made' was the Dutchman's motto. It was not an unusual thing for a farmer, a generation ago [that is during the 1850s], to be worth from $50,000 even up to $100,000 in cash, besides a fine farm to leave to his posterity."

As noted previously, the solidly Dutch, "very prosperous" agricultural community of Clarkstown in Rockland County was the state's leading Democratic unit (89.9 percent). In contrast, the "prosperous" agricultural town of Ramapo, settled largely by twice-transplanted Connecticut Yankees from Hempstead, Long Island, was the county's lowest ranking Democratic unit (56.5 percent). Another "very prosperous" Dutch agricultural community, Coeymans in Albany County, cast 71.4 percent of its vote for the Democrats. The predominantly Yankee "marginal" town of Knox in the same county cast only 34.0 percent for the Democrats. (It is worth noting here that the pattern of high Yorker and low Yankee support for the Democrats was not limited to Rockland and Albany, but tended to persist in almost all counties where "restless" Yankees came to disturb the peace of "conservative" Yorkers.)

Other "Dutch" towns heading their county's Democratic list were Lexington in Greene (79.1 percent), Deerpark in Orange (67.7 percent), Greenbush in Rensselaer (64.7 percent), Newton in Queens (60.3 percent), Shawangunk in Ulster (60.1 percent), and Sullivan in Madison (53.1 percent). In every case, these towns were "prosperous" or "very prosperous" agricultural communities. The two Yorker communities at the tail-end of their county's Democratic list were Catskill in Greene (42.3 percent) and Esopus in Ulster (32.7 percent). Catskill, a "very prosperous" commercial and agricultural town on the Hudson, was settled originally by the Dutch, but the heavy Yankee influx after the Revolution makes it difficult to determine whether the Yorker element actually predominated by 1844. Similarly, Esopus on the Hudson was a "prosperous" old Dutch agricultural town, but it contained many Huguenots who may have been responsible for its low Democratic vote.

Arriving in the lower Hudson Valley early in the eighteenth century, many of the "poor German Protestants" from the Palatine migrated soon afterwards to the "fat lands" along the Mohawk and Schoharie rivers. Although by 1844 the post-Revolutionary Yankee invasion had drastically changed the ethnocultural composition of Herkimer, Schoharie, and Montgomery counties, the Palatines still formed at least a substantial minority element in those reliably Democratic counties. Certainly they formed the numerically dominant element in the highest ranking Democratic towns in all three counties.

The town of Herkimer in the county of Herkimer, named after the Palatine's revolutionary hero (General Nicholas Herkimer), was "unusually prosperous" and contained the "German Flats," widely renowned for their enduring fertility. It gave the Democrats 70.5 percent of its vote, slightly more than the "prosperous" Palatine agricultural towns of Sharon in Schoharie (66.0 percent) and St. Johnsville in Montgomery (65.6 percent) gave them. Of the highest ranking Democratic towns dominated by the Palatines (and Dutch), Taghanic in Columbia County (70.1 percent) was the only one of "marginal" status.

As was true in general of the three Yorker groups we are now considering, not all Palatine towns voted heavily Democratic. For example, although the "very prosperous" town of Schoharie in Schoharie County strongly resembled Herkimer in socioeconomic composition and other characteristics, it voted only 52.0 percent Democratic. Schoharie shows that the group's voting pattern varied somewhat in different areas, but does not weaken the finding that Palatine communities characteristically gave the Democrats comfortable majorities.

Yonkers, an Old British (English) town, led the Democratic ranks in Westchester (70.3 percent). Nearness to New York City had long given its farmers an excellent market for produce, and land values soared after 1842 as Yonkers increasingly became a suburban community. The "marginal" town of Putnam Valley in adjoining Putnam County presented an exception to the general rule of Yorker prosperity, but it was another Old British community long devoted to the Democratic cause (83.2 percent). Across the Hudson in Orange County, the flourishing agricultural towns of Crawford (Scotch-Irish), Hamptonburg (English and Scotch-Irish), and New Windsor (English and Scotch-Irish) also registered comfortable Democratic majorities (65.8, 59.3, and 57.5 percent, respectively).

Although I estimate that the three groups voted about 60 percent Democratic, undoubtedly differences existed among the Dutch, Palatine, and Old British patterns. The significant point, however, is that those groups enjoyed relatively high socioeconomic status in their communities and definitely sided with the Democrats in the political wars.

D. Penn-Jerseyites

Like the Old British, the last ethnocultural group to be considered here is a composite one. Particularly after the Revolution, Scotch-Irish, Germans, and Dutch from Pennsylvania and New Jersey came to take up unoccupied lands in New York. Although they tended to locate in southeastern and Southern Tier counties, many of them pushed farther north. Seneca County in western New York, for example, was as much a Penn-Jersey center as Chemung on the Pennsylvania line and Orange on the New Jersey line.

Analysis of county and town statistics leads to the conclusion that the Penn-Jerseyites tended to divide evenly between the parties. Unlike the Yankees, however, this native group leaned to the Democratic side, and I estimate that about 55 percent of them voted "Locofoco." Thus the Democrats had a majority in counties such as Chemung (58.1 percent) and Steuben (55.0 percent), and the Whigs had a majority in no Penn-

Jersey county. Even in Seneca, where the Antimasonic "blessed spirit" had manifested itself, the Democrats received 51.6 percent of the total vote. Nevertheless, both the highest and the lowest ranking Democratic towns in Seneca, Tioga, and Tompkins counties were Penn-Jersey centers that resembled each other in many respects; it seems clear, therefore, that the group was closely divided politically.

Summary

Perhaps the most dramatic way to summarize and delineate the ethnocultural basis of party divisions in New York in 1844 is to bring together the estimated group voting percentages. Table I illustrates the main point: party affiliations were extremely polarized among immigrants, and native voters tended to be relatively evenly divided. It is worth noting that the "deviant" behavior of Negroes and Huguenots strengthens rather than weakens the conclusion that native groups had not yet developed polarized voting patterns. Like the immigrants, members of those two groups were influenced by certain ethnic and religious factors that differentiated them from the great bulk of the native electorate.

TABLE I

Estimated party percentages, New York ethnocultural groups, 1844

| | "NATIVES" | | | "IMMIGRANTS" | |
	WHIG %	DEM. %		WHIG%	DEM. %
Negroes	95.0	5.0	Catholic Irish	5.0	95.0
Huguenots	75.0	25.0	French Canadian	5.0	95.0
Yankees	55.0	45.0	French	10.0	90.0
			New German	20.0	80.0
Penn-Jerseyites	45.0	55.0			
Old British	40.0	60.0	English	75.0	25.0
Dutch	40.0	60.0	Scots	90.0	10.0
Old German	40.0	60.0	Welsh	90.0	10.0
			Protestant Irish	90.0	10.0

14. ALEXANDRA McCOY
"Political Affiliation of American Economic Elites"

In *The Concept of Jacksonian Democracy*, Lee Benson argued that, contrary to our usual view, members of America's wealthiest groups were to be found among the leaders of both the Democratic and Whig parties. But his analysis left open whether, despite the Democrats in their ranks, the upper classes as a whole disproportionately supported the

Whigs. In the following selection from her unpublished Wayne State University doctoral dissertation, "Political Affiliation of American Economic Elites: Wayne County, Michigan, 1844, 1860 As A Test Case," (Wayne State University, 1965), Alexandra McCoy, a student of Benson's, carefully examines the political affiliation of economic elites in Wayne County, Michigan, in the Jacksonian period and finds that certain ethno-cultural factors are a much surer predictor of party membership than wealth or class status. She also makes an important methodological point —that if there is a disproportionate number of one ethnocultural group in a particular economic class, misleading conclusions may result unless other variables are carefully considered. Reprinted, with most footnotes omitted, by permission of Alexandra McCoy.

Ninety-seven individuals made up the economic elite of Wayne County, Michigan, in 1844. These men were selected primarily on the basis of their known wealth with important economic roles as a secondary consideration. Tax assessment rolls for real and personal property for the city of Detroit and Wayne County provided the comprehensive measurement by which the men were ranked. Wealth figures were based on the assessment formula then in operation, which was to rate property at 30 percent of actual cash value. Therefore, Lewis Cass, whose real and personal property was assessed at $73,383, was considered to be worth $244,365.

. . . The systematic selection of an economic elite makes it possible to determine partially the relationship between political affiliations and economic class positions. Whether in Michigan the "vast majority" . . . of the Whig party . . . "were well-to-do and conservative men or those who, for some reason, upheld the interest of this class" and whether the Democrats were "composed mainly of the poor and uneducated people in the cities and the rural districts," will not be known until a thorough study has been made of the voting patterns for the entire state by county and ward. Districts voting Whig and Democrat have to be analyzed as to composition in an effort to determine whether voting reflects membership in economic, ethnic, religious or other groups. Through this method of multivariate analysis it will be possible to develop a solid basis for hypothesis about the nature of "those [Whigs] who, for some reason upheld the interest of this [well-to-do] class."[1]

The overall study of voting behavior by district, ward or county cannot by itself settle the question of economic class as a determinant. A separate study of economic elites must be made because voting statistics cannot be used to ascertain the political affiliations of men who, by

---

[1] Floyd B. Streeter, *Political Parties in Michigan, 1837–1860* (Lansing: Michigan Historical Commission, 1918), 5–6.

definition, constitute only a small proportion of any aggregate political unit. Lee Benson cites the example of the Fifteenth Ward in New York City in *The Concept of Jacksonian Democracy*. It was known as "aristocratic," yet, since it "probably contained only a small proportion of voters who belonged to the upper classes," . . . "its strong support for the Whigs fails to discredit the post-election estimate of a leading anti-Whig newspaper that 'a large portion of the monied men and capitalists of this city and throughout the State, voted the Democratic ticket.' "[2]

Clearly what is needed to test the relationships between class and political affiliation is a systematic study of how men assigned to different economic classes actually voted. Once the political affiliations of the elite have been ascertained and subjected to multivariate analysis, the results can be examined against the pattern of mass voting behavior for the same unit. If the voting pattern of rich men of one ethnocultural group follows the same pattern as that of the lower class of the same group, then we have strong evidence to support the thesis that "ethnic and religious differences have tended to be *relatively* the most important sources of political differences."[3] If, on the other hand, the elite members of an ethnic group show a tendency to adopt different political affiliations, class cannot be ruled out as an important influence on political behavior.

The political affiliations of the economic elite of Wayne County in 1844 were not difficult to ascertain. Members of this group tended to be active in politics, so that their names appear continually in the newspapers as candidates for office, delegates to ward, county or state party meetings or as signers of petitions. Newspaper references provided a check against party designations in biographical sources which were usually corroborated. Since it was not possible to find data directly referring to all men's party affiliations in the year 1844, evidence was taken from accounts dated as far back as 1839 when both the Democratic and Whig parties had become established organizations.

The assumption made in this study, which was born out by the evidence, is that men remained loyal to a political party. Although Floyd B. Streeter's description of parties in the late 1830s would seem to dispute the hypothesis of party loyalty, he does not document with names men who actually changed parties. Streeter claimed that well-to-do Democrats in the central tier of Michigan counties became disgusted with their party over internal improvements—the Democrats wanted to splurge on railroads outside the central tier—and united with the Whigs. He also claimed that "each party was so utterly broken up into factions in the

2 Benson, *Concept of Jacksonian Democracy*, 146.
3 *Ibid.*, 165.

thirties and forties that it might almost he said that the name Whig or Democrat represented an idea rather than an actuality."[4] What is suggested here is that factions worked together for particular immediate goals. It does not necessarily contradict continuing allegiance to party on the part of individuals.

We found strong support for the continuance of party membership. Although more than one source has been found to document political affiliations for seventy-five of the elite, only two cases of a party switch before the 1850s turned up. H. N. (elsewhere H. P.) Baldwin, who was later a Whig, was a member of a Democratic First Ward Committee of Vigilance in a charter election in 1839, and William K. Coyl (not a member of the elite until 1860), designated as an "earnest Whig in early life," was Democratic nominee for assessor in 1839. That party loyalty was a customary mode of behavior during this period is suggested by Lee Benson's exhaustive analysis of voting patterns in New York. He found that "secular trends appear to have stemmed more from shifts to minor parties and from changes in the composition of the electorate than from a sizeable number of voters gradually deserting one major party to support another."

On the basis of available evidence, and assuming constancy in political affiliations, the Wayne County elite in 1844 can be described as follows: sixty Whigs, twenty-eight Democrats, five Liberty Party and four unknown.

TABLE I

Political affiliations of the elite—1844

Whigs	60	62% of the Elite
Democrats	28	29% of the Elite
Liberty	5	5% of the Elite
Unknown	4	4% of the Elite
	97	100%

Although Whigs predominate, Streeter's characterization of the Whigs as the party of the well-to-do cannot be regarded as definitive. Clearly, we ought not to accept an economic explanation of party which leaves 40 percent of the group as an exception. What is essential, then, is to examine other factors which might reasonably influence men's political affiliations. Streeter, along with other historians, suggests ethnocultural as well as economic factors as possible influences on Whig membership: "a large number of the Whigs had been reared in homes in New England and

4 Streeter, 12.

eastern New York where they had enjoyed the advantages of wealth and education." By the use of multivariate analysis we hope to be able to relate ethno-cultural and economic characteristics to party membership with greater precision. . . .

. . . Assigning specific economic roles to the elite made it possible to determine whether there were any patterns of party affiliation according to occupation. Some occupations showed a marked concentration of the same political adherents. Merchants and non-specialized entrepreneurs were preponderantly Whig (87 percent and 89 percent) with manufacturers showing a marked tendency to the same party (68 percent).

Landowners were the only group showing a marked Democratic concentration, although not to the degree that merchants and entrepreneurs were Whigs (66 percent of landowners Democrats, 34 percent Whigs). Whigs led among the lawyers and Democrats among bankers, but here the smaller numbers involved makes the correlation seem less significant. The pattern for bankers is in line with a study of New York bankers who were found not to be "prone to be Whigs any more than they were to be Democrats."[5]

. . . Any study of the political behavior of men in nineteenth-century America would be completely superficial without the investigation of one of their dominating concerns—religion. Despite separation of church and state, religion had thrived on an institutional basis and "by 1860 the clergy had recovered whatever influence over public affairs they had lost in the generations of Thomas Jefferson and Andrew Jackson."[6] The Great Protestant revivals had not only transformed the mode of religious experience but had brought about expanded church membership. By 1855 15 percent of the population were members of a Protestant congregation compared with the 10 percent including both Catholic and Protestants who were members in 1790.

. . . It will be noted on Table II that 76 percent of the Presbyterians were Whigs compared with 16 percent who were Democrats. The Whig-Presbyterian correlation makes sense when we investigate Presbyterian attitudes and note the congruence with Whig positions. Both Whigs and Presbyterians were antipathetic to Catholics. Although George Duffield's anti-Catholicism took an extreme theological form, his attitudes conformed to the outlook of the Michigan Presbyterian Synod. One of the Synod's chief preoccupations was the preservation of the sanctity of the sabbath, the desecration of which was blamed on Roman Catholics,

5 Leonard Zivits, "The Political Affiliations of Bankers in New York State in 1844" (Unpublished seminar paper, Columbia College, 1958), 3, and *passim*, cited in Benson, *Concept of Jacksonian Democracy*, 160.

6 Timothy L. Smith, *Revivalism and Social Reform in Mid-Nineteenth America* (New York: Abingdon Press, 1957), 38.

TABLE II

Percentage of major religious groups according to party — 1844

	PRESBYTERIAN		EPISCOPALIAN		CATHOLIC		NO RELIGION	
	No.	*%*	*No.*	*%*	*No.*	*%*	*No.*	*%*
Whig	28	76	18	64	4	57	7	35
Democrat	6	16	10	36	3	43	9	45
Liberty	2	5	–	–	2	10	–	–
Unknown	1	3	–	–	–	–	2	10
Totals	37	100	28	100	7	100	20	100

Omitted: 5

European immigrants, increasing ties with Europe, Sunday newspapers, and railroads. In the political sphere Whig newspapers and politicians echoed the Presbyterians. The *Detroit Advertiser* did not give unqualified support to the Know-Nothings, but clearly revealed its anti-Catholic bias in describing them as native born who would "use any honorable means to counteract the secret and jesuitical influence of the Pope." Although it is difficult to separate the strands, anti-Catholicism among Whig-Presbyterians may have been inspired by religious prejudice rather than racism. A letter written in 1853 by the widow of prominent Whig and Presbyterian, Robert Stuart, gives voice to the intensity of anti-popery:

You are right in thinking the Catholic question an important one, it is the only one, which should at this moment occupy the American mind—They for the last 20 yrs. have been moving all their powers to enslave our beautiful Republic, but they have gone too fast . . . Every Christian has to buckle on his Armour & keep it Bright—The Battle of the Lord of Hosts has begun—In this struggle, the German and French Catholics have behaved most nobly—the Irish and Belgians were his Satanic Majesty's Standard Bearers.

In 1844 Episcopalianism did not identify as closely with one party as did Presbyterianism. Although it represented the largest affiliation of Democrats (36 percent of them Episcopalian), 31 percent of the Whigs also embraced the fashionable faith (see Table III). Furthermore, because Whigs were preponderant they accounted for 64 percent of the Episcopal group (36 percent Democratic; see Table II above). Despite their small numbers Democrats did lead, however, in the number of men who were not found to be affiliated with any religion (they account for 45 percent to Whig 35 percent of all nonaffiliated men). Joseph Campau was reputed to have left the Catholic church for political reasons—he was

TABLE III

Percentage of each party according to religion, 1844

	WHIG		DEMOCRAT		LIBERTY		UNKNOWN	
	No.	*%*	*No.*	*%*	*No.*	*%*	*No.*	*%*
Presbyterian	28	48	6	21	2	40	1	25
Episcopalian	18	31	10	36	–	–	–	–
Catholic	4	6	3	11	–	–	–	–
No Religion	7	9	9	32	2	40	2	50
Congregational	1	2	–	–	1	20	–	–
Baptists	1	2	–	–	–	–	1	25
Methodist	1	2	–	–	–	–	–	–
Unitarian	–	–	–	–	–	–	–	–
Church of Christ	–	–	–	–	–	–	–	–
Totals	60	100	28	100	5	100	4	100

outraged when Father Gabriel Richard ran for territorial delegate against his nephew, John R. Williams. Williams himself was baptised a Catholic but was not found to be a member of any church, although most of his children were Episcopalians.

The voting pattern of the seven Catholics among the Wayne County elite of 1844 is perhaps one of the more interesting findings of this study. Four, or 57 percent of the Catholics have been identified as Whigs and three, or 43 percent of the Catholics were Democrats. The first conclusion suggested by the Whig preponderance among Catholics is that economically successful Catholics were subjected to "cross pressures" as they distanced their co-religionists and abandoned the Democratic party, the overwhelming favorite of Catholic voters. However, the ethnocultural characteristics of these Wayne County Catholics present complicating factors. They were all French, but only one family among them, the Desnoyers, could be called "immigrants," and two of the three Desnoyers, Peter J. Desnoyers and one of his sons, Charles, were Whigs. Peter J. Desnoyers, the father, became a successful merchant, having started out in Detroit in the early 1800s as a silversmith, financed by his father in Paris. His Whig orientation could easily be explained as an identification away from (negative reference group reaction) the native French whose separation from the invading Yankees was based on their ethnocultural differences as much as upon their religion. Two of the richest French members of the elite, Antoine Beaubien and Joseph Campau, were distinctly "peasant" types. Beaubien was illiterate and Joseph Campau (ex-Catholic and Democrat) was "a picturesque French gentlemen" and shrewd peasant landlord who conversed "colorfully" in broken English.

Beaubien's Whig affiliation was a weak one. The only evidence for it was his signature on a broadside for one of the first organizational meetings of the Whig Party, signed also by Joseph Campau, who has been classified as a Democrat because of his close connection with his nephew, John R. Williams. If the political affiliations are considered from the point of view of ethnocultural similarity rather than religion, then the pattern is more in conformity with New York and elsewhere. Of eleven of French descent, five were Democrats, four Whigs and two no party. It should be noted in connection with religion that four, or 36 percent, of the French members of the elite were not found to be practicing Catholics. This may also represent a negative reference group reaction.

No significant pattern of political identification can be read from the two Baptists (Whig and no party) and one Methodist in the 1844 group because of their numbers. That so few of the elite embraced these sects conforms to the class patterns of Methodism and Baptism. From the nineteenth century through the twentieth they were the Protestant sects of the common man with Baptists having their greatest success in the rural South and Methodism in the Eastern cities.

. . .

An investigation of the ethnic and geographical origins of the elite is essential in order to clarify the role religion played in influencing political affiliation. Since religion tended to coincide with ethnic origin as in the case of French Catholics, it might be assumed that a separate investigation of ethnocultural origin is superfluous. We shall discover, however, that by separating out ethnic background from religion we are able to pinpoint more sharply the determining role of religion. As Lee Benson discovered in New York, religion separated Irish voters: the Protestants voted Whig, the Catholics Democratic.[7] One of the values of an elite study is that available sources make it possible to check religious affiliation against ethnocultural background with a certain degree of exactitude. Benson's study enabled him to estimate percentages of party affiliation according to ethnocultural groups, but the religious affiliations of the same groups could not be examined except where the religion and ethnic component created the total group character as in the case of Irish Catholics and French Huguenots. His study indicated that Yankees, who also dominated the Wayne County elite in 1844 and 1860, could be expected to show much greater variations in politics than immigrant groups. . . .

[7] Benson, *Concept of Jacksonian Democracy,* 167, 171.

. . . The dominance of New Englanders among the elite becomes marked when a comparison is made with the general population of Michigan. Next to natives of Michigan, New Yorkers in 1850 constituted

Native born	341,591		Slave states	3,266	
Foreigner	54,852	(14%)	Michigan	140,648	(35%)
	396,443		Northwest	17,567	
			New York	133,756	(34%)
			New England	30,923	

the largest group of the general population, accounting for 34 percent. Among the elite the New York (English) contingent represented 20 percent in 1844 and 23 percent in 1860. In the case of the New Englanders the situation was reversed: as opposed to 8 percent of the general population in 1850, New Englanders constituted 27 percent of the elite in 1844 and 1860. The proportion of immigrants among the elite, however, was close to the foreign born among the general population: 12 percent in 1844 and 16 percent in 1860 compared with 14 percent for the entire population in 1850.

Having found Yankees to be the largest ethnocultural group in both elites (47 percent in 1844, 50 percent in 1860) and Whigs and Republicans the major parties (62 percent and 58 percent), it is not surprising to find Yankees dominating the leading parties. It is interesting to note

TABLE IV

Percentage of each major party according to ethnocultural origin

| | 1844 | | | | 1860 | | | |
| | WHIGS | | DEMOCRATS | | REPUBLICANS | | DEMOCRATS | |
	No.	*%*	*No.*	*%*	*No.*	*%*	*No.*	*%*
New England English	22	36	4	14	22	38	10	21
New York English (Yankee)	11	18	5	18	19	32	6	13
Totals Other Native	33	54	9	32	41	70	16	34
English	2	5	1	4	1	2	7	14
Native French	3	5	5	18	2	3.5	8	17
Other Native	11	18	6	21	5	9	7	14
Immigrants	7	12	4	14	7	12	7	14
No known origin	4	6	3	11	2	3.5	3	7
Totals	60	100	28	100	58	100	48	100

that the Republican Party showed an even greater proportion of Yankees (70 percent) than did the Whigs in 1844 (54 percent).

TABLE V

Percentages of Yankee English and New York English according to party, 1844

	NEW ENGLAND ENGLISH (26)		NEW YORK ENGLISH (19)	
	No.	%	*No.*	%
Whigs	22	84	11	58
Democrats	4	16	5	26
Liberty	–	–	3	16
Totals	26	100	19	100

The increased Yankee majority among Republicans, it should be noted, represents a larger proportion of New York English. In 1844 the greatest concentration was New Englanders in the Whig party.

The greater cohesion of New Englanders in 1844 (84 percent of them Whigs) compared with New Yorkers (58 percent of them Whigs), which bears out the observations of Fox and Benson on New York Yankees, would seem to hold only for 1844.

The high Yankee correlation with the Whig and Republican parties would seem to suggest a strong ethnocultural influence on political affiliation. If the ethnocultural factor were decisive, however, it would follow that Yankees were hardly ever Democrats. This was indeed not the case. Yankees (again both New England English and New York English) made up the largest ethnocultural grouping in the Democratic Party (32 percent in 1844 and 34 percent in 1860). All we can say from these figures is that Yankees tended to be Whigs and Republicans to a much greater extent than they were Democrats.

Can we then find any variable presented in this study which seems to be definitive as to party? On the basis of simple cross tabulations of one variable against political affiliation we have found tendencies for certain groupings to favor one party but in no case has the relationship been exclusive as to party. By using multivariate analysis—in this instance by combining both religion and ethnocultural origin—we have been able to isolate religion, already noted above, as a dividing factor between Democrats and Whig-Republicans. When Presbyterianism is combined with Yankee origin and tested against political affiliation there is a marked polarization between the two parties which holds for both 1844 and 1860. Yankees who were Democrats were not Presbyterians. The fact that Lewis Cass was the sole Presbyterian Yankee Democrat in 1844 and 1860

TABLE VI

Yankee Presbyterians according to
political affiliation

	1844 (23)		1869 (26)	
	No.	%	No.	%
Whigs	20	87	–	–
Democrats	1	4	1	3
Liberty	2	9	–	–
Republicans	–	–	21	81
No Party	–	–	4	16

makes the non-Presbyterianism of Yankee Democrats seem almost 100 percent, because Cass's Democratic politics were determined by the circumstances of his early career in the territory.

Non-Presbyterianism applied only to Yankee Democrats. When we examine non-Yankee Presbyterians as to political affiliation we no longer find a sharp demarcation. The non-Yankee Presbyterian Democrats were of heterogeneous ethnocultural background: George Russel (Scotch-Irish), Jonathan Kearsley (Scotch-Irish) and Jacob Beeson (English), all from Pennsylvania; William Barclay from Scotland, Theodore Romeyn of Dutch Reformed antecedants from New Jersey, and Edward Orr and John Hurlburt, origins unknown.

Is there any possible explanation for the non-Presbyterianism of Yankee Democrats? Robert Dahl's study of New Haven and Dixon Ryan

TABLE VII

Non-Yankee Presbyterians according
to political affiliation

	1844 (14)		1860 (16)	
	No.	%	No.	%
Whigs	8	57	–	–
Democrats	5	35	5	31
No Party	1	8	4	25
Republicans	–	–	7	44

Fox's of Yankees in New York are suggestive. Dahl found that "patrician" Episcopalians were Democrats because their religion put them in opposition to the political control of the Congregational Church, the "Standing Order" of Connecticut "consisting of Congregational ministers, lawyers and men of business of whom the ministers had historically furnished most of the leadership." (It should be reemphasized here that Congregationalism was the fount of western Presbyterianism. Of the few Congregationalists among the elite none was a Democrat). Fox attributed the westward migration of New England Baptists as well as Connecticut Episcopalians to their desire to escape their disadvantages under the church-state system.

Religion, in the case of Presbyterianism, the predominant faith among the elite, showed a more constant correlation with political affiliation than did any economic role. What makes this relationship impressive is that religion presents a much more clear-cut designation than economic role. Many who were merchants or capitalists were also landowners but no one was a Presbyterian and an Episcopalian simultaneously. Furthermore, the continuity of Presbyterianism among Whigs and Republicans was matched by the consistency of non-Presbyterianism among Democrats.

15. RONALD P. FORMISANO
"Michigan and the Party System, Mass Party Loyalty, 1835–1852"

No discussion of mass political ideology or actual voting behavior can get very far without an appreciation of the persistent stability and structure found in electoral behavior. Most popular voting is determined by habit, tradition, and party label, rarely by rational evaluation of the great issues of the day. One means of demonstrating this is by measuring the regularity of voting patterns in a given area through statistical time series and inter-election correlations, tools of great potential for political historians. In the following chapter from his book, *The Birth of Mass Political Parties, Michigan, 1827–1861*, Ronald Formisano, another of Lee Benson's students, uses these methods, among others, to establish the strength of the politics of habit and tradition during the Jacksonian period. From Ronald P. Formisano, *The Birth of Mass Political Parties; Michigan, 1827–1861* (copyright © 1971 by Princeton University Press), pp. 21–30. Reprinted by permission of Princeton University Press. [Footnotes omitted and Table III corrected.]

In the 1830s mass party loyalty on a stable basis came into being for the first time in American history. If a political party is defined as having three major areas of being, namely legislative, organizational, and electoral, then the latter at least had not characterized party structure previously. Studies of the Federalist and Republican parties suggest that they achieved most of their rootedness in the electorate after 1800, and stable, large-scale citizen support proved at best transitory in the individual states. Studies of the "first party system" have not yet provided the data to show the existence of stable voting patterns among freely attached electoral followings.

The second party system—or by this definition the first—created a "party-in-the-electorate," and thus resembles the political scene today in distribution and intensity of partisanship. Political scientists have shown the great extent to which party loyalty has shaped voting behavior in this century. The "role of basic partisan dispositions" has been called perhaps "the most impressive element" in American political life. While short-run influences are not trivial "each election is not a fresh toss of the coin; like all good prejudices, the electorate's basic dispositions have a tremendous capacity to keep people behaving in accustomed ways."

Actually, party loyalty is probably less widespread now than during the nineteenth century when, according to Professor Walter Dean Burnham, the "voting universe was marked by a more complete and intensely party oriented voting participation among the American electorate than ever before or since." Comparing the period from 1854 to 1872 with six subsequent periods between 1878 and 1962 Burnham found stronger party voting by every measure for the earlier years. In Michigan during the Civil War scarcely 15 percent of the potential electorate appeared to have been outside the voting universe. About 7 percent could be classified as "peripheral voters," who participated during "surge" elections of high excitement, while more than three-quarters of the total appear to have been core voters, or party loyalists.

The conditions of electoral mobilization just described came into being in the 1830s. For most of its Territorial Period, from 1805 to 1837, Michigan did not know party politics. In 1819 territorial elections began in which taxpayers chose a Delegate to Congress every two years. In 1823 voters could also elect a nine-man Council to legislate for the territory. These steps toward self-government often resulted in spirited battles for office among competing Republican factions, but did not bring parties into the arena. Political participation was low. In 1829 Antimasons organized the first party, and the rival Republican factions, whose ideological distinctions have thus far escaped detection, quickly emulated the Antimasons. But these organizational trial runs possessed little continuity, let alone measurable support among voters. The fragmentary state of the data, however, makes identification of voting patterns almost impossible. Before 1835 stable alignments cannot be discerned in a confusing thicket of leadership factions, a growing and barely rooted electorate, and shifting civil division boundaries. Demographic and socioeconomic conditions, undeveloped communications, and political practices all suggest that persisting patterns of voter alignment did not divide Michigan's territorial electorate.

In 1835 the first true Whig-Democratic contest mobilized much of the electorate along party lines. Then after a two-year hiatus during which party competition vanished, organizational cadres and the voters finally rallied in 1837. For state and presidential elections virtually all adult white males soon participated. And the vast majority divided along lines that would endure. Nevertheless, party loyalty should not be treated as a "given," but rather as a variable with at least two kinds of fluctuation: defections and conversions. Defecting voters temporarily leave their traditional party to vote for another and return when the specific causes of their departure relax. Converting voters switch their vote and their party allegiance.

Evidence for the party attachment of the electorate by 1837 is of three kinds: aggregate returns, studies of elite affiliations, and contemporary testimony. Returns for the presidential elections from 1840 to 1852 show that voters divided fairly evenly between the Democrats and their combined opponents (Table I). The Democratic vote ranged from 47.2 to 51.0 percent. In off-year contests after 1840 the distribution was not so even. However, the Democratic vote displayed relative stability. The one near landslide of the period (1851) occurred not because of an outpouring of Democratic voters but resulted from a depression in turnout affecting largely the anti-Democrats. That party loyalty was weaker among the latter is the subject of a later chapter.

TABLE I

Major state elections, party vote, 1837-1852

YEAR	OFFICE	DEMOCRAT		WHIG		LIBERTY	
		Vote	*Percent*	*Vote*	*Percent*	*Vote*	*Percent*
1837	Gov.	15,314	51.0	14,546	49.0		
1838	Cong.	16,255	50.3	16,051	49.7		
1839	Gov.	17,037	48.3	18,195	51.7		
1840	Pres.	21,096	47.6	22,933	51.7	321	0.7
1841	Gov.	20,993	55.7	15,449	41.0	1,223	3.2
1843	Gov.	21,392	54.7	14,899	38.1	2,776	7.1
1844	Pres.	27,737	49.7	24,375	43.8	3,639	6.5
1845	Gov.	20,123	50.9	16,316	41.3	3,023	7.6
1847	Gov.	24,639	53.3	18,990	41.1	2,585	5.6
1848	Pres.	30,677	47.2	23,930	36.8	10,393	16.0
1849	Gov.	27,837	54.2	23,540	45.8		
1850	Cong.[a]	29,259	48.7	30,872	51.3		
1851	Gov.	23,827	58.5	16,901	41.5		
1852	Pres.	41,842	50.5	33,860	40.8	7,237	8.7

[a]Equals total of Congressional districts

If returns for major elections are examined by county it is clear that most of those units established a partisan loyalty by 1840. Similarly, inspection of voting profiles for townships in 32 counties throughout the period suggests that most townships, once population stabilized, took on a fairly predictable pattern of vote distribution. Many townships fluctuated widely in the degree to which they preferred a particular party, but major changes of basic disposition usually could be traced to demographic changes.

Another way of inferring party loyalty consists of statistical correlation of party percentage strength over a series of elections. Returns for 30 counties in 1840, for example, were available. The Democratic percentages in each election could be correlated with the Democratic percentages in all other presidential elections. The Pearson coefficients of correlation (Table II) suggest the high stability of the 1840–52 period, at least for every four-year interval.

In Wayne, Livingston, and Calhoun counties, interyear correlations for *townships* produced results of overall similarity. These three counties provided a rough sectional sample and different patterns of voting. Wayne, in the east, maintained a consistent Democratic loyalty until 1860. Livingston, north and west, voted Democratic in the 1840s but went Republican in 1856. Calhoun, further west and south, returned a low Democratic vote throughout. The correlations also suggest that the

TABLE II

Interyear correlations of Democratic percentage strength of counties, 1840–1860, presidential, and 1854 gubernatorial elections

	1840	1844	1848	1852	1854	1856
1844	.622					
1848	.385	.786				
1852	.345	.810	.858			
1854	.079	.611	.562	.827		
1856	.242	.280	.389	.063	.228	
1860	.106	.603	.551	.589	.066	.482

basic Democratic and anti-Democratic divisions of the electorate in the 1840s probably continued into the 1850s. One result of the turmoil of the 1850s may have been to *increase* the tendency to identify with a major party.

Political researchers using aggregate data often rely on measurement of split ticket voting as an index of party loyalty. Burnham has suggested that the 99 percent levels of straight ticket and complete ballot voting that he found in the nineteenth century "may have been partly an arti-

TABLE III

Interyear correlations of Democratic percentage strength in 3 selected counties, 1840-1852

| | WAYNE COUNTY | | | | | | |
	1837	1840	1844	1848	1852	1854	1856
1840	.755						
1844	.642	.672					
1848	.662	.385	.656				
1852	.547	.605	.718	.849			
1854	.364	.227	.546	.801	.837		
1856	.476	.237	.569	.880	.887	.914	
1860	.420	.244	.496	.834	.902	.856	.912

| | LIVINGSTON COUNTY | | | | | |
	1844	1848	1850	1852	1854	1856
1848	.556					
1850	.802	.634				
1852	.706	.653	.668			
1854	.519	.662	.588	.471		
1856	.489	.484	.730	.498	.704	
1860	.593	.563	.696	.667	.385	.797

| | CALHOUN COUNTY | | | | | |
	1840	1844	1848	1852	1854	1856
1844	.166					
1848	.002	.565				
1852	.097	.601	.868			
1854	.040	.511	.863	.957		
1856	.361	.515	.643	.787	.787	
1860	.147	.429	.728	.786	.870	.708

fact of the party ballots then in use. " Michigan law provided that voting "shall be by ballot in writing, or on a paper ticket, containing the names of the persons for whom the elector intends to vote." Newspapers, or their printing presses, were vital to party organization because they usually distributed printed ballots, often of bright colors, to their party's faithful. The convenience of such ballots undoubtedly encouraged straight ticket voting. Ticket splitting did occur, however, and political observers regarded it as a deliberate display of independence of party. However, in township after township, county after county, from the late 1830s on, manuscript and newspaper tallies of votes given for groups of federal, state, or local offices, presented in tabular form, usually looked like an intricate design consisting of vertical columns of numbers. Some idiosyncratic breaks in the symmetry could be observed, but the overwhelming impression was of straight ticket voting, especially in rural townships.

Elite behavior also suggests a high degree of party loyalty. Men mentioned frequently in newspapers as political activists broadly represented party leaderships. From 1848 to 1856 in Wayne County of the 743 men who appeared as active in one or more elections only 174 changed their allegiance and only 11 shifted more than once. When one considers that the Republican party replaced the Whig and Free Soil parties during these years the overall stability is more impressive. Professor Alexandra McCoy's study of Wayne County's economic elite observed the party loyalty of 97 elite members from 1837 to 1854. McCoy found that the elite displayed almost uniform party loyalty up to 1854. Only two of these prominent men switched parties.

No wonder contemporaries described "heredity in politics" as "stronger even than in religion" and that "It was expected as a matter of course that partisan politics would descend from sires to sons with unbroken regularity." One pioneer told of how a strong Jackson man typically had carried his Democratic principles from New York state into the Michigan woods where he raised his sons: "It was natural for his young family, to claim to be Democrats in principle, in their isolated home."

Finally, campaign styles prevalent in Michigan by the late 1830s also bolster the proposition that intense partisanship characterized the disposition of the mass of voters. Parades, wagon trains, marches, rallies, singing, floats, transparencies, flags, and a variety of quasi-military activities directed toward mobilizing opposing "armies" implied mass party loyalty. Such practices assume that the hosts to be marshalled for voting were already committed partisans.

IMPACT OF THE LIBERTY AND FREE SOIL PARTIES

The Liberty party's entrance into the political lists in 1840 did not disturb the unity of the 1837–52 period because the new party drew its votes overwhelmingly from Whiggery. Thus, Democratic and anti-Democratic divisions remained about the same, much to the advantage of the Democrats. Whigs, naturally did not take a calm, analytical view of this. Astute Whig observers recognized that "political abolitionists" came from both parties but that "the majority in our state, heretofore has been [sic] of the opponents of the Locos." Indeed, one major Liberty-ite goal was to seize the balance of power between parties. Whigs were thus more vulnerable and Libertyites expected more from Whigs. Many had been Whigs, their old party had pretensions to morality while the

Democrats had always been pro-Southern, proslavery, and of dubious virtue. Liberty leaders felt justified in punishing the Whigs even if the loss of votes and elections did not push them to antislavery.

The aggregate state vote from 1837 to 1841 suggests that most abolition votes came from the Whigs. In major elections from 1837 to 1840 Whigs kept pace with and surpassed the Democrats, but fell drastically behind in 1841, as the Liberty vote climbed to 1,223. The Whig vote fell from 22,933 to 15,449 (Table I). Obviously, in addition to defections and conversions, nonvoting also caused the Whig decline. In the 1840 Congressional voting, 17 counties out of 31 gave one or more votes to the Libertyites. Of these 17, 13 had voted Whig in 1839. By 1841 only two of those 13 remained Whig. In the others the Liberty vote had increased and the Democrats now enjoyed a majority or plurality.

Many causes produced Whig nonvoting in 1841. Before the election one Democrat observed that the Whig party "manifests a most astonishing apathy and I do not believe they can drag their force to the polls." The first Whig President, William Henry Harrison, had taken office only to die soon after in April 1841. His successor, John Tyler, dismayed Whigs everywhere by revealing himself to be more of a States' rights Southern Democrat than a Whig. Michigan Whig leaders reacted to Tyler's "apostasy" with rage, disgust, and frustration.

In Michigan itself political apathy received a boost from hard times, while Whiggery had been racked by internal feuds and had been deprived of its most prominent leader. The party controlled the legislature in 1841 but could not agree on a choice for United States Senator. After an intraparty fight, the Democratic minority joined one Whig faction to elect William Woodbridge, incumbent Whig governor elected in the Whig triumph of 1839. The departure of the popular Woodbridge could not have helped Whig morale. Meanwhile the Bank of Michigan, which the Whigs had made state fiscal agent, failed, and many Whigs privately predicted that the "monster's" mishaps would cost the party votes.

The Liberty party's presence probably increased nonvoting among Whigs. Since they were more vulnerable to political antislavery, it follows that more Whigs than Democrats would be caught undecided between their old party loyalty and the abolition appeal, and might resolve their indecision by not voting. Many of the Whigs who failed to vote in 1841 probably voted Liberty in 1844. In 12 counties in 1844 the Liberty party received more than 6.5 percent of the vote, its statewide percent. In only 3 of the 12 counties did the Democratic percentage strength decline from 1840. In 2 of these, Genesee and Kalamazoo, the Democratic percentage fell slightly while the Whig tumbled much more (Table IV). In only one, Van Buren, did the Democrats lose more percentage points than the Whigs between 1840 and 1844.

TABLE IV

Party percentages in 1840 and 1844 presidential elections in counties giving the Liberty party 6.5 percent or more in 1844

			DEM.	WHIG	LIBERTY
EAST	Oakland	1840	44.9	50.1	
		1844	52.1	40.9	6.9
	Washtenaw	1840	44.9	55.1	
		1844	48.2	44.4	7.3
	Hillsdale	1840	46.1	53.9	
		1844	48.0	42.7	9.3
	Jackson	1840	42.7	57.3	
		1844	43.9	41.1	15.0
	Eaton	1840	40.5	59.5	
		1844	44.4	48.4	7.2
NORTH	Lapeer	1840	45.6	54.4	
		1844	50.8	40.3	8.9
	Genesee	1840	42.6	57.4	
		1844	42.5	46.0	11.5
	Shiawasee	1840	36.0	64.0	
		1844	40.1	45.1	14.4
	Ionia	1840	45.2	54.8	
		1844	45.5	47.8	6.7
WEST	Kalamazoo	1840	43.8	56.2	
		1844	40.7	45.8	13.6
	Van Buren	1840	58.0	42.0	
		1844	52.3	40.8	6.9
	Ottawa	1840	52.1	47.9	
		1844	66.3	24.0	9.7

In most townships Whig and Liberty voters can be regarded as the approximate sum of anti-Democratic strength, particularly in units, where, were it not for the abolitionists, Whiggery would have enjoyed a majority. The most common pattern observed was the Liberty party taking votes from Whigs. The social bases of this will be explored later.

In 1848 the Liberty party merged into a broad political antislavery movement which nationally brought together Conscience Whigs, New York's Barnburners, and a variety of supporters from the antislavery-abolition spectrum of politics. In Michigan prominent Democrats for the first time joined political antislavery. The national Free Soil Party nominated Martin Van Buren, former Democratic president, to head the coalition's ticket. It appeared that Michigan Democrats with antislavery tendencies were being given strong incentives to set aside party loyalty. At first Michigan politicians expected that Van Buren's candidacy would help the Whig nominee, General Taylor, and Whig leaders encouraged Free Soilism. However, it became clear that "multitudes of Whigs also were joining" Free Soil, and regular Whigs called for a halt to any efforts to aid the independents. In some areas, however, Whigs and Free Soilers formed coalitions.

More Michigan Democrats do appear to have defected to Free Soil in 1848 than had ever deserted earlier to the Liberty camp. Yet it is surprising how few Democrats did vote Free Soil. Of course, the Democrats were running Michigan's favorite son, Lewis Cass, for President, and this must have offset somewhat the pull of Van Buren. Open Whig-Free Soil fusion in some districts also repelled Democrats from Free Soil.

The Democratic percentage of the state vote fell by 2.5 percentage points between 1844 and 1848, while the Whig fell by 7 points. The number of Democratic votes rose by 3,000 with the Whig falling by 400. In 1852, with Van Buren absent from the ticket and the sectional crisis quiet, the Free Soil vote declined sharply. The Whigs increased their percentage strength between 1848 and 1852 far more than the Democrats: they had far more to regain. County and minor civil division returns show the same patterns, with this difference: slightly increased Democratic defections occurred mostly in units already disposed to cast some antislavery votes. Whig defection or conversion to Free Soil still greatly surpassed that of the Democrats.

Thus, in the period from 1837 to 1852 most of the electorate identified with a party, and most voters obeyed the norm of party loyalty. Antislavery parties upset very little the gross divisions of voting strength because they drew votes largely from the Whigs. In 1844 probably 90 percent of Liberty men were ex-Whigs and in 1848 perhaps 80 percent or more of Free Soilers were ex-Whigs. The general continuity of party loyalty simplifies the task of identifying Whig and Democratic social groups.

16. ROBERT KELLEY
"Presbyterianism, Jacksonianism and Grover Cleveland"

As we cut from the measurement of political behavior to the substance underlying it, we ultimately must return to the surviving documents of the age—but with a difference. At its best, quantitative analysis of voting patterns allows us to pose new questions and gain new understanding of the material available. In the following essay, Robert Kelley skillfully combines the fruits of quantitative research and more traditional material to probe long-surviving belief patterns and attitudes towards politics and the government of the nineteenth-century Democrat. From Robert Kelley, "Presbyterianism, Jacksonianism, and Grover

Cleveland," *American Quarterly,* XVIII (1966), 615–36. Copyright, 1966, Trustees of the University of Pennsylvania. Reprinted by permission of the author, the *American Quarterly,* and the University of Pennsylvania. [Footnotes omitted.]

Grover Cleveland was a minister's son, and a Democrat whose political lineage went back to the Jacksonians. Curiously enough, his biographies have left these matters largely unexplored. The aim of this essay is to examine them at some length. What was the nature of the Presbyterianism within which he was reared? Set beside his larger view of politics, does the profile of the one resemble that of the other? Similarly, what was there in the Jacksonian outlook which may be found in his own as well? Congruence, of course, does not prove causation. As William Dray has pointed out, it rather provides a basis for understanding a man's actions as reasonable and appropriate. My purpose is to suggest, in this spirit, a new rationale for understanding Cleveland's character and policies. Seen from the vantage points here utilized, Cleveland seems certainly to look rather different from the picture of him given to us by the standard accounts.

Cleveland's own testimony pointed to the religious line of analysis. "I was reared and taught in the strictest school of Presbyterianism," he once said of his childhood years, which were spent near Syracuse, in the heart of western New York. To the "precious precepts and examples of my early days," he went on, "I owe every faculty of usefulness I possess, and every just apprehension of the duties and obligations of life." During noontimes, in Sabbath school, in three church sessions every Sunday and in a family circle "Hallowed and sanctified by the spirit of Presbyterianism," he was rigorously taught the faith. Though the Shorter Catechism, he said, was difficult for a boy to understand, "those are not apt to be the worst citizens who were early taught, 'what is the chief end of man?'"

He was not a churchgoing man in mature life. He was the kind of minister's son who veers away from the childhood pattern of life, enjoying the saloons and the songs. Buffalo, to which he moved to spend 25 years in law practice, was a rough and tumble port city, and Cleveland loved to sit on a sanded floor, drinking beer with the Germans. Yet there was another side to his nature that showed the strong persistence of his early training. All his life his friends saw two Clevelands, one jovial and fun-loving, the other stern and unbending in his work and responsibilities, beclouded, as it were, by a pall of duty. Cleveland's case is another example of the fact that it is what is learned early that must be examined, despite later appearances.

What did it mean to be a Presbyterian in western New York in the years of Cleveland's youth? It meant being reared in the Burned-Over District, one of the great battlegrounds of American religion. Here took place in the Jacksonian years that explosion of revivalistic fervor which spawned, among other faiths, the Adventist churches, the Mormon churches and John Humphrey Noyes' Perfectionism. Methodists, Baptists, Christians, Universalists, Presbyterians and many others crossed and re-crossed western New York, setting off holocausts of evangelistic religion. As Whitney R. Cross describes it, a "veritable host of evangelists . . . swarmed over Yankeedom, old and new, preaching every shade of gospel, heresy, and reform to a people who for a generation had been saturated with spiritual and moral intensity. The impulse to eccentricity and radicalism was thus broadly and deeply planted."

What grew to dominate all of this was the "ultra" cast of mind. True believers who were charged with the fire that a conviction of direct contact with God can give were triumphantly confident that they were the agents of the operation of the Holy Spirit in the here and now. Moved by an urgent belief that Christ was soon coming to usher in the millennium and called upon imperiously by their faith to purify the world in preparation for that Coming, ultras set off clamorous reform crusades. The concept of sin was expanded far beyond its normal human boundaries. The slightest transgression now became a stench in the nostrils of God. Men of solid reputation for probity and good will found themselves accused of radical sinfulness for petty acts. At the same time, the ultra was typically convinced that all the world's ills could be solved by one or another great and simple reform to be achieved now, immediately, by one bold cleansing stroke.

They were determined to use governments—as in the days of the Puritan past—as divine instruments to reshape American life in accordance with the imperatives of the newly recharged faith. As Franklin Hamlin Littell has observed, the churches of New England were only partially out of the frame of mind induced by generations of existence as state churches. "Again and again," he writes; "confronted by special problems or opportunities, they reverted to the old custom of using government or tax monies to support church work." Antimasonry, temperance campaigns, agitation for Sunday laws and similar ultra crusades swelled the turbulence of the Jacksonian years. So vigorous and thrusting did this new Yankee clericalism become that an outcry began against a suspected new linkup of church and state. The temperance campaign in particular led many to cry "Priestcraft! Church and State!" A labor paper charged that "political Anti-Masonry is neither more nor less than a Church and State intrigue." In time, this political activism, frustrated in the temperance crusade, moved on into the long campaign for abolition of slavery.

All of this had been largely begun by the Presbyterians in western New York, and it caused their fellow churchmen elsewhere painful concern. Presbyterians in the Burned-Over District, in fact, were a special type quite unlike the ruggedly orthodox Scotch-Irish Presbyterians in Pennsylvania and to the south. They were rather ex-New England Congregationalists of the more enthusiastic and religiously liberal sort who, by the Plan of Union, became Presbyterians when they entered New York. They led the early revivals, and continued to add fuel to the flames in a new outburst of self-conscious, inspired and triumphant puritanism.

Presbyterians outside of the "infected" area, however, reacted in distaste. They detested religious enthusiasm. "Dignified clergymen, whatever their theology, objected to being called antichristian merely because they hesitated to act like common ranters." More than this, they were outraged by unorthodox theology. Leading Presbyterian revivalists like Charles Finney were not trained ministers, carefully schooled in the creedal beliefs, the scholastic distinctions and the fundamental theology of Presbyterianism. Finney did not even know the Westminister Confession of Faith. He worked instead directly from the Scriptures. Since the revival situation seemed to demand an assumption of personal choice, Finney and others unconsciously moved toward free will. The rigorous determinism of traditional Calvinism disappeared, and the emphasis thereafter in this branch of the Presbyterian church was toward Perfectionism, with all the radical changes in theological world-view that this implied.

The Princeton divines—the theologians for American Presbyterianism —were deeply aroused at this heresy. They and the Scotch-Irish Presbyterians had long believed that they had opened the gates to heretical beliefs when they had agreed in 1801 to the Plan of Union, and now their fears were confirmed. They set off an outraged counterattack. By heresy trials and annual battles in the General Assembly the conflict was carried on for years within the church. By 1837 the Old School had a clear majority at the Philadelphia meeting, and four synods in western New York containing almost half the membership of the church were bodily excluded. The American Home Missionary Society—long the arm of the church in western New York—shifted wholly to the conservative side, and many congregations split off from the infected synods to join orthodoxy. Eventually many Presbyterian ultras moved out of the church and erected Congregational bodies, making that sect as large in the Burned-Over District as the Presbyterian.

Ultraism, meanwhile, was in process of collapse. In reaction, disillusioned ultras were finding their way back to orthodoxy, where strict fundamentalism and an exclusive concern for simply saving souls and not transforming the world was the mode. The "radicalism of the reform movements and the heresy of perfectionism," Cross writes, "turned moderates into conservatives and prepared a substantial portion of each major denomination for a contest to determine which could best prove its utter orthodoxy."

This is the context into which the Cleveland family came in 1841. It explains, in fact, two things left largely unexplained by the Cleveland biographies—one apparently unimportant, the other of central concern: the move of the Cleveland family from New Jersey to western New York; and why the Clevelands, father and son, were Democrats. Richard Falley Cleveland was a firmly orthodox Presbyterian minister. He was clearly part of the counterattack against heresy. He was sent to the Syracuse region as an emissary of sanity, of the true faith, to train his congregation in the stern doctrines of the Shorter Catechism.

Furthermore, the ultras against whom the long campaign for the true faith was mounted were Whigs, attracted to that party by its activist ideas about government and its friendliness to religion in politics. Many in New York seem to have become Democrats because they did not like the ultras. As Lee Benson has shown, in a persuasive use of the negative reference group concept, much of New York politics can be explained by the instinctive reaction of the Dutch, the Irish Catholics and the workingmen's movements against the puritans of the Burned-Over District. The latter wanted to attack the Masons, free the slaves, end drinking, rail against Catholic infidels and create a collectivist atmosphere of active government intervention in private morals. Their whole style of life—righteous, sin-hating, abstemious, austere—warred with the life-style of such laboring groups as, for example, the lumbermen, whom Benson finds voting largely Democratic in consequence. One suspects that the same could be said of Cleveland's Germans, with their beer-drinking and boisterous conviviality. In many ways, the new puritans polarized New York politics.

There is every reason to explain the political behavior of orthodox presbyterians in similar fashion. The "enemy" in the lives of the Clevelands was Whig, enthusiastic and activist in politics and religion, and abolitionist. In reacting against abolitionism and the flamboyance of the Frémont campaign, Cleveland, like his father, was reacting not against single issues, but against a whole complex of negative associations and cherished dislikes. The irony, of course, lies in the fact that the ultras drove orthodox Presbyterians and agnostic New York City intellectuals and workingmen into the same party. It was never a comfortable working partnership, as Cleveland's later bitter battles with Tammany make clear, but it was in any event a partnership which illustrates again the classic observation that in politics as in war, "The enemy of my enemy. . . ."

The Presbyterianism of Cleveland's youth, therefore, was in a state of victorious, energetic orthodoxy. Creed, doctrine and dogma were emphasized, not vitalism. In Cleveland's time the teacher was the key figure in the church, not the preacher. Parishioners were drilled in the specifics of doctrine, not led to apply them to the ills of the larger world. "Instruction in the Catechism," Charles A. Briggs of Union Theological Seminary later observed, "was almost universal. Lectures upon the Confession of Faith, and in exposition of the Scriptures, on Sabbath morning and at the weekly lecture, were heard gladly by the people." The reigning mode of Biblical interpretation was sternly fundamentalist. When many years later the dramatic discoveries of higher criticism excited the religious world, Cleveland's reaction was revealing: the "Bible is good enough for me, just the old book under which I was brought up. I do not want notes, or criticism, or explanations about authorship or origin, or even cross-references. I do not need or understand them, and they confuse me."

It says much about American Presbyterianism that the key document utilized in its teaching was the Shorter Catechism. The other fundamental statements prepared by the Westminster Assembly of Divines in the 1640s—the Confession of Faith and the Larger Catechism—have a different temper to them. They are relatively flexible, subtle and qualified. It is possible in them to see not only the sterner attributes of God, but also to see in Him a deity concerned about the fate of mankind, lively in His appreciation of the complexities of the human condition, and ready to enter into a many-sided relationship with man in which love would be a major element. The Shorter Catechism, however, through its brevity, contains a much more austere, simplistic and demanding Calvinism. American Presbyterianism from time to time modified the Confession and the Larger Catechism, but the Shorter Catechism, upon which it concentrated, was retained without change. The result was to make American Presbyterianism perhaps the most conservative of all branches of the Calvinist world.

The consuming object of concern in the Shorter Catechism is the awesome, blazing, transcendent sovereignty of God, not His saving concern for mankind nor His vitality. He is depicted as stern, demanding, unbending. Twin to His sovereignty is man's duty, which is inexorable, imperative, inescapable. One must worship God not through gratitude or love or adoration, but because of duty. "The scriptures principally teach," says the Third Answer, "what man is to believe concerning God, and what duty God requires of man." The most important section in the Catechism is that concerned with morals, for the first rule revealed to man by God, the Catechism states, "was the moral law." No mere man "is able in this life," the Catechism warns after scores of forbidding questions and answers developing all the nuances of sin and the moral law, "perfectly to keep the commandments. . . ." Furthermore, "Every sin deserveth God's wrath and curse, both in this life and that which is to come." So imperative was this punishment, indeed, that two of the major Presbyterian theologians of Princeton orthodoxy, Charles and A. A. Hodge, held that God is *bound* to practice justice by punishing sin, thus denying him the freedom to love and to forgive. "Christian love," wrote Briggs despairingly, "has been overwhelmed by law."

Briggs' despair, however, was the grief of a liberal theologian at Union, not at Princeton, who was trying to change the temper of his church. The measure of his failure may be seen in the publication in 1901, by the Presbyterian Committee of Publication, of E. W. Smith's triumphantly orthodox *The Creed of Presbyterians,* the book which by the 1920s had become much the most widely read book ever written in America on Presbyterianism.

Smith proclaimed the Presbyterian as "pronouncedly and preeminently" a doctrinal church. What was the most prominent and pervading quality of its basic documents? Ethical concern, expressed as "the practical 'duty which God requires of man.' " God's holy laws, Smith warned, cover every aspect of life; we are forever accountable to them. No other creed was so devoted to divine law. Nowhere else but in the Westminster Standards could be found "such an unfolding of the heart-searching claims of that law," especially in the stern Shorter Catechism, the "consummate flower" of the Westminster Assembly. Why is the Shorter Catechism so demanding, so filled with hard sayings? Because "there are hard sayings in the Bible." The Standards, therefore, have never been popular with "the rationalistic and unregenerate world."

The dominant theme of Presbyterian faith, Smith observed, was its "exaltation of God." He is "the Absolute and Ever-Blessed Sovereign, infinitely worthy of love, worship, and obedience. . . ." At the peril of the soul, God's will and order must be obeyed. "Not," Smith warned, "is it pleasant, or popular, or profitable; but, is it right? Is it what God would have me do? This is Calvinism's first question."

God being great and glorious, man's sins are "heinous and fatal." The enormity of them and the punishment they deserve "are beyond man's calculation and conception." Sin is utterly loathsome and deadly. Left to himself, man is hopelessly condemned, hopelessly miserable. Only God's inscrutable decision—made, as the Shorter Catechism puts it, "out of his mere good pleasure"—can save degraded man. But the feeling of salvation, when it comes, places a man's feet upon rock. He is sure; he is confident; he has in him a divine energy springing from the confidence that "through him is working out eternal purposes of good. . . ." Thus he has invincible strength, the strength of a man who knows himself to be a man of destiny. "Alone among men he may be, but only more consciously allied with God." Steeled with the conviction that he is working out God's commands, the Presbyterian can go to his work and troubles "shielded by a panoply more invulnerable, and nerved by a courage more unconquerable, than any other faith could bestow."

Predestination and Providence were the core doctrines to this faith. They meant that God has a plan for the world (predestination), and moves to carry it out (providence). Instinct in Calvinism, in short, was the belief that God *rules*. He has authority; He "has a right to exercise dominion; [and] for the good of the universe that right should be exercised. . . ." He was "no absentee Deity, sitting outside the universe. . . . He is 'everywhere present,' 'upholding, directing, disposing, and governing' all creatures, actions, and things from the greatest even to the last."

Official creeds and their explanations have imbedded in them an ideal character type. Presbyterianism, as Smith's explanation of it clearly shows, aimed at the creation of a particular kind of man. He should have a preternaturally strong and imperious sense of duty, joined to a conviction that law (creed, doctrine, principle) is preeminent, is fundamental to the order of the universe, and must be both obeyed and preserved. Strength, stability and a readiness to act vigorously in this world in carrying out God's wishes should go together with personal humility, probity and a stiff-necked insistence upon just dealing. Precisely because it was centered upon the moral law, Presbyterianism, Smith wrote, was "admirably fitted to be . . . the spiritual food of stalwart souls, the nurse of a supremely massive and masculine type of piety." Presbyterians should make good businessmen, through their trustworthiness and diligent hard work. They should also make energetic public officials, for they would see the universe as held together by the active will of a vigorous God who acts through them. They would certainly be monolithic in character. "Calvinism," wrote Smith, "plies men with hammer and with chisel . . . and the result is monumental marble. Other systems leave men soft and dirty; Calvinism makes them of white marble, to endure forever."

It would be absurd to hold that all Presbyterians were of this character. But whatever its failure or success in producing its ideal type in the mass of its members, Presbyterianism would seem to have had much success with Cleveland. Using William Dray's terminology, the appropriateness of the one for the other makes it reasonable to conclude that Cleveland's faith helped shape his character. He fits the archetype. Not only do Smith's words above describe him perfectly, but so do those of the French historian Hippolyte Taine, who described Calvinists as "Strict in every duty . . . attentive to the least requirements; disdaining the equivocations of worldly morality; inexhaustible in patience, courage, sacrifice. . . ." Carl Schurz may be taken as typical when he said that people saw in Cleveland "a man conscientiously devoted to his duties, honest in his zeal to understand and to perform them without regard to personal advantage, and maintaining with dauntless courage what he thought right against friend and foe alike—a personality of exceptional strength and trustworthiness, commanding confidence."

The word "duty" runs throughout Cleveland's letters and speeches. "I have often thought," he wrote an intimate friend in 1885, "how solemn a thing it is to live and feel the pressure of the duties which life—the mere existence in a social state—imposes. . . ." Upon leaving office in 1889, he said "We know that we have espoused the cause of right and justice. We know that we have not permitted duty to country to wait upon expediency." In 1892, aroused by the turmoil within his party and convinced that he must run again for office, he wrote that "it is an exceedingly high duty to do all that is within legitimate human reach to win success in November." Embattled and downcast in 1894, he wrote a close companion, "I am sure I never was more completely in the right path of duty than I am now. . . ." What rewards wait for the self-made man who considers the welfare of society, he asked in an 1897 Princeton address? Not wealth nor fame, though they may come, but a much more valuable reward: "consciousness of duty well and faithfully performed. Popular applause is, of course, gratifying; but there are times when a man's own satisfaction with his conduct is a better criterion of real merit." The last words which came from him were, "I have tried so hard to do right."

Furthermore, he *knew* he was right. In Smith's words, his feet were on the rock. In the work of "public life and effort, God has never failed to clearly make known to me the path of duty," he wrote to his friend Richard Watson Gilder. "Do you know," he wrote another friend in 1895, "that I have never been so sure that there is a high and unseen Power that guides and sustains the weak efforts of man? I feel it all the time. . . ." In seeming obedience to Smith's injunction to ask not whether something was pleasant, or popular, or profitable, but rather whether it was right, Cleveland was notable not only for taking steps which he was warned against as being unpopular, but because he delighted in them. Gilder said he had never seen Cleveland more pleased than he was after writing his anti-free silver letter in 1892, thereby supposedly throwing the presidency out of the window. It showed that "he cared more for principle than for the Presidency." He always insisted that his native obstinacy was his principal virtue, once saying that "if every other man in the country abandons this issue, I shall stick to it." Speaking of how he and John G. Carlisle, his secretary of the treasury, had struggled together to save the currency, he observed, "We were just right for each other; he knows all I ought to know, *and I can bear all we have to bear.*"

Cleveland's Presbyterianism was congruent not only with his character, but with his presidency as well. It was in the nature of Presbyterianism, for example, to assume the rightful existence of power and the necessity for its use. The active sovereignty of God, one of Calvinism's key concepts, implies that what is needed in the world is energy, direction, authority, decisiveness, used primarily by reference to a divine plan or to values rather than to human purposes or considerations. Cleveland respected authority. He held its symbols in awe. He often spoke of the feelings called up in him when he thought of the sovereignty embodied in the office of the presidency. It is a thing, he said, "full of solemnity; for this sovereignty I conceive to be the working out or enforcement of the divine right of man to govern himself and a manifestation of God's plan concerning the human race."

From the beginning of his meteoric career, therefore, and throughout it—as mayor, as governor and as president—he showed a vigorous executive temper. His characteristic mode of leadership was that of interposing an uncompromising negative in the spirit of the "thou shalt not's" of the Decalogue and the Shorter Catechism image of God. Like Andrew Jackson—interestingly enough, also a Presbyterian—he built his presidency, just as he had built his governorship and mayoralty, primarily upon a long series of vetoes.

There was more to it, however, than just a string of vetoes. He took pains in one of his longest messages as governor of New York fulsomely to praise a bill giving major executive powers to the mayor of New York City. Almost as soon as he became president he fought a successful struggle with the Senate over the power of the president to withhold certain papers from the Congress on the grounds of executive privilege. He was delighted with Albert Bushnell Hart's book, *The Coercive Powers of the Government of the United States of America,* taking the unusual step of writing Hart to praise the work. It is revealing that the four *Presidential Problems* upon which he chose to write after his final exit from office were essentially crises in which he could display executive power. His whole discussion of the Chicago strikes and riots in this book displayed a bone-and-marrow instinct for the rightfulness and the transcendent necessity of authority and of obedience to that authority. He was absolutely undivided in his mind as to the imperative need for the national executive to move in swiftly and powerfully to assure obedience to duly constituted authority, in this case the injunctions of the courts.

Most of all, however, Cleveland showed his appetite for the use of power in his battles for a lowered tariff and sound money. The tariff battle was Cleveland's Bank War. He began the fight in 1886, issued his famous Tariff Message in 1887, campaigned for it vigorously through the years of his interregnum, and forced his party to a climactic struggle, and failure, in 1894. Similarly in the extended silver controversy he actively led the struggle to fight off free silver, shattering his party on the issue. No president since Lincoln bestrode the stage of national politics as Cleveland did in his two terms. He was more man than partisan, Woodrow Wilson observed—in easily the most acute assessment of Cleveland as president, written in 1897—"with an independent executive will of his own; hardly a colleague of the Houses so much as an individual servant of the country; exercising his powers like a chief magistrate rather than like a party leader." He staffed his second cabinet entirely out of the circle of his close friends and associates, choosing them as if he intended openly to show his independence of party. "It was singular," Wilson observed, "how politics began at once to centre in the President, waiting for his initiative, and how the air at Washington filled with murmurs against the domineering and usurping temper and practice of the Executive. Power had somehow gone the length of the avenue, and seemed lodged in one man."

Thus, in Cleveland's mind and character: duty, certainty and vigorous authority. There was also a veneration of law. To the Shorter Catechism mind, God is seen as organizing and ordering the world through law. Such divine injunctions, expressed in creeds, principles and rules, hold the world together. They discipline man, aid him in the dark scramble of life and save him from his natural selfishness and cupidity. It is vital to preserve such principles in their original purity as they are passed across the generations. To ignore, to replace, to attack the creed is heresy, a damnable crime.

When placed against this background, Cleveland's behavior in the long currency crisis of the 1880s and 1890s takes on a new aspect. In his party there was a deeply rooted traditional creed, and a highly elaborated one, on money matters. Developed by the radical wing of the Jacksonians, it came down to Cleveland largely through the influence of the old Jacksonian Samuel J. Tilden, whose genius in financial matters Cleveland intensely admired.

Radical Jacksonians were convinced that sound money—that is, money convertible to gold upon call—was the only protection of the "Democratic masses" against the grasping speculations of bankers and other capitalists. The wild price fluctuations of the age of Jackson they explained primarily by the operation of evil forces which, through the Bank of the United States, utilized the pliable and insubstantial medium of paper money to keep prices fantastically fluctuating so that at each rise and fall clever men could profit. Some leading Jacksonians even declared that only hard money, metallic coin, should be utilized as currency. In whatever form, sound money was firmly believed by Jacksonians to be the only means of protecting the working man, whose wages were not within his control. When prices moved upward with inflated currencies, the urban masses suffered cruelly.

It is important to note that the sound money position was also the internationalist position, as against the implicit nationalism of the silver campaign. The existence of an international pool of gold was a key concept of British economists, notably David Ricardo, who described its function as being the equalizer of price throughout the commercial world. Samuel Tilden had long since learned this theory intimately, and had written extensively upon its operation. In brief, the theory ran that the international gold pool would keep prices stable and prevent disastrous inflation or deflation. As prices rose in one country above that of others, gold would flee as overseas creditors demanded payment in gold rather than in depreciated currency. This would create currency contraction, and a subsidence of the price level. If deflation took place, gold would flow inward to the nation to seek the higher profits there to be made, since gold would be at a premium, and prices would rise.

From his first message on the problem until his last, the creed-minded Cleveland never questioned these orthodox principles, received so directly from the sainted Jacksonians. He persistently held—probably accurately, for that matter—that the United States could not maintain a bimetallic currency alone in the world, and that the two metals would part company entirely as gold was drained from the Treasury by panic. This would be disastrous, for gold was "still the standard of value and necessary in our dealings with other countries. . . ." Furthermore, bankers and speculators would get richer, for clever men at the seats of power could always profit from price rises and declines, but "the laboring men and women of the land, most defenseless of all, will find that the dollar received for the wage of their toil has sadly shrunk in its purchasing power." Eight years later, locked in the silver struggle of 1893, he directly quoted Tilden, "one of the greatest statesmen our country has known," who had insisted that "the very man of all others who has the deepest interest in a sound currency and who suffers most by mischievous legislation in money matters is the man who earns his daily bread by his daily toil."

In holding doggedly to the sound money creed, Cleveland was confident that he was saving what he called the "ark of the convenant," the true principles of the Democratic party. "Is it ordained," he asked a Southern friend, "that I am to be the instrument through which Democratic principles can be saved . . .? I shall be obedient to the call of my country and my party. Whatever happens no one shall say that I refused to serve in a time of evil . . . [when the nation was faced by] the free-coinage heresy."

What followed was a long and bitter struggle, stretching out over many months, in which he exerted every ounce of executive power that he could bring to bear upon Congress to secure repeal of the Sherman Silver Purchase Act. "It was the President's victory," Woodrow Wilson later observed, "and every one knew it. . . . Such a stroke settled what the course of congressional politics should be throughout the four years of Mr. Cleveland's term, and made it certain that at the end of that term he should either have won his party to himself or lost it altogether."

As it turned out, Cleveland lost it. Prosperity did not return, as he had said it would, with the repeal of silver purchase. All the calamities of severe depression which later afflicted Herbert Hoover came to rest upon Cleveland's head, and he grew increasingly alienated from his party, friendless, bitter and depressed. He found it impossible to credit Silver Democrats with any sincerity or real convictions. In his eyes they were charlatans, chameleons, opportunists playing upon the ignorant credulity of a sorely distracted people. "I am near the point," he wrote in 1897, "of believing them to be conspirators and traitors and, in their relations with the honest masses, as confidence sharks and swindlers." He considered Bryanism a "sort of disease in the body politics." The silverites had "burglarized and befouled the Democratic home."

The somber temper of his later years was in reality a deepening of the mood in which he had all along viewed the nation. True to his Calvinism, and perhaps also to the Jacksonian world view which he inherited, he looked upon the world as a place dominated by sensual greed, grasping egoism and a callous disregard of one's fellows. It was this concern which led to his great accomplishment, the substantial establishment of the civil service system. But he was concerned with much more than this. "Selfish" and "sordid" were the key words in his vocabulary. The elaborate mechanism of government aids to business, the rape of the western territories by land grabbers and railroads—all these and more, to Cleveland, grew out of the selfishness and sordidness which he saw blighting American life.

After he lost the tariff battle of 1888—which he had presented as a battle against privilege and exploitation—he issued one of the most radically leftist annual messages ever to come from the White House. Nothing less than a violent attack upon the power elite of the nation for their corrupting of a once-innocent society, it was a pungent restatement of the Jacksonian social analysis. It also sounded like nothing so much as the evangelist Jeremiah crying woe, the land is defiled, its inheritance is made an abomination. America, Cleveland said, had originally been a place in which government looked only to see that each man left the other alone, and had a clear field ahead for individual achievement. It was a frugal government because the people were frugal. Combinations, monopolies and great aggregations of capital were sternly prevented or controlled. The people were not attracted by the pomp and glitter of undemocratic nations. Their lives were plain and simple, they enjoyed sturdy competition, and they worked hard to ennoble man, to solve the problem of free government and to achieve the God-given destiny which awaited them.

After a century, what sat upon the land? Great and wealthy cities, filled with luxury; immense factories which poured out undreamed-of fortunes; and a mad race for riches leading to enormous aggregations of capital in the hands of the few. Beneath the glitter, the land was sick. City wealth and luxurious living mingled with poverty, wretchedness and unending toil which returned a pittance. The cities were crowded and constantly growing, for the countryside was afflicted with a distaste for farming. Farmers' sons left the "simple and laborious life" of their fathers and joined the frenzied chase for easily acquired wealth.

Great fortunes were no longer gained by honest toil, by enlightened foresight and sturdy enterprise, but by corrupt arrangements in which the government discriminated in favor of manufacturers. Huge profits came largely from exploiting the masses. Workers, meanwhile, found themselves steadily more remote from their employers as corporations grew into great, distended creatures. Classes were rapidly forming, "one comprising the very rich and powerful while in another are found the toiling poor." Trusts, combinations and monopolies ruled the land, "while the citizen is struggling far in the rear or is trampled to death beneath an iron heel." The corporations which laws should carefully control so that they served society were swiftly becoming the masters of the people who had allowed their appearance.

Throughout the unhappy land, therefore, the kind of patriotism which represented a simple affection and trust which the people earlier had felt for their government was being replaced by "selfish greed and grasping avarice." In unconcealed arrogance, men sordidly disregarded anything but their own personal interest. They jealously kept every inch of selfish advantage they had, and by combining together perpetuated their advantages by controlling legislation or intimidating and corrupting the people into misuse of the sacred ballot.

"Communism," he said, "is a hateful thing and a menace to peace and organized government; but the communism of combined wealth and capital, the outgrowth of overweening cupidity and selfishness . . . is not less dangerous than the communism of oppressed poverty and toil, which, exasperated by injustice and discontent, attacks with wild disorder the citadel of rule." Those who said that the government would care for the rich, and the rich for the poor, mocked the people. The boast of free institutions was that they cared for the humblest. Giving into wealthy hands the care of society would make free institutions "a glittering delusion and the pretended boon of American citizenship a shameless imposition."

He began going back and forth across the country condemning these evidences of a new life-style in American society. He called out again and again for a new model of citizenship in a society which had become egoistically personalist to an extreme degree. It is not too much to say that the theme of national decay became his grand obsession—though he protested again and again his faith in the people. Look to the past, he urged Boston merchants, and see how far they and their kind had fallen from original innocence. The businessmen of the early Republic were sturdily self-reliant, wanting no favors for themselves or for others. But now businessmen were invited to become the dependents of the government's favor, and beneficiaries of its taxing power. The "spirit of selfishness is abroad in the land," he said, and it filled the air with clamorous demands for special privilege from the government. "Vile, unsavory forms rise to the surface of our agitated political waters, and gleefully anticipate, in the anxiety of selfish interest, their opportunity to fatten upon corruption and debauched suffrage."

We have forgotten the past, he said in New York City, and the great labors and sacrifices which had made the country. Why? Because of the "impetuous race after wealth which has become a characteristic of our people." The growing "selfishness and sordidness," the cynical attitude toward patriotism and morality in government, the attitude that politics was a career for personal gain like any other, had all combined to create a fatal departure from the principles upon which the very system of government rested. "Point to your immense fortunes," he said, "to your national growth and prosperity; boast of the day of practical politics, and discard as obsolete all sentiment and all conception of morality and patriotism in public life," but do not for a moment entertain the delusion that these things meant that the nation was on a safe course.

The American government was in fact only suited to a frugal and economical people, he said in Ohio. It could only survive if it was in the hands of men who had acquired strength and self-reliance by self-denial and by living in circumstances in which they had been forced to acquire economical habits. Such a thrifty and careful people would make the government in their image. Tragically, however, the Republicans derided cheapness and economy within the home in their drive for higher tariffs and higher prices, and were reckless and wasteful with the public money, showering it upon businessmen. This showed, he warned, that "something is wrong with us. . . ." "We, who are proud to call ourselves Jacksonian Democrats," he said in New York City, were also, like Jackson, "boldly and aggressively [attacking] a political heresy opposed to the best interests of the people and defended by an arrogant and unscrupulous party."

It was in this spirit that he gave his Second Inaugural Address. The nation, he warned, was like a strong man who could be confident in his strength yet find hidden within him a terrible disease which could lead to collapse. The very strength and robustness of the nation had given rise to a heedlessness about the laws which governed its national existence. Americans could no longer enjoy the corrupt luxury of a belief that they could expect from the government "especial and direct individual advantages." This spirit degraded to a mechanism of wily craft the great system established by the fathers. Honest patriotism had been perverted into self interest. Men no longer admired and supported their sacred government out of a sense of duty, but instead because of a "pitiful calculation of the sordid gain to be derived from their Government's maintenance." The love of a sovereign, he might have said as a good Calvinist, is a duty, not something given in the expectation of a return.

What must be done? All bounties and subsidies must be refused. There must be no more wild and reckless scramble for unearned pensions from the government. Frugality and economy must again reign, for the opposite simply encouraged personal lives of prodigality and extravagance. The tariff must be lowered without question, for the six-year campaign he had launched in 1887 had finally been won, and the people had given their clear mandate. They now demanded the lifting from their lives of the "inordinate and unequal advantages too long enjoyed by the few." Furthermore, the enormous trusts and combinations which were formed for the purpose of limiting production and fixing prices, those exploitive and unnatural conspiracies, must be attacked to "the extent that they can be reached and restrained by Federal power. . . ."

He concluded that the currency problem was the more dangerous one, however, in light of the alarming drop in the gold reserves. By the time he had finished the silver repeal fight and could turn to tariff reform, he had created too many enemies and lost the momentum of his early administration. When it became clear that the Senate would eviscerate the bill he had got from the House, he lashed out desperately against "party perfidy and party dishonor." How could the Democratic party face the people, he said, "after indulging in such outrageous discriminations and violations of principles"? If thorough tariff reduction were only achieved, he pleaded, there would be a "quick and certain return of prosperity. . . ."

But he had failed utterly, and his administration entered upon the endless dog days which made the next three years a hell for him. "The trusts and combinations—the communism of pelf—whose machinations have prevented us from reaching the success we deserved," he wrote a friend, "should not be forgotten nor forgiven." The trust prosecutions he began, however, were frustrated by the courts, and save for a blistering attack upon the trusts contained in his last message, he was powerless.

His last years were not easy for him. While in time he was pleased to find himself reinstated in popular affections, the rush and roar of Bryanism, imperialism and the America of Theodore Roosevelt dismayed him. The popular enthusiasm over imperialism left him aghast; he could never understand it. "It seems to me," he said in 1898, "that the ears of our people are closed to reason." "My pride and self-conceit have had a terrible fall," he said in the following year. "I thought I understood the American people." The way Roosevelt had acquired the Panama Canal route, he said in Carnegie Hall in 1904, had shamed America, violating "our national honor . . . good name . . . and, above all, our national morality." Roosevelt's election in 1904 staggered him. The whole thing so surprised him that "for a moment, the idea has entered my mind that a change in the character of our countrymen has taken place." When his close friend Richard Watson Gilder, editor of the *Century* magazine, suggested the preparation of a biography in 1905, he replied that "I am by no means sure that it would be in tune with the vaudeville that attracts our people and wins their applause."

Paradoxically, however, he clung to the faith in the Whole People which he had repeatedly expressed throughout his career. They might be afflicted by selfishness, sordidness and a delight in carnival attractions, yet they were still sound. In his last year he wrote that "I have always been such an optimistic American and have always had such complete faith in the saving power of American good sense, that I cannot make myself believe but that we shall weather all storms and find the bright daylight in due time. Though occasionally a feeling of discouragement comes over me, I am glad to say it is only temporary."

To the end, therefore, the essential paradoxes in Cleveland—the ambivalences inherent in his faith and in his political world view—persisted. He was torn between an optimism induced by the conviction that America was carrying out God's plan, and a pessimism characteristic of the Calvinist conviction that mankind is degraded. Devoted to a grimly determinist faith, he yet derived from that same faith the stimulus to be a vigorous and strong-willed executive. His appetite for active power led him to reinvigorate the American presidency, yet he was content to devote his vast energies to only a few campaigns. It is true that it was not yet in the tradition of the presidency for him to be a prolific creator of proposed legislation, and that in contrast to most of his predecessors he was remarkably active. Yet the fact that this immensely vigorous presidency produced so little of major consequence, save his great achievement in cleaning up the government, must be accounted for. The explanation must in part lie in the fact that he had long ago rejected the kind of Presbyterianism which might have led him to fight many-sided humanitarian crusades. The message of active love for others, as Charles A. Briggs had complained, was muted and indistinct in orthodox Presbyterianism. It enjoined denial, not creation.

Therefore, though he was a relentless social critic, inspired by the biting social analysis of Calvinism, his jeremiads on the increasingly greedy life-style which marred his era were only that; they were followed by little action. This makes understandable another facet of the Cleveland paradoxes: the contrast between his contemporary popularity—he got the popular vote majority in three successive presidential elections, and in 1892 brought in the first Democratic sweep of presidency and Congress since 1856—and the fact that he has faded into the background of our historical memories.

It is not too much to say that his career embodied the paradoxes not only of Presbyterianism, but of the Jacksonian political world view as well. Jackson and Cleveland spent much of their presidencies attacking unearned wealth, grasping monopolies and social exploitation, yet both were satisfied with surprisingly little in the way of program. Out of all the sound and fury of Jacksonianism, its endless attacks upon the corrupting of an innocent society by evil men, what emerged as the Jacksonian agenda? Destroy the U.S. Bank and establish sound money. Cleveland's Fourth Annual Message in 1888 depicted a nation sick to its core, defiled, shallow, led astray by false gods, ground under the iron heel of wealth and power. What was the answer? Lower the tariff. This would supposedly end the monopolies, terminate special privilege and clarify American life, bringing prosperity and honest toil in its wake.

It was doubtless this disparity between diagnosis and prescription which led so many then and since to see Cleveland as the front man for the moneyed interests. Such an interpretation, however, misses the essential point: Cleveland operated within a political tradition which was devoted to only a few large and essentially negative goals. Cleveland and the Jacksonians shared the obsession introduced into American political thought by the founder of the left wing, Thomas Jefferson. The root cause for social oppression, Thomas Jefferson was convinced, lay in a corrupt relationship between business and government. To the Jacksonians and to Cleveland, the ills from which America suffered sprang primarily from this cause: the corruption introduced into American life by governments which lavishly distributed special privileges to business enterprise. The United States Bank was the large and visible symbol of this alliance in Jackson's day, and the tariff in Cleveland's. Unfortunately for Cleveland, the tariff was a much more impregnable institution to assault than the U.S. Bank, and in the half-century since Jackson the Democrats had grown deeply divided on the money issue. The result was a shattered party, an ineffective presidency and a flat historical image.

After his failures, which came with much of his second presidency yet to run, why did he not respond with innovation, with new proposals to get at the national sickness? Possibly because, as an orthodox Presbyterian, his mind was encapsulated within creed. His faith had dwelt upon immutable principles and inflexible catechisms; there was no place within it for growth and change. The order of the universe was fixed. For Cleveland, what was not perceived within the original vision was not part of the divine plan. His mission, to use his own revealing words, was to preserve "the ark of the covenant," the received principles of his party. All else, as he put it, was heresy. Given the massiveness of his character and the care with which he chose his words, it is clear that he meant just that. Heresy fighters, however, are unhappily miscast when forced to play roles in which success can be achieved only by innovation. When Cleveland failed in his tariff battle, he had nothing else to offer. The stock was exhausted.

5

---

conclusion: unsolved problems and new directions

Clearly, as historians of Jacksonian America systematically collect vast quantities of numerical data and employ new methods to order and elaborate their evidence, our perspective of the age must change. It is too early to suggest that an all-encompassing new synthesis has emerged, but some of its elements are discernible. First, to many voters Jackson and his party were an ambiguous symbol of democratic practice and ideology. More to the point, class divisions were usually not central to the political conflicts of the time. Voting behavior may not be explained by any single one-to-one relationship between material well-being (or social status) and party choice. The mass of men at the grass roots who surged to the polls in the mid-nineteenth century political world were more influenced by a set of values rising out of deep-seated ethnocultural tensions than they were by economic issues and class consciousness. These hostilities affected party formation, the conduct of politics, perceptions of issues, parties, and political leaders, and actual voting behavior.

The "rediscovery of complexity" in mass political behavior, to use Richard Hofstadter's apt phrase, has been the major consequence of the application of interdisciplinary methods to Jacksonian era politics.[1] Nevertheless, the work of the historians using these methods has only

[1] Richard Hofstadter, *The Progressive Historians* (New York, 1968), p. 442.

begun to unravel the complexities present. Our area and time coverage is limited, our case studies few in number. Lee Benson's research focuses on New York state voting in one year, 1844, Ronald Formisano's on the period after 1837, although both studies consider Jackson's presidency in constructing their interpretations. In addition, Thomas P. Alexander and his students have analyzed voting patterns in two southern states, Alabama and Mississippi, and have found there the same absence of economic class distinctions as in New York and Michigan.[2] All of these investigations are very suggestive of larger patterns, but they are not enough. Research into different time periods is needed, particularly in those elections in which Jackson was a candidate or still an active factor; studies of states and localities with different social and economic configurations would also be most useful. It is clear that economic matters affected the partisan stance of the upper classes in Jacksonian America at certain times. Frank Gatell has shown that, whatever their previous affiliations, a preponderance of New York's wealthiest citizens were Whigs in the mid-forties, apparently as a result of their negative reaction to the vigorous economic programs of the Jacksonians.[3] But had their affiliation changed? And did such issues affect the mass electorate too in moments and places not yet analyzed? Only when we have dealt with a wider range of cases and periods of electoral behavior will we have the systematic coverage necessary to build a new interpretation of the nature of the Jacksonian political process.

As we have noted earlier, however, for the kind of systematic coverage of Jacksonian era politics that is desirable, we lack much of the necessary electoral and social data. Despite the most assiduous searching, for example, Alexander and his students could locate electoral returns for only a very few of the smallest political units in Alabama (the beats, comparable to wards, precincts, and townships elsewhere) before 1860, although all of the county-level returns were at hand. In New York, a state very well endowed in historical archives, researchers have been able to turn up about two-thirds of the minor civil division election returns for the Jacksonian and pre-Civil War period. Social and economic data is similarly difficult to locate. Although much evidence is available, and more is turning up all the time, such limitations severely hamper research.

These data limitations are a particularly severe impediment to quanti-

---

2 Thomas B. Alexander, *et al.*, "The Basis of Alabama's Ante-Bellum Two Party System," *Alabama Review*, XIX (October, 1966), 243–76; David Young, "The Mississippi Whigs, 1834–1860" (Ph. D. dissertation, University of Alabama, 1968).

3 Frank Otto Gatell, "Money and Party in Jacksonian America: A Quantitative Look at New York City's Men of Quality," *Political Science Quarterly*, LXXXII (June, 1967), 232–52. See also, Robert Rich, " 'A Wilderness of Whigs,' The Wealthy Men of Boston," *Journal of Social History*, V (July, 1971), 263–76.

tative analysis. A commitment to multivariate analysis—the testing of all possible determinants of voting decisions—is the central component of the systematic investigation of political phenomena. But without the information necessary for such comprehensiveness the chance of missing crucial factors is severe, and the danger of accepting plausible but potentially incorrect correlations is high. This data problem is made even more critical by what a social analyst has called the "ecological fallacy," that is, the interpretation of individual and group behavior from aggregate geographic characteristics.[4] We are always, at best, describing gross relationships between the social characteristics of particular geographic areas and group patterns of voting, not how any specific individual actually cast his ballot. But statistical associations, even at the township level, presuppose regularities in the distribution of characteristics over a unit, something which may not actually exist. Furthermore these small units never went 100 percent for one party, and there is no way of knowing from the information available who in the unit did not conform to the prevailing pattern of electoral behavior. Thus the possibility of establishing a spurious relationship between demographic characteristics and voting remains a critical problem, even when we use the smallest geographic units for which we have data. Of course, as we have argued before, the smaller the unit of analysis, the less likely a significant distortion will occur; once again the need for comprehensive social and electoral data is underscored.

Not only do historians of Jacksonian politics lack important descriptive data, but they also have insufficient information about social structure, value systems, and the psychology of voter choice in the communities they are studying. Although social scientists are learning more about these matters in a contemporary setting, our knowledge of the past is still incomplete. We need studies that describe and assess the patterns of settlement and mobility, the distribution of wealth, relationships between classes, social contact between different groups, and the nature of social integration existing in Jacksonian America. A number of historians have begun to investigate these problems in systematic fashion. But we need to know still more about them and particularly about their impact on political beliefs and electoral behavior. Why do people perceive politics as they do? Why do they make the choices they do from the multitude of political cues offered by society? And why do they retain their partisan identification as long as they do?

Some of these problems can be tackled in accustomed ways. As noted in the introduction, nothing in quantitative analysis eliminates the

---

[4] W. S. Robinson, "Ecological Correlations and the Behavior of Individuals," *American Sociological Review*, XV (June, 1950), 351–56.

need for the sensitive use of surviving documents. They, whatever their limitations, can recapture the mood and political attitudes of an era as well as illuminate critical problems about its political culture. The most rewarding approach combines statistical data, when available, with detailed study of documentary materials. Colonial historians have learned through quantitative investigations, for example, that widespread suffrage existed in America before the Constitution, but that few changes in traditional patterns of upper class political leadership came about as a result. Analyses of the pertinent documents suggest that a great deal of deference to the "natural" leaders of society, a deference rooted in a traditional belief system, remained central to the colonists even in the New World. A political scientist has also demonstrated how, by examining changes in ballot forms in the late nineteenth century, we can illuminate the reasons for quantitative changes in voter turnout. Richard McCormick in his *The Second American Party System* brilliantly combines statistics of voter turnout with examinations of partisan documents, legislative debates, and legal and constitutional records to analyze party development in the Jacksonian period. A number of related studies of the era suggest themselves from these examples. All would be best realized through the use of quantification necessarily combined with a range of documentary materials.

The integration of the ideas and methods of the social sciences with historical phenomena has significantly altered our view of a number of important facets of Jacksonian era politics. We are still just beginning to use systematic quantitative analysis and are beset by many problems and limitations, but the payoff appears to have been worth the costs incurred. We hope that as more historians adopt this approach, we will uncover new data, continue to rethink traditional problems, discover new directions, and ultimately produce the synthesis of Jacksonian political culture that we still lack.

6

suggestions for further reading

An excellent introductory bibliography to the extensive available literature on Jacksonian era politics is in Edward Pessen, *Jacksonian America: Society, Personality and Politics* (Homewood, Ill., 1969), pp. 352–94. Charles Sellers, "Andrew Jackson Versus the Historians," *Mississippi Valley Historical Review*, XLIX (March, 1958), 615–34, and Alfred A. Cave, *Jacksonian Democracy and the Historians* (Gainesville, Fla., 1964) place this literature in historiographic perspective. Richard Hofstadter, *The Progressive Historians* (New York, 1968), and Lee Benson, *Turner and Beard: American Historical Writing Reconsidered* (Glencoe, Ill., 1960), are the best introductions to that most influential group of scholars. Hofstadter and Benson should be supplemented by John Higham's two studies of twentieth-century American historiography, *History* (Englewood Cliffs, N.J., 1965), and *Writing American History: Essays in Modern Scholarship* (Bloomington, Ind., 1970).

Lee Benson's call to political historians to incorporate systematic quantitative data when studying popular voting is in "Research Problems in American Political Historiography," first published in Mirra Komarovsky, ed., *Common Frontiers in the Social Sciences* (Glencoe, Ill., 1957), pp. 113–83; and reprinted above on pp. 70–101. The development of Benson's ideas can be seen in "An Approach to the Scientific Study of Past Public Opinion," *Public Opinion Quarterly*, XXXI

(Winter, 1967–1968), 522–67. Both essays are reprinted along with others of a similar nature in Lee Benson, *Essays Towards the Scientific Study of History* (Philadelphia, 1971). Samuel P. Hays, "New Possibilities in American Political History: The Social Analysis of Political Life," in Seymour Martin Lipset and Richard Hofstadter, eds., *Sociology and History: Methods* (New York, 1968), 181–227; and William O. Aydelotte, *Quantification in History* (Boston, 1971), also cogently argue the value of systematic quantitative methods in political history. Richard Jensen traces the connection between those Progressive historians who used quantitative data (Turner, Beard, Arthur C. Cole, *The Whig Party in the South* [Washington, 1913], and Dixon Ryan Fox, *The Decline of the Aristocracy in the Politics of New York, 1790–1840* [New York, 1919], among others), and the modern quantitative political historians in "American Election Analysis: A Case History of Methodological Innovation and Diffusion," in Seymour Martin Lipset, ed., *Politics and the Social Sciences* (New York, 1969), 226–43.

The work in political science that has most influenced American political historians is in Angus Campbell et al., *The American Voter* (New York, 1960) and in their *Elections and the Political Order* (New York, 1966). Other influential studies include V. O. Key, "A Theory of Critical Elections," *Journal of Politics,* XVII (February, 1955), 3–18 and his "Secular Realignment and the Party System," *Journal of Politics,* XXI (May, 1959), 198–210. Gerald Pomper, "Classification of Presidential Elections," *Journal of Politics,* XXIX (August, 1967), 535–66; Charles Sellers, "The Equilibrium Cycle in Two-Party Politics," *Public Opinion Quarterly,* XXIX (Spring, 1965), 16–38; Thomas Jahnige, "Critical Elections and Social Change: Towards A Dynamic Explanation of National Party Competition in the United States," *Polity,* III (Summer, 1971), 465–500; Walter Dean Burnham, *Critical Elections and the Mainsprings of American Politics* (New York, 1970), and Jerome Clubb and Howard Allen, *Electoral Change and Stability in American Political History* (New York, 1971), all deal with the structural and cyclical aspects of American popular voting over time. These cycles are employed to describe specific eras of political party history in Walter Dean Burnham and William Nisbet Chambers, *The American Party Systems* (New York, 1968). This book is an excellent introduction to understanding the role played by parties in structuring popular voting.

Theoretical statements concerning the political ideology of present-day Americans are to be found in Donald Stokes, "The Nature of Belief Systems in Mass Publics," in David Apter, ed., Ideology and Discontent (Glencoe, Ill., 1964), 206–61; Lloyd Free and Hadley Cantril, *The Political Beliefs of Americans* (New York, 1968); Robert Lane, *Political Life* (New York, 1959); Lane, *Political Ideology* (New York, 1967),

Everett C. Ladd, *Ideology in America* (Ithaca, 1969); and in the ency-
clopedic Bernard Berelson and Gary Steiner, *Human Behavior: An
Inventory of Scientific Findings* (New York, 1964). Robert Merton's interpretation of the importance of reference group attitudes in influencing
voting behavior in *Social Theory and Social Structure* (Enlarged edition,
New York, 1968) provides the theoretical underpinning used by Lee
Benson in "Outline for a Theory of American Voting Behavior," in *The
Concept of Jacksonian Democracy: New York as a Test Case* (Princeton,
1961), 270–328. Much of our knowledge about political ideologies and
how they affect election campaigns is entertainingly presented in Nelson
Polsby and Aaron Wildavsky, *Presidential Elections,* 3rd ed. (New York,
1972).

The results of the quantitative research that has gone on in American
political history is reprinted and surveyed in a number of books and
articles. See especially, Allan G. Bogue, "The United States: The New
Political History," in Walter Lacqueur and George Mosse, eds., *The
New History: Trends in Historical Research and Writing Since World
War II* (New York, 1966); Morton Rothstein, Philip Greven, Samuel
McSeveney, Robert Zemsky and Joel Silbey, "Quantification in American
History: An Assessment," in Herbert Bass, ed., *The State of American
History* (Chicago, 1970), 298–329; Robert Swierenga, ed., *Quantification
in American History: Theory and Research* (New York, 1970), and
"Clio and Computers: A Survey of Computerized Research in History,"
Computers and the Humanities, V (September, 1970), 1–22. The results
of the application of such techniques specifically to popular voting behavior throughout American history are reprinted in Joel H. Silbey and
Samuel T. McSeveney, *Voters, Parties and Elections* (Waltham, Mass.,
1972). The many problems involved in doing such research for mid-
nineteenth century America are discussed in Ronald Formisano, "Analyzing American Voting, 1830–1860: Methods," *Historical Methods Newsletter,* II (March, 1969), 1–12.

Our knowledge of the importance of ethnocultural factors in influencing popular voting throughout our history is intelligently summarized
in Robert Swierenga, "Ethnocultural Political Analysis: A New Approach
to American Ethnic Studies," *Journal of American Studies,* V (April,
1971), 59–79, and in Samuel T. McSeveney, "Ethnic Groups, Ethnic
Conflicts and Recent Quantitative Research in American Political History," *International Migration Review* (forthcoming). See also, Seymour
Martin Lipset, "Religion and Politics in the American Past and Present,"
in Robert Lee and Martin Marty, eds., *Religion and Social Conflict* (New
York, 1964), 69–126; and Lawrence Fuchs, ed., *American Ethnic Politics*
(New York, 1968).

A number of useful compilations of historical electoral statistics have been published. Walter Dean Burnham, *Presidential Ballots, 1836–1892* (Baltimore, 1955), and Sven Petersen, *A Statistical History of the American Presidential Elections* (New York, 1963), are particularly useful if limited in coverage. The Inter-University Consortium for Political Research at the University of Michigan has collected all election returns since 1824 for certain national and state offices in every state at the county level as well as the available social data in the federal censuses. Unfortunately, no one has yet collected or published similar amounts of election returns at the township and ward level, or state census materials. The methods used by political scientists and historians to organize, arrange and interpret these vast amounts of data are described in V. O. Key, *A Primer of Statistics for Social Scientists* (New York, 1954), and in Richard Jensen and Charles Dollar, *A Historian's Guide to Statistics* (New York, 1971).

J. R. Pole has led the way in using statistical time series to work out the patterns of voter eligibility and participation in elections in the first part of the nineteenth century. See, for example, his "Suffrage and Representation in Maryland from 1776 to 1810: A Statistical Note and Some Reflections," *The Journal of Southern History,* XXIV (May, 1958), 218–25; "Election Statistics in North Carolina To 1861," *Journal of Southern History,* XXIV (May, 1958), 225–28; and "The Suffrage in New Jersey, 1790–1807," *Proceedings of the New Jersey Historical Society,* LXXI (January, 1953), 54–61. He places his findings in larger context in *Political Representation in England and the Origins of the American Republic* (New York, 1966). In addition to his article reprinted in this volume, Richard McCormick has utilized statistics of turnout and party competition to study *The Second American Party System* (Chapel Hill, 1966) which traces the formation of the Democratic and Whig parties in every state in the 1820s and 1830s.

Most recent quantitative studies of Jacksonian era politics have focussed on the structure and distribution of the vote. Lee Benson, *The Concept of Jacksonian Democracy: New York as a Test Case* (Princeton, 1961), holds a seminal position among these recent reinterpretations of Jacksonian era voting and political belief patterns. Ronald Formisano, *The Birth of Mass Political Parties: Michigan, 1827–1861* (Princeton, 1971), adds depth and another state. Thomas Alexander, et al., have studied "Who Were the Alabama Whigs," *Alabama Review,* XVI (January, 1963), 5–19 and, "The Basis of Alabama's Antebellum Two-Party System," XIX (October, 1966), 243–76. Edward Pessen, "Did Labor Support Jackson?: The Boston Story," *Political Science Quarterly,* LXIV (June, 1949), 262–74; and William Sullivan, "Did Labor Support Andrew Jackson?" *Political Science Quarterly,* LXII (December, 1947), 569–80, long ago raised challenges to the Progressive interpretation of Jacksonian voting through the use of quantitative techniques. (But also see Robert Bowers, "Note on 'Did Labor Support Jackson?: The Boston Story,' " *Political Science Quarterly,* LXV [September, 1950], 441–44.) Lynn L. Marshall, "The Genesis of Grass-Roots Democracy in Kentucky," *Mid-America,* XLVII (October, 1965), 269–87; John L. Stanley, "Majority Tyranny in Tocqueville's America: The Failure of Negro Suffrage in 1846," *Political Science Quarterly,* LXXXIV (September, 1969), 412–35; and Herbert Doherty, *The Whigs of Florida,* 1845–1854 (Gainesville, 1959), all usefully add to our knowledge of the voting patterns in the era. A number of studies remain unpublished. David N. Young, "The Whig Party in Mississippi" (Ph.D. dissertation, University of Alabama, 1968), and Roger Petersen, "The Reaction to a Heterogeneous Society: A Behavioral and Quantitative Analysis of Northern Voting Behavior, 1845–1870, Pennsylvania A Test Case (Ph.D. dissertation, University of Pittsburgh, 1970), both follow in the path Benson first surveyed. Michael Holt, *Forging a Majority, The Formation of the Republican Party in Pittsburgh,* 1848–1860 (New Haven, 1969), although focusing on a slightly later period, contains much of importance to students of the Jacksonian period. Donald B. Cole, *Jacksonian Democracy in New Hampshire* (Cambridge, 1970), uses quantitative electoral data to argue a more traditional interpretation of the nature of voting behavior.

The most extensive quantitative literature on the Jacksonian era, after studies of voting patterns, has been of the partisan preferences of economic and political elites. Grady McWhiney, "Were The Whigs a Class Party in Alabama?," *Journal of Southern History,* XXIII (November, 1957), 510–21; and Charles Sellers, "Who Were The Southern Whigs?," *American Historical Review,* LIX (January, 1954), 335–46, were early attempts to investigate the problem systematically and quantitatively. More recent attempts include Alexandra McCoy, "Political Affiliation of American Economic Elites: Wayne County, Michigan, 1844, 1860 As A Test Case" (Ph.D. dissertation, Wayne State University, 1965), part of which is reprinted above. Sidney Arenson, *Status and Kinship in the Higher Civil Service* (Cambridge, 1964), focusses on the related problem of whether the Jacksonians democratized the civil service by appointing more representatives from the lower classes of society than had earlier presidents. In a series of articles Edward Pessen has addressed himself both to investigating the problem of elites and politics and to refining some of the source material necessary to study the subject. See his "A Social and Economic Portrait of Jacksonian Brooklyn," *New York Historical Society Quarterly,* LV (October, 1971), 318–53; "The Wealthiest New Yorkers of the Jacksonian Era: A New List," *New York Historical Society Quarterly,* LIV (April, 1970), 145–72; "Moses Beach Revisited: A Critical Examination of His Wealthy Citizens Pamphlets," *Journal of*

American History, LVIII (September, 1971), 415–26; "Did Fortunes Rise and Fall Mercurially in Antebellum America? The Tale of Two Cities: Boston and New York," *Journal of Social History,* V (October, 1971), 339–59; "The Egalitarian Myth and the American Social Reality: Wealth, Mobility, and Equality in the 'Era of the Common Man,'" *American Historical Review,* LXXI (October, 1971), 989–1034. Finally, Frank Otto Gatell has criticized the findings of Benson and others who have found few economic or class differences between Jackson and Whig leaders. See his "Money and Party in Jacksonian America: A Quantitative Look At New York City's Men of Quality," *Political Science Quarterly,* LXXXII (June, 1967), 235–52. Also see Robert Rich, "'A Wilderness of Whigs,' The Wealthy Men of Boston," *Journal of Social History,* V (July, 1971), 263–76.

There are still very few studies of political ideology in the era which utilize the findings of quantitative and behavioral electoral research. Ronald Formisano, "Political Character, Antipartyism and the Second Party System," *American Quarterly,* XXI (Winter, 1969), 683–709; and Robert Kelley, "The Thought and Character of Samuel J. Tilden: The Democrat as Inheritor," *Historian,* XXVI (February, 1964), 176–205, stand lonely and alone. Herbert Ershkowitz and William G. Shade, "Consensus or Conflict? Political Behavior in the State Legislatures During the Jacksonian Era," *Journal of American History,* LVIII (December, 1971), 591–621, while focussing on legislative roll-call voting and not election behavior, adds considerable substance to our understanding of the nature of political beliefs in the era.

Many historians remain critical of the whole quantitative enterprise both generally and as applied to the Jacksonian era specifically. Arthur M. Schlesinger, Jr., "The Humanist Looks at Empirical Social Research," *American Sociological Review,* XXVII (December, 1962), 768–71 and Oscar Handlin, "History: A Discipline in Crisis?," *American Scholar* (Summer, 1971), 447–64 stand out as general attacks. On Jacksonian era quantification see Edward Pessen, "Jacksonian Quantification: On Asking the Right Questions," in Herbert Bass, ed., *The State of American History* (Chicago, 1970), 362–72. The critics are themselves criticized in Philip M. Hauser, "Schlesinger on Humanism and Empirical Research," *American Sociological Review,* XXVIII (February, 1963), 97–99; in the exchange between William O. Aydelotte and J. H. Hexter reprinted in Aydelotte's, *Quantification in History* (Boston, 1971), 155–80, and most specifically in Gene Wise, "'Reality in Recent American Scholarship: Progressives Versus Symbolists," *American Quarterly,* XIX (Summer, 1967), 303–28, which compares the interpretation of Jacksonian politics of Arthur M. Schlesinger, Jr. and Lee Benson.